Science and the UFOs

Jenny Randles
and
Peter Warrington

Basil Blackwell

First published 1985

Basil Blackwell Ltd
108 Cowley Road, Oxford OX4 1JF, UK

Basil Blackwell Inc.
432 Park Avenue South, Suite 1505,
New York, NY 10016, USA

British Library Cataloguing in Publication Data

Randles, Jenny
    Science and the UFOs.
    1. Unidentified flying objects
    I. Title   II. Warrington, Peter
    001.9′42   TL789
    ISBN 0-631-13563-4

Library of Congress Cataloging in Publication Data

Randles, Jenny.
  Science and the UFOs.

  Bibliography: p.
  Includes index.
  1. Unidentified flying objects.   I. Warrington,
  Peter.   II. Title.   III. Title: Science and the U.F.O.s.
  TL789.R325 1985   001.9′42   84-20319
  ISBN 0-631-13563-4

Plates can be found between pages 88 and 89

Typeset by Freeman Graphic, Tonbridge, Kent
Printed in Great Britain by The Camelot Press, Southampton

Contents

The greatest scientific problem of our times.

Professor James E. McDonald,
address to the American Association
for the Advancement of Science, 1969

Preface

Until 1947 the world had hardly heard of UFOs. They had been seen in some quantity but sightings rarely became public knowledge. Then, in June of that year, came a report of 'saucer-like' objects over the Cascade Mountains in the USA. An astonishing chain reaction began that was to turn UFOs into subjects of everyday conversation throughout the world. But what is almost as astonishing is that the subject of UFOs has been shunned for the most part by the scientific establishment. The reasons for this curious behaviour are many and varied, and it would be dishonest to suggest that all are invalid, considering the bizarre, but common, interpretations of UFO reports. However, even in the early days after 1947, a few professional scientists took a serious interest, and in more recent years the numbers who have ventured to examine aspects of the UFO phenomenon have grown at an encouraging pace. Indeed it is the involvement of these workers which has established the underlying principle of this book and made its conception both possible and essential. This principle, simply stated, is that between the two extremes of the total sceptic and the committed believer lies some middle ground – ground which offers much of interest for a wide range of scientific disciplines. The study of UFOs (ufology) can provide material of direct relevance and potential importance to both the physical and the social sciences. Beneath the mask of the popular mystery there is a puzzle which should fascinate any genuine scientist. And yet, just as those who believe in UFOs fail to pose all the questions, so there are those at the other end of the opinion scale who refuse to look at such answers as there are.

They ignore the evidence, rely heavily on sweeping assumptions, and thus get rid of the proverbial baby along with the bathwater.

We are not writing only for people new to the subject, but we have tried to write at a level understandable to all. Nor do we intend this to be the definitive volume on ufology, because at this stage of our knowledge that would be both presumptuous and impossible. Rather, we are aiming to show how recent work has proved that a hard core of evidence does exist among the numerous incidents which are now regarded as the UFO phenomenon. For many years it was suspected that this central core, if it really existed, was too nebulous for objective examination and investigation. Time and again this excuse has been used by scientists, who have not studied the data, as an honest way to avoid responsibility for reviewing the UFO phenomenon. It is now becoming clear that after discarding the useless or misleading material which tends to cloud the issue, one can see distinct signs of cohesion within. It seems likely that several different phenomena are involved, some physical and some psychological.

Scientific respectability is something which the UFO enthusiast has sought unsuccessfully for over 30 years. Doubtless there are scientists who would gladly see this search last, equally fruitlessly, for another 30 years. Obviously respect must be earned, and the fact is that the UFO community in general has failed to earn respect. They have all too frequently been gullible and undisciplined in their approach; they have earned themselves a place in the 'lunatic fringe'. In so doing they have damaged the prospects for serious research and slowed ufology's progress.

This book is not an appeal for ufology's acceptance into the scientific community, nor is it a request to make the criteria for acceptance more malleable. It aims to show that there are sound reasons for scientists to investigate the subject for themselves.

PART 1 · THE PAST

1

A Historical Perspective

When were UFOs first seen? The answer to this rather depends upon your definition of the term. If by UFO you mean a supposedly anomalous, often disc-like, object that is frequently interpreted as a spacecraft of unknown origin (usually alien), then the starting-point is probably June 1947, although one might be tempted to stretch this to a year earlier, when there were some sightings in Scandinavia. On the other hand, if you really want to talk about any unknown phenomenon observed in the atmosphere, the starting-point would be the dawn of civilization, because to primitive man every sky phenomenon was at first inexplicable.

Consider a rainbow, for instance. This must have seemed miraculous to those who knew nothing of physics. It would take a very long time to appreciate, by observing many rainbows, that whatever these things were they tended to appear when there were drops of moisture in the atmosphere. And it required an understanding of the laws of physics, which did not come for thousands of years, before the nature of rainbows could be understood. While this analogy may well be useful in grasping the fundamental problem the UFO poses, it is hardly helpful to regard the history of UFOs as the history of man's observation of things in the sky!

Probably the most reasonable approach is to consider reports of phenomena for which unambiguous and non-controversial explanations have yet to be found. Even in this sense, sightings of UFO-like phenomena go back for thousands of years, possibly as far as the beginning of written records.

Kenneth Arnold, an American businessman, observed a formation of disc-like objects over Mount Rainier, Washington State, USA on 24 June 1947. He described them to intrigued journalists as 'flying like saucers skipping over water'. From this innocent statement the phrase 'flying saucer' was born and UFO-hunting became all the rage. People looked for them and staged hoaxes using models. Newspapers played journalistic ping-pong with the subject. From then on UFOs were to be forever of interest. However, the sighting by Kenneth Arnold is now seen as neither especially interesting nor particularly strange. Formations of UFOs, as in this case, are very rare, but were it to happen tomorrow it would be unlikely to raise the eyebrows of even the most enthusiastic ufologist. Indeed, dozens of much better substantiated cases take place in every country every year, yet generally speaking, few of these now create much media excitement, except possibly in the local newspaper.

The Arnold UFOs are probably explicable. Several theories that seem to make sense have been proposed. In other words, it is likely that this case falls into the category of report usually termed an IFO (identified flying object). The plain fact is that about 90 per cent of submitted UFO sightings can be readily explained as cases of mistaken identity. Culprits range from Venus (arch-enemy number one to most working ufologists), stars, satellites, plane-lights, balloons, luminous owls, granny's windborne hat and many other unlikely objects. The list of explanations grows each year. And while outright hoaxes do, of course, happen, they are actually rather rare.

It was quickly discovered that the Washington State sighting had not been the first. Reports of anomalous objects were frequent in an American 'wave' (as such cyclical periods of intense UFO activity are called). This began around May and continued through into August. The Arnold case was but one of hundreds, and simply happened to be the first to capture newspaper publicity. It is hard to tell whether this was genuinely the start of the modern UFO era. A long list of sightings which had supposedly taken place before 1947 have been investigated. The earliest photographic case, for example, occurred in the last century. The witnesses involved in these early cases usually claim that they had no background against which to view their encounter when it happened and so were incapable of appreciating its nature. Only when a convenient way of categorizing the occurrence was created by Kenneth Arnold did they know to whom to report and how. This contention sounds reasonable, although one can suspect some accounts because they post-date Arnold's in their reporting. But, if one goes further and examines the events, there seems little doubt that some others must refer to real encounters well before 1947. The following is a typical report.

Mr F. Price (a pseudonym) was a building foreman in November 1939, contracted to do essential war work at what was to become an airfield in Gloucestershire, England, for test flying Meteor jets. Early on Monday mornings he would drive from London across country to his lodgings in the village of Brockworth. In making this journey Mr Price had to pass a farm, which on the day in question (13 November 1939) was deserted. This is not all that surprising in view of the national emergency. As he drove past he became aware of a high-pitched humming sound (like a finely tuned electrical motor), and then confronted a very strange object hovering over a field at the rear of the farm. It was bell-shaped and dull grey in colour, with dark shadings or window-like patches in a line part of the way up the body. Most curious of all, however, was the curtain of greenish light that emanated from its underside, creating the impression that it had a skirt. Mr Price stopped his car and got out to watch. In two minutes the light curtain vanished. It retracted upwards into the base of the object, disappearing as if it were something solid rather than composed of beams of light. As it rose it thinned out and dissipated. This 'solid-light' phenomenon is actually a rare, but significant, aspect in a number of UFO accounts. A hoaxer would have to be well-read to know about it. When the light curtain disappeared the UFO tilted to an angle of about 80 degrees and then moved away in total silence. Mr Price was, needless to say, frightened and left the scene with some haste.[1]

This type of object, the glowing skirt, the tilting manoeuvre and other features have all been described on many other occasions. A 1972 case from Oldham, Greater Manchester, for example, virtually duplicates the above case but in somewhat

[1] Case report 3901 by Mark Brown, BUFORA files.

different circumstances. However, according to ufologist Mark Brown, who conducted an excellent retrospective investigation at Brockworth, Mr Price was most unlikely to know anything about the Oldham case.[2]

Clearly, if any of these stories are to be given credence, they must have a major impact on our thinking about UFOs. And this is without taking into consideration any of the waves of phantom airships (the USA, 1896; Denmark, 1909; Great Britain, 1913), pilotless aircraft (the USA, 1930s) or ghost rockets (Scandinavia, 1946).[3] While these are verifiable from contemporary newspaper records, they are felt by UFO researchers to be of largely socio-logical importance. This means that the initial explanation which was at first presumed viable in 1947 (that of secret military weapons) could have been proved untenable right from the outset. But the collation of these past records took time, and by then the secret-weapons hypothesis had been established as a non-runner by other means.

As report piled upon report the next significant steps came in the early 1950s. Science-fiction films began to incorporate UFO imagery and in some cases (e.g. *Earth Versus the Flying Saucers,* 1955) were even built around UFO books originally written as 'fact' but here dramatized as 'fiction'. This trend continued into the modern day with the Steven Spielberg film *Close Encounters of the Third Kind* (1977). Popular knowledge of UFOs had increased so much that the title (taken from UFO researcher Dr J. Allen Hynek's classification scheme for UFOs) was not felt to be too extraordinary. This film was also built as fiction around real UFO sightings, culled from the UFO literature by Spielberg. As the wave of imitators, Spielberg's immensely popular 'sequel', *ET,* and the plethora of television commercials with a UFO theme all serve to demonstrate, the UFO phenomenon continues to be of great public interest. From the outset these films have had one very serious effect: the dividing line between fact and fiction has been blurred. This may have had more damaging

[2] J. Randles and P. Warrington, *UFOs: A British Viewpoint* (Robert Hale, 1979), pp. 108–10.

[3] See: C. Grove, 'The Airship Wave of 1909', *Flying Saucer Review,* 16 (6), and 17 (1), 1970; 'Ghost Bombs over Sweden', *FSR,* vol. 15, nos. 2 and 3, 1969; G. Adamski and D. Leslie, *Flying Saucers have Landed* (Spearman, 1970).

impact on serious UFO investigation than any other single factor.

The early 1950s brought another new facet to the problem – the contactees. George Adamski, Truman Bethurum and Cedric Allingham, plus many others, seized upon growing UFO interest to spin fantastic yarns about voyages to the moon (where there were trees and rivers, of course) and even to other planets (inhabited by peace-loving aliens and sexy space sirens with names like Aura Rhanes). The world was back in the days of Buck Rogers and Flash Gordon, with the difference that it was all in the guise of truth. On a planet emerging from a horrific war, one where space travel was still a dream (but a much vaunted one), all of this was welcomed by both public and publishers. Thirty years on, these stories seem quaintly amusing and ludicrous. It is hard to conceive of anyone being taken in by them, but people were – and indeed they still are. Elaborate theories to explain the contactee experiences are occasionally put forward. Adamski in particular has his champions, even in a computer age which has cruelly demolished his assorted, blotchy photographs of 'spaceships'. Adamski's spaceships evidently existed in his mind, but probably not in reality. His pictures of them just cannot be taken seriously. The use of spotlighting and small models is obvious even to a casual observer, and technology from the space programme has enabled photographic analysis to prove this beyond all doubt.

Perhaps some of these contactees were genuinely misguided. Others were undoubtedly clever tricksters with an eye for some fun and a quick way to make money. Still others might well have been hoaxers with rather more dubious motives. We have been shown irrefutable evidence, collated by a remarkably persistent ufologist, that one of the contactees mentioned in this chapter did not even exist. His book about space voyages was written by a person who later became famous and highly respectable. The hoax has not yet been admitted to. This example does illustrate the problem with these early tales. We also know about a much more recent contactee-style book which was hoaxed in a similar way and is still on sale as genuine. This craze of contactees died quickly in the late 1950s, but left its scars on UFO investigation. It could well have set back serious study by 15 years.

With all the silliness of the contactees, and media inventions of phrases such as 'little green men' (a curious one as UFO entities have hardly ever been reported as green), discussion of the problem soon descended into carnival. When UFO societies sprang up in the wake of the contactee wave they became infuriated by what they thought was a government cover-up (see p. 18). The train of their reasoning went something like this: these things are appearing in the sky. It is obvious they must be alien craft. We suspect it, and so the government with their resources must know it. Yet they not only deny this; they invent ridiculous explanations that are more fantastic than the truth. Looked at this way, it was easy to presume that governments knew what was happening but were afraid to admit it. Of course, this reasoning is fraught with presumptions and misunderstanding. However, the belief in cover-ups and repeated attacks on governments (especially in the USA) became virtually a crusade for early ufologists. It was one more factor which convinced most ordinary people (and more importantly most scientists) that UFOs were childish illusions.

Ufology went through what has been called a 'Dark Age' as a result of all these problems and did not emerge until the beginning of the 1970s. The founding in the USA, in 1973, of CUFOS (the Center for UFO Studies) was a symbol of the new vigour injected into what had become a stagnant subject. CUFOS, pioneered by astronomer Dr J. Allen Hynek, was the first all-scientist UFO group, which started with brave ambitions, even if in fact it found itself up against many of the difficulties of the older amateur groups. CUFOS and sister groups around the world began to push their investigators into achieving higher standards. Inevitably this led to a considerable drop-out rate as promising cases crumbled beneath unprecedented research efforts. But those cases that did not crumble (and in real terms, if not percentage terms, there were still many) stood out all the more strongly.

Higher standards of investigation went hand-in-hand with greater concern about ethics. Serious British UFO groups met together in 1981 and 1982 to devise a code of practice (see appendix). This defined obligations (rather like a doctor's oath). Self-regulation of one's work is, we hope, a sign of advancing maturity. Respectable and serious UFO books have begun to outweigh the light-hearted (and decidedly misleading) nonsense that had hitherto been typical. Hack writers used to read a few newspapers and make up a book by stringing stories together with some curious hypothesis, such as the human race having been genetically engineered by Martians holidaying on Earth. Now students of the subject who are willing to be sceptical, open-minded and thoroughly perceptive are becoming the authors. The decade leading up to 1984 saw the publication of far more truly important UFO books than all the previous years. As the writer of some of this work, Hilary Evans, once remarked, 'Ufology has come of age.'

2

The Evidence for UFOs

There is something unusual going on here.

Dr Bruce Maccabee,
US Navy physicist

How can we decide whether UFOs really exist? The most obvious method is to consider the sheer wealth of case material which forms the body of UFO knowledge. We do not here refer to stories with alluring titles such as 'Annie sees a spaceship' or 'Jim flies on Martian craft', which form the staple diet of the UFO media. The real UFO data is something quite different. This is a small sample of cases from the UFO records, illustrating how the phenomenon has been manifested through half a century.[1]

Date: August 1920
Time: 3 p.m.
Place: Dawlish, Devon, England

Some children stealing tomatoes from a field spotted two red spheres in the western sky. These moved at great speed and then stopped. They hovered in this new position for two minutes and as the frightened youngsters looked on, they sped away, at a tremendous speed and at right angles to their previous course. They vanished over Dartmoor into a clear blue sky.

---

[1] Information on these cases comes from the *Daily Express* UFO Bureau, which was organized by the newspaper for two weeks in order to obtain details of old cases which had not been previously reported. Serious UFO researchers throughout Britain then investigated them.

Date: Unknown, 1927
Time: 10 p.m.
Place: Near Wexford, Ireland

Two friends were returning home down a narrow country lane when they saw what they thought was a car approaching round a bend. It illuminated the whole road in front of it. As it silently came closer they marvelled at the brilliance of its lights, so out of keeping for cars of that day, especially in a still-backward part of the world. But then the object rose into the air! Traversing a ditch, moving off at right-angles and flying over a field, it began to travel away. The light beam was projecting out of nowhere. There was certainly no car behind it. It bypassed a quarry and turned again on reaching a railway line. It then followed the tracks, still travelling near the ground, until it was lost to sight in the distance.

Date: June 1940
Time: Afternoon
Place: Hoy Island, The Orkneys, Scotland

On a bright, sunny afternoon a team of artillery gunners received an air-raid alert. This was common as it was wartime, but on this occasion the alert proved a false alarm. However, the reporter of these events was responsible for using a height- and range-finder to track any incoming aircraft and, with radar back-up, direct the gunners. Reacting swiftly to the alert, he faintly perceived, and then focused in on, a strange object in the sky. For ten seconds he had an excellent view of an oblate spheroid moving in swift, level flight. Its height was recorded as 38,000 feet – in excess of the capabilities of aircraft of the day. A full enquiry was launched but no explanation was forthcoming. The witness does not know if the radar tracked anything, which is a pity as it would have been one of the first radar visuals on record if so.

Date: 22 January 1945
Time: 3 p.m.
Place: Heydebreck, Upper Silesia, Poland

A British prisoner of war was being paraded by the Germans, with other people of several nationalities, in preparation for

leaving camp on what was to prove a four-month trek away from
the invading Russian army. Their tanks were plainly audible just
a few miles away. Overhead a four-engined bomber plane trundled
across the sky at about 18,000 feet and all those on the ground
looked up, seeing what they thought was a fire at its rear. Soon
they recognized this error. The next suggestion aired among the
onlookers was that a parachute flare had been caught up in the
slipstream of the aircraft, but this too was quickly seen to be
untrue. A brilliant glowing sphere of white light tailed the plane
wherever it went, visible for several minutes as it passed across
the sky. This seems to have been a rare example of a 'foo fighter'
(as they were called during wartime) seen by ground observers.
(A number of reliable accounts from pilots and their crews were
collated during and after the hostilities. Both the Allied and Axis
powers saw them.)

Date: Summer 1955
Time: 5 a.m.
Place: Glasgow, Scotland

Three members of a jazz band were returning home from a late-
night session when they saw a stationary object in the sky. It was
cigar-shaped, with a line of dark 'windows' along its edge and a
short orange glow or flame emerging from one end. They got out
of their car for a better view and watched in amazement as the
object accelerated from a standing start to a terrific speed in a
startlingly short time. It then hovered for several seconds over a
golf-course before shooting out of sight above the Campsie Hills.

Date: August 1958
Time: Evening
Place: Kuching, Malaysia

Five people, including two government officials, were enjoying
the warm evening and admiring the view over a golf-course
towards Mount Matang when suddenly an orange ball of light
appeared in the west. It was just smaller than the full moon. It
travelled slowly and silently on a horizontal path and pulsated
every few seconds. These pulsations consisted of the object

emitting three 'brackets' of light to the fore and three feathery-white trails to the rear. After a few minutes' passage the object suddenly fell from the sky into the jungle. The authorities launched an investigation and sent an army patrol into the trees but nothing was found. All the witnesses had seen meteors before and said the phenomenon was totally unlike one.

Date: 5 December 1977
Time: Noon
Place: Isle of Dogs, Greater London, England

The witness was working inside a grocery warehouse when a strange object flew in through the large, open doors. It was small and white and the size of a butterfly, but with a kind of jellyish texture. It darted about across the room in swift, evasive motions. At first the witness thought he must be seeing a 'floater' (a piece of dead matter in the eye), but, to his astonishment, the warehouse cat then saw the UFO too. It proceeded to chase the object all over the building, leaping from crate to crate. At one point the thing passed by the man within six feet, giving him a few seconds' perfect view before it simply disappeared into thin air.

These seven accounts are each fascinating in their own way; we could relate others for a few more hundred pages and we would still be far short of exhausting the scope of the testimony. Few specifically describe anything which might reasonably be termed a craft. Indeed one might have to start pondering extraterrestrial midges if one seriously considered the last case to be a piloted device! Usually the label 'atmospheric phenomenon' applies rather better than UFO. It certainly involves less presumption.

Clearly, if even one or two of these stories describe what has actually been observed, with a reasonable degree of accuracy, then there *are* scientific mysteries here. For these phenomena, whatever their explanation, do not appear to be presently understood within the normal province of science. As this collection shows, UFO events have occurred for a very long time (perhaps throughout time) and are seen by all manner of people without warning, in all manner of situations. All that has changed with the times is the cultural context in which we interpret them. It also

shows that UFOs are not restricted to any one nation, but occur
all over the world.

The seven accounts are important for one other reason. In each
case the phenomenon observed has since repeated itself, in
different circumstances and with witnesses who, so far as it is
possible to tell, had no idea that anybody else had previously
reported what they were now seeing. 'Foo fighters' still tail the
occasional aircraft.[2] Mini-UFOs have been reported flying about
inside rooms.[3] The event seen at Glasgow all those years ago was
almost precisely duplicated at Abram, Greater Manchester,
England, in August 1982.[4] And so on for UFO type after UFO
type. This reproducibility of the phenomenon is very significant,
and it is commonly overlooked. Of course, most UFO sightings
do differ from one another. There seem to be many sorts of UFO.
But it is well known too that witnesses tend to add personal
touches to their observations.

Imagine a totally uneducated person interested in the sky. He
may collect reports by witnesses of all the things they see and will
find he has thousands of complicated descriptions which seem to
form a meaningless jumble. When he looks deeper he can sift and
classify, just as ufologists try to do. He may then realize that he
has many reports that refer to clouds – phenomena that vary in
shape but are usually white or grey in colour. He also has reports
of seemingly animate objects that float by, often in groups. These
may be black, brown or sometimes other colours. Occasionally
they make strange noises. These are, of course, birds. In this way
a picture can be built up of all the various phenomena in the sky.
He may then isolate out those which specifically interest him.
Ufology suffers from the same fundamental problems, which
explains its apparent complexity. Some of the things reported as
UFOs are irrelevant, just as birds are unimportant to the meteor-
ologist. Researchers need to sort out these non-UFOs first. The
rest of the data falls into several distinct groups, some of which
may be phenomena whose manifestation is fairly rigid and consis-

[2] See J. Randles, *UFO Reality* (Robert Hale, 1983), pp. 21–4.
[3] See J. Randles, *The Pennine UFO Mystery* (Granada, 1983), pp. 72–3.
[4] *Northern UFO News*, no. 100, Jan./Feb. 1983. See chapter 8 for a description.

tent, whereas others may describe phenomena which are the ufological equivalent of clouds – always changing and only loosely consistent in appearance.

Unfortunately our UFO classifications, based as they often are upon misconceptions, do not aid this quest. To study, as a group, 'UFOs that land' may be very misleading. Our sky-watcher, for example, would find in this category reports of birds, aircraft, helicopters, the setting sun and snowflakes, when snowflakes may be the only thing he is really concerned about. There is much discussion in contemporary ufology about the right classification and strict definition of the term UFO.[5] This is premature and possibly harmful, since to classify on the strength of such incomplete knowledge could lead to much effort being wasted.

The consistencies between different accounts are among the most exciting features of the UFO hunt. They will leap suddenly from the pages of an investigation report, making one backtrack to another case where the same specific detail was recorded. For instance, on the evening of 10 December 1982 a husband and wife had a strange encounter on a country road in the Rossendale Valley, near Bacup, Lancashire, England. The object passed directly overhead on a still, silent night. It looked like two semicircles of white light separated by two bars of red light, so that the whole phenomenon was almost circular, but with flattened sides. This is a precise and unusual description. Not four months later, on 22 March 1983, at almost exactly the same time of day but miles away across the Irish Sea in Lurgan, Northern Ireland, two men (*knowing nothing* of the unpublicized Bacup events) saw an object with 'two rectangular red lights on each side and a large circle of white light between the red lights'. It buzzed them on a country road. The UFO and the situation were virtually identical to those at Bacup. In both cases there were investigations (by the British army at Lurgan) that produced no explanation.[6]

Sometimes the similarities can be even more precise, although the events occur thousands of miles apart. They are all the more interesting if the object described does not seem likely to

---

[5] See *Zetetic Scholar*, nos. 10 and 11, 1983.
[6] *Northern UFO News*, no. 103, July/Aug. 1983, pp. 11–13.

be an atmospheric phenomenon but is much more akin to a physical craft. The following report from Tittensor, Staffordshire, England, in early December 1977 offers a typical illustration. The witness was cattle farmer Arthur Johnson. As he drove along a quiet lane one night at about 9 p.m. he saw two brilliant lights coming towards him across a field. His car window was open but he could hear no sound apart from the engine, so he had to reject the helicopter explanation which first occurred to him. He stopped the car, switched off the engine and got out. Climbing up an embankment, he watched as the object turned towards him and crossed the road, travelling very near the ground and hedge-hopping. It went down the side of the field, turned around a tree and flew out of sight. Johnson had an excellent view of the object. It was light grey, metallic, with a flat base and small, dome-like turret on top. This top was transparent but with struts down it. In the centre of the base was a grill-like device. Light emerged from two spots – the dome and the grill – projecting forward in beams. Despite its passing very close to him, he heard no sound.[7]

This is a well-observed close encounter, but when you look at it in conjunction with the following account it becomes fascinating. This sighting happened at a similar time of night (9.30 p.m.), at nearly the same time of year (late November) and also on a country road. But it took place four years after the Tittensor events, in 1981, at Marshall, Texas, USA. This time there were two occupants of the car – Dale Spurlock and his girlfriend. They too saw a bright light heading towards them, which then resolved into two forward-projecting beams. These came from an object moving so low down that it was hedge-hopping. Eventually they stopped their vehicle for a closer sight and the UFO tilted towards them before moving off. It changed direction sharply, keeping low. It made no noise at all.[8] As the witness sketch shows, the Texas and Tittensor UFOs are almost identical, certainly within the limits of observer error. All the previously noted features crop up again: flat bottom, small turret-like dome, grill-

[7] *FSR*, vol. 24, no. 3, 1978, p. 29.

[8] *International UFO Reporter*, May/June 1982, pp. 5–7. Spurlock's girlfriend wished to remain anonymous and did not talk to investigators about the experience.

like patches at the base and lights shining through the transparency of the turret. The colour was the same and the estimated size in both cases was similar.

Such remarkable similarities do not happen frequently but they certainly occur often enough for the alert ufologist to feel fairly sure that some real object is being seen in different places. (The ufologist cannot draw any conclusions about just what that object is, of course, but coincidence seems a feeble explanation.) The only alternatives are either that some psychological effect is involved, or that information about UFOs is very widely spread so that people imagine things in similar ways. Closer investigation of reports is necessary, but it is unscientific to dismiss the likelihood that Arthur Johnson and Dale Spurlock, and all the others in similar circumstances, just happened to observe the same basic phenomenon. In effect that would mean that UFOs are real.

One can range other evidence against disbelief in UFOs. Animal disturbance, for instance, where the consistent behaviour displayed by wildlife and domestic animals (dogs in particular) argues strongly that they are responding to a truly anomalous event. Gordon Creighton researched the connection between animal disturbance and UFOs, compiling statistics for over 200 cases recorded before 1970. Of these 50.9 per cent involved dogs, with horses the second most commonly affected animals (15.6 per cent), and other cases concerned sheep, cats, birds etc. (even an elephant!). Typical was a Canadian case which occurred on the morning of 19 February 1968. A glowing object (almost certainly a UAP (see p. 88)) hovered over an electrical transformer and caused a mild electric shock to the skin of a woman farmer nearby. A high-pitched hum or whining noise was emitted and the farm dog suffered greatly, apparently much more upset by this noise than by electricity. It cowered on the frozen ground and desperately tried to protect its ears by pawing snow over them.[9]

There is also evidence of gross physical effects on witnesses. There are now dozens of cases on file where witnesses have had to go into hospital following a close encounter. Burns, nausea and other ill effects, often thought to be like radiation sickness, are

---

[9] A summarized case catalogue of the reports was published in *FSR*, vol. 18, no. 3, 1970, and for the following two years.

common symptoms displayed in such circumstances. One of the
classic cases of severe witness disability resulting from a UFO
close encounter involved prospector Stephen Michalak. He was
inspecting a quartz vein near Falcon Lake, Canada, on 20 May
1967, when a dome-shaped object landed nearby. He claims that
he went right up to it and inspected 'machinery' inside what he
imagined to be a secret experimental aircraft. 'Warm air' was
radiating from it and a painful purple (ultra-violet?) light was
emitted. Stepping back in panic, he accidentally put his gloved
hand on to the metal surface of the 'craft' and his glove partially
melted. Then a searing blast of hot air came from a vent beside
him as the object rose into the sky (leaving a smell like ozone in
the air). His shirt and undershirt caught fire from the blast and he
had to tear these off.

After struggling back to civilization Michalak was taken to the
general hospital at Winnipeg, where he was found to have a
substantial burn-mark on his chest. This was photographed and
treated and is consistent with the checked pattern of his undershirt. Michalak was in hospital for several weeks (having to be
readmitted later). He displayed symptoms of nausea, tiredness,
weight loss and muscular pains. Doctors thought he might be
suffering from mild radiation poisoning, especially when a temporary change in his blood lymphocyte count was recorded. But
his illness cleared of its own accord and no explanation was
found.[10]

There *are* photographs, cine films, physical traces on the
ground, radar trackings and other direct evidence implying the
existence of a real anomaly.[11] To be fair, this evidence is nothing
like as substantial as UFO enthusiasts might hope, but it nevertheless exists, and cannot be wished away by the sceptic who
insists upon total honesty. It is in keeping with essentially rare
phenomena.

Finally, we might consider the extremely useful 'experimental
situations' which have occurred. These involve the chance introduction into the environment of a strange phenomenon which can

[10] See the account of the investigation by Chris Rutkowski in 'The Falcon
Lake Incident', *FSR,* vol. 27, nos. 1, 2 and 3, 1981.
[11] See 'A Critical Look at the Physical Evidence' in Randles, *UFO Reality.*

be witnessed by many (who think it is a UFO), and yet whose real nature is known to researchers. Principally we find bright fireball meteors or satellite-debris re-entries in this category. In 1968 a Russian Zond satellite booster re-entered the atmosphere over the USA. Scientists studied eyewitness reports of it. This was one of the earliest re-entries to occur and so likely to have been one of the least understood by the ordinary person. Yet the results were broadly similar to those found ten years later when the booster from Cosmos 1068, another Russian satellite, came back in spectacular fashion on New Year's Eve over Great Britain.[12] Various studies demonstrate that eyewitnesses generally describe the phenomenon well. Certain factors are badly gauged, e.g. height, size and speed, but the description of the appearance of the stimulus, in most cases, is close to reality, though varying in details. Very few, even mild, associated effects were recorded: nobody suffered burns; no motor-car engines and lights failed; and no animals had their personalities altered. Hundreds of witnesses gave a fairly accurate picture of the essence of the event. If we extrapolate this to the data of genuinely puzzling UFO reports it implies that the evidence is, at least often, closely aligned with the reality of the original stimulus.

UFOs, in some form or another, do exist. Therefore ufology, the study of UFOs, is a valid area of scientific exploration.

---

[12] *Zond IV:* Condon (ed.), *The Scientific Study of UFOs* (Bantam Press, 1969), pp. 571–7. Cosmos 1068: Randles, *UFO Reality*, pp. 44–9.

3

The Official Line:
Science in the Shadows

*Our consultant panel stated that these solutions would
probably be found on the margins, or just beyond, the
frontiers of our present knowledge in the fields of atmospheric
and extraterrestrial phenomena . . .*

Part of a secret report sent by the Office of Special
Investigations to the CIA (September 1952)

The history of official UFO study throughout the world would fill
a large book on its own. It would be quite a tale, involving as it
does political manœuvrings, intrigue, allegations of cover-up and
sometimes panic at the highest of levels. We only have room here
for a basic outline, but the area is an important one, because,
first, these projects (especially those involving the US government) have had a profound effect on scientific and public attitudes. Indeed the current status of the subject is dictated in large
part by decisions taken many years ago in the upper echelons of
the US government, often with scientific considerations the very
last thing on their minds! Second, it must be realized that these
government projects frequently do involve scientists, as consultants, debunkers and (it has to be said) occasionally as puppets
through whom the official version of the truth is expressed. This
last statement may sound rather extreme, but it can be amply
supported by the reams of official documentation which has
recently come into the open thanks to the Freedom of Information Act in the USA.

What might seem undue emphasis will be laid on the USA in
the following pages. This should certainly not be taken to mean

that official UFO study programmes have not been initiated in many countries. Undoubtedly they have, but, generally speaking, we know little about them. The Soviet Union for instance is known to have taken measures such as official suppression of private UFO groups. Such research as there may be remains under strict state control. What they have discovered through this process may be known to certain Western intelligence authorities, but any comment on our part would be mere speculation. China, on the other hand, has emerged as a very open-minded nation in this area. Over the past few years it has expanded its research into UFOs, although this work is very much in its infancy.[1]

As for other Western countries, they seem to have followed the USA's lead. Until recently they have not initiated much activity on their own. It is crucial to realize that in almost every instance UFOs are treated as a defence matter, in other words as unidentified aircraft. In the current state of international relations, were an enemy to invade, its unfamiliar aircraft might possibly be reported as UFOs. In view of the world's political situation it is reasonable to anticipate that western European countries would fall in with whatever plans their US allies determined, as Europe's defence has to a certain extent been handed over to the USA. It would be rather naïve to assume that there have not been discussions and mutual agreements between NATO countries on the subject of UFOs. Whether or not UFOs exist, *per se*, really has little to do with this, because UFO reports certainly *do* exist and in great abundance. In military terms a UFO report is as significant as any UFO which may or may not lie behind it (see p. 42).

France

France is probably the one developed nation in Europe which does not toe the US line so markedly. We shall look a little later

[1] See G. Creighton, 'The Development of Ufology in Russia', *FSR*, vol. 27, nos. 3, 4 and 5 1982; Paul Dong, *The Four Mysteries of Mainland China* (Prentice-Hall, 1984).

(see p. 61) at the world's only openly government-funded and scientifically staffed UFO project which operates on a permanent basis.

(see p. 61)

Britain

It is not known when government investigations of UFOs began in Britain, but ufologists have spoken to many witnesses who claim to have had significant encounters (often involving radar tracking or aircraft interception) while they were in the armed services, and were interviewed about them. This strongly indicates that some authority was responsible for UFO investigations at least as far back as 1948. Usually the participants were reminded of the British Official Secrets Act, and told not to discuss what had happened to them. Thinking that they had observed our own secret weaponry, a good many of them complied. It is quite likely that dozens of impressive UFO events have not been reported to ufologists or publicized in the press because of this, in view of the number which have emerged despite such obstacles.

Officially, the Ministry of Defence has a small clerical unit which deals with UFO reports, department DS8 (standing for Defence Secretariat). It is in fact primarily responsible for other types of air incident, such as complaints about low-flying military jets. DS8 staff receive reports of UFOs direct from the public and from police stations, civil and military airports and other governmental bodies. They claim that their files date back only to 1962 and that therefore there is no information on the radar cases, the interceptor jet incidents and other military contacts referred to above. Nor is there apparently any file on the many publicly admitted cases, such as one of August 1956 when there were multiple radar echoes and ground and airborne sightings. It is possible that some other government agency (or several agencies) has these files. Certainly it would seem odd that no record is kept of such major events. But then the MOD may very well not regard many reports for filing as 'UFOs'. There may be files somewhere for 'anomalous radar returns' or 'transient atmospheric events' – and one wonders just how claims of strange alien entities might be recorded!

The following is a typical example of the sort of incident the MOD says it has no file about. This is quoted from an official US Air Force reference, suggesting that some information at least was collected in the past: 'Then, on November 3 [1953], about 2.30 in the afternoon, radar in the London area again picked up targets. This time two Vampire jets were scrambled and the pilots saw "a strange aerial object". The men at the radar site saw it too; through their telescope it looked like a "flat, white-coloured tennis ball".'[2]

The public relations efforts of the MOD have always been low-key, and some would doubtless term them inept. Statements about UFOs have rarely been proffered and witnesses writing to the MOD (reporting something they consider to be of significance to national security or at least of potential interest to it) commonly receive either no reply or simply a stock response. The wording of this response has hardly changed over the years. Here is the September 1978 version:

I regret, however, that I cannot help you over the incident you mention. We are grateful for the reports sent to us and these are referred to specialist authorities in the department to see if they have any bearing on the defence of this country. But we are unable to carry out investigation beyond our defence interest either to establish the positive identity of the object seen or to treat unidentified flying objects as the subject of independent study. I should add that investigations over a number of years have so far produced no evidence that UFOs represent a threat to the air defences of this country.

On the one level – a departmental one – this reply is reasonable. After all the MOD is charged with our defence, not with finding out what UFOs are, if they prove not to be of relevance to that defence. Where this acceptable position has fallen down is in the authorities' apparent insensitivity to there being a problem worthy of investigation. Their own figures (which show many thousands of examined reports) refer to 10 per cent of them as unexplained.[3] If the system used for investigation is as arbitrary

---

[2] E. Ruppelt, *The Report on Unidentified Flying Objects* (Ace Books, 1956), p. 310.

[3] J. Randles, *FSR,* vol. 24, no. 3, 1978.

as that adopted by the US Air Force (where any vaguely feasible answer is taken as an identification) or even just as inadequate as the MOD's own statement admits it to be, then this 10 per cent will be the *minimum* figure. Indeed in an interview with us in August 1983 it was admitted that these UFO/IFO statistics are meaningless and that they had stopped issuing them for that reason.

Considering the quality of the reports that flood into the authorities, at the rate of many hundreds a year, it seems somewhat baffling (especially to the worried or frightened witness) to find that the government professes no interest. Indeed, David Mason, who, with his family, saw a UFO in South Wales in October 1982, wrote a report which was passed to the MOD. In March 1984 he told the British newspaper, the *Observer,* that 'I do not understand how the Ministry of Defence could have investigated the case without contacting me with further queries.' This response was generated because the MOD, admitting to the possession of a report on the case, told the newspaper, 'we are satisfied that there were no defence implications.'[4] What this effectively comes down to is the official line: a UFO (whatever one of those is) can come down on top of your car, cut out its engine and lights, burn your skin, possibly leave radiation traces and then zip off into the night, and so long as it can be reasonably concluded that it has not come to invade us then no government body is interested. Many people find that position either very hard to believe or, if true, then very unsatisfactory.

Fortunately there seems to have been a small change in attitudes since the late 1970s (which quite possibly relates to events in the USA which we will shortly discuss). It began when countries such as Italy and Spain began to offer military case histories (usually involving radar tracking and jet-plane chases) to rather amazed UFO investigators. Certain officials of these governments also made public statements on the subject. One Italian general suggested that there had been a global study programme which had proved the reality of UFOs and that the world would soon be told the truth. A Spanish minister of transport ventured his view that there was now no doubt that UFOs were real. This

[4] *Observer,* 4 March 1984.

last pronouncement followed a case where a UFO forced a civil jet liner to make an unscheduled landing, the said UFO having been tracked on radar and chased by air-force planes. After these revelations there was a sudden turnaround in Australia. Veteran ufologist Bill Chalker was advised that he could visit the Air Force offices where he would be cleared to see all the UFO files. In early 1982 he made the first of several visits and was positively encouraged to report on their content to the UFO community. They contained fascinating material.[5] The Freedom of Information Act passed in Australia for 1983 implementation was probably instrumental in this decision.

However, all this was happening during a period when the number of UFO events reported all over the world seemed to have fallen to an all-time low. The *Daily Express* newspaper carried a story from Italy, where ufologists were decrying the lack of cases, apparently unaware that in Great Britain reports received by the British UFO Research Association (BUFORA) had fallen from 700 in 1977 to almost 200 in 1979, and to just 60 in 1982. This change seems likely to be significant and some UFO experts are eager to link it with alterations in government policy. Yet MOD figures for their investigations in the period do *not* show this trend. Aside from one year (1982), when the figure dropped below 300 cases, the total varied between 390 and 600 – exactly as it had in all previous years. This is a curious anomaly, probably suggesting that the true number of UFO experiences has *not* gone down, although public desire to report them to the media or UFO societies has.

Has there been any change in Great Britain? The MOD have been rather inconsistent. Jenny Randles has been urging the MOD to release their files since 1978, pointing out that they themselves do not see the reports of UFO events as a defence matter, but a scientific one. She reminded them that the withholding of information enhanced people's suspicions that they were party to a cover-up, and if that was not true the best way to demonstrate it was to 'come clean'. However, they refused her suggestion that in future people with reports of experiences

---

[5] A complete summary is provided by Chalker in *UFO Research Australia Newsletter*, vol. 4, no. 2, 1983.

should be referred to a scientific institute rather than the MOD. No doubt they feared that they might miss just the one case that did have 'defence implications'. They also commented that the cases ufologists talk about are in a different league to those which interest the MOD; however when they were offered examples of much stranger cases than any they professed to hold, they declined to investigate.

In late 1982, Jenny received a most unexpected reply to one of her letters. The MOD informed her that they *had* now decided to make the reports generally available. The department was considering the best way to do this, an operation which might take a little while as there were thousands of reports. This news was withheld from the media for fear that press attention might lead to a reversal in policy. The MOD more recently told us that the policy had not changed. They added that the MOD 'certainly has no evidence that alien spacecraft have landed on this planet'. To justify this claim several sample reports were enclosed!

In releasing reports rather than files, the MOD avoid giving the public access to any policy outlines which might exist. The ones we received are disappointing: they contain no investigation and evaluation data and consist merely of several lines of information recording the bare bones of an observation. It is hardly conceivable that they would be considered adequate to judge matters of potential importance to national defence.

A few other similar MOD 'reports' emerged during 1983 and 1984, although there is now no sign of any move to release all the data. In fact, when the *Observer* decided to run a story about the MOD policy on UFOs, and were assisted in this by us, they found the MOD were talking of only releasing selected reports to *bona fide* inquirers. However, the shift in attitude expressed by the release of *any* reports was good news for those interested in the scientific study of UFOs. While the MOD data would be of limited value to anyone undertaking detailed research, it would have some merit, and it would be important if only to diminish the unnecessary secrecy which governments seem to find so valuable when considering UFOs.

However, the latest MOD statement offered to Jenny Randles as this book went to press is disturbing. A reversal of policy seems to have occurred. Lack of money to undertake the extensive

editing of the thousands of files available for release is given as
explanation for a decision *not* to release anything further. Yet, at
the same time, Ralph Noyes, a former head of the DS8 'UFO'
department at the MOD, has become a public supporter of the
UFO movement. His speculative novel *A Secret Property* (to be
published in 1985 by Quartet Books) is based on the premiss,
which he has since discussed with us, that the major world powers
are guilty of a cover-up because they are quite simply baffled by
UFOs. Noyes claims personal knowledge of certain aspects of this
conspiracy, including the withholding of many probative cases
from the public and scientists. These apparently include gun-
camera movie films of numerous strange luminous objects which
were taken from RAF jets. The phenomena (which in his view
are more likely to be atmospheric UAPs than exotic UFOs) have
demonstrated remarkable abilities and are being treated as of
potential value to military scientists – they are seen as the
'property' of the military.

UFOs and Defence

In order to comprehend why it is assumed that UFOs must be
dealt with as a security matter, we must go back to the days
immediately after the Kenneth Arnold sighting above Washington State, USA. Such was the press sensation about this and
hundreds of other sightings which followed it that no government
could have withstood the pressure to investigate. With the second
world war only 20 months in the past, and the nightmare slip-up
of Pearl Harbour still vivid in many minds, the UFOs were seen
as a great potential threat, and so instantly given priority as a
security matter. The still unexplained 'Foo fighters' (pacing wartime aircraft) and the spate of ghost rockets in Europe immediately after the end of the war must have had an effect on those
who determined US military policy. It was strongly suspected that
they, and thus by inference the newly reported 'flying discs', were
Russian weapons of an advanced design, probably captured from
the Nazis who were, of course, noted for their proficiency at
making weapons of destruction. To worried military chiefs the
timing and behaviour of these UFOs were just too coincidental,

and this thought totally dominated all thinking during the first few post-war months. This is where the cover-up originated. Nobody was seriously speculating about what the discs might be, but everybody in authority was seriously concerned about what it was widely believed they were.

As intelligence officer Edward J. Ruppelt, later to head the US Air Force secret UFO project, said when he left the service, 'there is a world-wide interest in flying saucers; people want to know the facts. But more often than not these facts have been obscured by secrecy and confusion, a situation that has led to wild speculation on one end of the scale and an almost dangerously blasé attitude on the other.'[6] With commendable honesty Ruppelt set out the facts as he saw them in a book published in 1956. He described military consternation about an unknown phenomenon apparently able to fly about in our air-space at will. He said: 'the public also is entitled to know the details.'[7] But within a few years, he made a rather odd and radical about-face, completely altering key statements in a reprint of his book. He died soon afterwards without contributing further to the UFO debates. Dr J. Allen Hynek, who worked with all the US Air Force UFO project leaders, told us that he wished Ruppelt had lived longer and continued to contribute to ufology. He could have done a lot of good. But at least he left behind one of the classics of the UFO literature in the first edition of his book.

The USA

Ruppelt's memoirs have assisted us considerably in putting together the following history of official UFO study in the USA. We have also used the extensive files from the various Air Force projects, made available through the 1977 US Freedom of Information Act. That same act has also been used to squeeze out documents on UFOs held by the CIA and the FBA. Many more are still held, as are files at other agencies such as the NSA (National Security Agency). Attempts have been made to obtain

[6] Ruppelt, *Report*, pp. 5–6.
[7] Ibid., p. 25.

these by a band of pioneers (including lawyers and scientists) who call themselves CAUS (Citizens Against UFO Secrecy). So far they have achieved little – most documents are still retained 'on grounds of national security'. The NSA files went as far as the US Supreme Court in 1982 but the application for their release was rejected because it would have had too great an impact on national security. The security-cleared judge made his ruling after seeing not the 130-plus documents admitted to, as is usually the case, but 21 pages giving reasons for withholding them! One might wonder just what the files themselves contain if it takes 21 pages to justify not releasing them. This affidavit was applied for under the Act and it was eventually obtained in a 'sanitized' form. It is an amazing document. It consists largely of deletions. The only significant thing one can find among the thick black lines is the NSA advice that the speculations of their agents on the UFO phenomenon were so controversial that if released and then proved wrong the credibility of the NSA might suffer. It seems reasonable to wonder what it is that causes security agents from one of the most sophisticated investigatory bodies in the world to make such extreme speculations about UFOs that they are afraid to make them public.

Project Sign

Study by the US government of UFOs (then called flying discs) was conducted in a very haphazard manner during 1947. But a memorandum to the Pentagon from Lieutenant-General Nathan F. Twining, in charge of the UFO data collection, dated 23 September, stating that 'the phenomenon reported is something real and not visionary or fictitious', led to high-level orders for an evaluatory project that would be given top-security rating. Project Sign came to life on 22 January 1948. The project already had some preliminary statistical data to work with. As early as July 1947 (just a month after Kenneth Arnold's sighting) an Air Force evaluation of 16 cases had been produced internally. This inevitably had some effect on the policy of Sign, even though it was kept secret until 1977. Indeed both the Twining memo and the detailed results of Sign were kept secret for many years. The July 1947 appraisal listed certain typical characteristics for the phenomena investigated, which included a metallic, disc-like object which moved with snaking motions. It concluded that 'Something is really flying around.' Sign seems to have taken its work very seriously and contacted the FBI (and no doubt other security bodies) to assist in the assessment of witness credibility. As a memo to the FBI (dated 4 February 1948) put the matter, 'Reports will be classified *at least* confidential.' No subsequent FBI memos for the year 1948 have been released. As far as Sign is concerned this is officially the sum total of their dealings with that security agency.

Sign called in several scientists to help them weed out cases of mistaken identity. A principal one was J. Allen Hynek, then a young astronomer from Ohio State University. Hynek admits that throughout this first project (which occupied much of 1948) he was a complete sceptic. He would try his hardest to find an answer (any answer) for every case, although if he found a report that was not explicable in astronomical terms he was willing to say so. Slowly it became clear to Hynek that some very remarkable things were being seen. This fact had struck home with the military leaders involved with Sign. The implausibility of the discs being foreign secret weapons had quickly been demonstrated, for what country would test such devices over enemy territory in such a brazen fashion? And this was but one consideration. On 7 January, Air Force Captain Thomas Mantell died from oxygen starvation as his plane climbed too high in pursuit of a large metallic object towards which he had been directed. He saw it; countless people on the ground saw it; air traffic controllers saw it – all in broad daylight. A hasty identification of the object as the planet Venus (with which Hynek never agreed) was issued by Sign in order to alleviate public fears. Much later a far more likely explanation emerged when the US Navy finally got round to telling the Air Force that they had been testing a classified balloon in the area. This did appear large and metallic. No doubt the incident much benefited inter-service liaison, especially in future dealings regarding UFOs, but the clarification came too late to save a needless death.[8] This fiasco so early in the life of

[8] Ibid., pp. 46–56. The Blue Book file on the case is summarized in B. Steiger, *Project Blue Book* (Ballantine Books, 1976), pp. 43–62.

Project Sign did little to aid public relations. There was inevitable ridicule of the frankly ludicrous claim that Venus had been the culprit. In mid-afternoon it just would not have been visible against a bright blue sky, let alone visible as a large metallic object! Talk of a cover-up for more sinister reasons for the crash became common. Much nonsense was talked about death rays disintegrating the metal structure of Mantell's plane. The truth was that there had indeed been a cover-up, but it happened through ignorance, rather than through any extraordinary knowledge. This was the first serious mistake the US government made.

Six months later, on 24 July, two aircrew on an Eastern Airlines DC-3 civil aircraft had a close encounter with a cigar-shaped UFO from which flames spouted. This nearly produced a mid-air disaster over Macon, Georgia. Despite sceptical suggestions that a meteor might have been responsible, Hynek and Sign decided otherwise. Ruppelt later commented, 'this report shook them worse than the Mantell incident.' For this had been 'the first time two reliable sources had really been close enough to anything resembling a UFO [to] get a good look and live to tell . . .'

The consequence of this, and the many less startling reports coming through to Sign, was an 'Estimate of Situation', written by staff from the project in August 1948 and given a 'Top Secret' rating. The team of military men and scientists now had no doubts that UFOs were real objects, and after dismissing the secret weapons hypothesis only two other ideas seemed viable. One was that all reports were mistaken perceptions of mundane things. Yet those cases which stood up to intense investigation seemed to refute this. So the other one seemed the only alternative and formed the basis of Sign's 'Estimate'. They suggested that UFOs were spaceships. This secret study went all the way to the top. It reached the Chief of Staff, General Hoyt S. Vandenberg, who refused to accept the conclusions without proof. A group from Project Sign actually went to the Pentagon to try to persuade him of the strength of their evidence. But Vandenberg would not budge. Soon afterwards the report was incinerated, except for a copy or two kept covertly by Sign. During the final few weeks of the project the Sign staff felt demoralized by this rejection of their findings. Their depression deepened when an

apparently classic case, involving multiple witnesses and an Air
Force pilot fighting a 'battle in the sky' with a lighted UFO,
crumbled upon investigation. The UFO turned out to be a
balloon. Even once-committed believers now began to wonder
whether, with hindsight, all the other 'classic' cases might not also
crumble. The life of a UFO investigator, swinging between belief
and scepticism according to the strength of each new case, remains just as difficult four decades later.

The final report of Project Sign was published in February
1949.[9] Of 243 cases analysed they considered 20 per cent to be
unexplained. The sightings were divided into four specific UFO
types (discs, cigars, spheres and balls of light) – thus generating
the first useful classification scheme. The fact that all four of these
UFO categories remain applicable in 1984 says something about
the consistency of the basic phenomenon. The report makes
interesting reading, especially when one understands the effect
the rejected 'Estimate' must have had on it. A lengthy appendix
by Dr J. E. Lipp of the Rand Corporation analysed the presumed
characteristics of an extra-terrestrial spaceship. This is of some
value in a historical, pre-space-age sense. But he concluded that
'the actions attributed to the "flying objects" . . . seem inconsistent with the requirements for space travel.' A rather technical
study of the flight capabilities of the various types of reported
UFO was also included, with various speculations about exotic
modes of propulsion (including anti-gravity). In all sections of the
report the spaceship hypothesis dominates, but it concludes that
present evidence is insufficient to prove or disprove this and adds,
'It is unlikely that positive proof of their existence will be obtained without examination of the remains of the crashed objects.'
The report ends by calling for more study of the psychological
process of misidentification and of the nature of ball lightning and
for better education in such things for military personnel. Overall
it recommends that proper (and full-time) study into the UFO
question be continued.

[9] The report is reproduced in ibid., pp. 170–216.

Project Grudge

On 11 February 1949, Grudge took over from Sign in the attempt to come to grips with the UFO phenomenon. Hynek stayed on as chief science consultant, but he was unsure of his position. He knew he must follow orders or be removed from the team. This had happened to many of those responsible for the pro-spaceship 'Estimate of situation' just six months before. Hynek tells us that the orders given to the project were to explain everything, even if a solution had to be forced onto a case. Ruppelt admits: 'Everything was being evaluated on the premise that UFOs could not exist.' This difference between Sign and Grudge is obviously significant. Some see hints that Vandenberg did *not* reject the results of the first project. Once it had been concluded that UFOs were even probably extraterrestrial it is quite likely that any real government study would have been made top secret. (Indeed, Canadian nuclear physicist Stanton Friedman argues that a classification above top secret exists for just such things. He tells us it is called 'cosmic'!) The aim of such secrecy would be to deflect both private scientific interest and potential research by hostile foreign powers. For the US government the potential military and technological advantage of amazingly advanced craft would be obvious. Grudge could thus be seen as nothing but a public-relations exercise to help create the illusion that the USA did not have any belief or interest in UFOs.

Of course, it is possible that the opposite decision was taken at high level: to get rid of the UFO problem at any cost. This too would explain the debunking. But it is difficult to equate this with the recently published results of the first project. In the circumstances of 1948–9, such a premature assessment (contrary to the recommendations of its own science researchers) would have been so risky for the US military that it almost seems unthinkable. Either an extraordinarily naïve mistake was made or UFO study *did* go below ground, probably without the staff of Grudge realizing that they had been set up as public-relations dummies. Some people began to suspect that this was the case (especially a few pioneer journalists) because the incoming data continued to build up and improve in quality. To conceive of the powers that be (who had to be aware of the sort of reports the newspapers were receiving) really ignoring it all seemed hard to accept. A retired major from the Marines, Donald Keyhoe, was familiar with military policy and had experience of UFO close encounters, both his own and other people's. He knew how the government responded. Through many books and articles he began a campaign against the cover-up. But he challenged Grudge, and its successors, which was almost certainly a mistake. He was arguing with people who knew little (if any) more than he did about any hypothetical secret study. They would follow policy and honestly deny the charges. He would see this as more evidence of a cover-up. They would then respond by casting Keyhoe in the role of credulous paranoiac. That all this is no fairy story is suggested by later CIA memos which refer to investigation dossiers, not just on Keyhoe (although he figures a good deal in them) but on 'key members of some of these [saucer] societies which have been instrumental in keeping the flying saucer craze before the public'.[10]

Once the cover-up began, and assuming there were no easy answers and continuing research merely made UFO study seem more complex, the arrival of protagonists like Keyhoe can only have dug the hole deeper. Initially, the pushing of the UFO mystery into the secret hiding places of government was done for basically honest and sensible reasons. This was a time of a very frosty 'cold war' and the aim was to get to the truth first. It is highly unlikely that any remarkable knowledge was being hidden, as the UFO enthusiasts claimed. But the cover-up became self-perpetuating, because the primary reasons for it came to be overlooked. The government could hardly admit that they knew something big was going on but had no idea what that something was. This would have only brought new allegations that they were *still* covering up!

Consider two released FBI memos, from 31 January and 14 March 1949, the time when Grudge was taking charge. While the FBI deny even today that they had active involvement in ufology, the first memo, from Project Sign, thanks them for their help on

[10] From a briefing to the CIA by the OSI (Air Force Office of Special Investigation), August 1952.

investigations! The later memo states that the UFO question 'is of sufficient importance to the internal security of the country that our field officers should secure as much information as possible'. The first memo is particularly important because it is a report on a regular intelligence conference on the subject of UFOs. It was held by the Air Force, with the FBI in attendance. Many sightings near 'vital installations' are noted and it states that 'this matter is considered top secret by intelligence officers of both the Army and the Air Force.' How can this be related to official policy which said that UFO reports were nonsense?

Accepting that Grudge operated under grave restrictions, what does it have to tell us? Its final report was produced very quickly – it was published on 30 April 1949. A summary was not made available to the media until December, and then it contained some interesting subtle emphasis. The most crucial fact (that 23 per cent of the reports were unexplained) was *not* mentioned. This was *more* than the previous project had found, despite the stricter controls. If anything was an indication that UFOs were a problem this surely was it, but few people spotted the fact, particularly since Grudge suggested to the Air Force that interest in UFOs should be reduced to a routine level because no evidence of a defence threat was indicated by the data. (This is precisely the line adopted by the British government more than three decades later.)

Any journalist who came to the Air Force at this time would be helped, provided he agreed to write an article that followed the debunking policy. But, as Ruppelt points out, this was never easy because 'All of the writers who were after saucer stories had made their own investigations of sightings and we couldn't convince them they were wrong.' When someone did agree to toe the line, the policy, again according to Ruppelt, was, 'I was continually being told to "tell them about the sighting reports we've solved – don't mention the unknowns".' Grudge was most adept at not mentioning the unknowns.

The final report did contain the studies requested by Project Sign on psychological factors and ball lightning. The psychological study is of little value, simply describing various types of possible misperception which could be found in standard textbooks. The ball-lightning paper, written by the US Department of Commerce Weather Bureau, is more useful.[11] It summarizes most of the features exhibited by this curious electrical phenomenon and suggests the sort of physical characteristics to look for, including electromagnetic interference and physiological effects on witnesses. These were not yet common in the UFO records (indeed mostly unheard-of) and yet they are now seen to be a part of the typical close-encounter report. In some respects this can therefore be seen as ufology's first scientifically predictive paper. Reading it in conjunction with subsequent cases must presumably have persuaded scientists involved in the official projects that certain UFO events *were* rare atmospheric phenomena.

Hynek was chiefly responsible for the statistical evaluation of the project reports. To his credit he reached the obvious conclusion from the increased percentage of unknowns. He recommended Grudge be upgraded and improved. He made his first in a long line of proposals for scientific methodology. But, to the Air Force's discredit, and not a few people's disbelief, they shut down the whole project. At least that is what they told the public.

Project Twinkle

You might be wondering by this point why the Air Force projects apparently sat around waiting for UFO reports to come to them. Why did they not try to conduct some kind of field research to obtain the hard data which the various project conclusions were all bemoaning the lack of? Well, the fact is that they did. Project Twinkle was another secret study (although this was so secret it was not known about outside the upper levels of government). Twinkle was an instrumentally aided field study into a recurrent type of UFO event. Our knowledge of it comes from papers released under the Freedom of Information Act, but it has been difficult to find out much, such as precise dates of its starting or closing down.

Sightings were very specific and very localized. The UFOs became known as 'green fireballs' and were seen almost exclusively in and around New Mexico. As this was the home of the

---

[11] The final report from Grudge is reproduced in Steiger, *Project Blue Book*, pp. 239–50.

atomic-weapons programme, with sensitive installations such as Los Alamos, military concern was great. In November 1948, when the first reports came in, the theory was that they were flares, because of their appearance and short duration. But a UFO was seen on 5 December by many witnesses, including aircrew, and the sighting led to the recruitment of Dr Lincoln La Paz, a meteor expert from the University of New Mexico. La Paz and his team decided that if they collected all the reports and made accurate plots on to a map they could trace the path of any fireball and find the spot where it must have hit the ground. Then they could go out and look for it. They had successfully used such techniques on many occasions with meteor impacts, and the 5 December reports, collected after many hours of interviewing and trekking, were ideal for their methods. They plotted the assumed impact points and went there – again and again. They found nothing. La Paz began to doubt that they were dealing with meteors.

A 31 January 1949 FBI memo describes a distillation of the numerous reports. They tended to move from east to west (La Paz later told Hynek north to south). Their mean speed was 7.5 miles per second and their estimated height was 6–10 miles. They looked like bright-green lights, about one-quarter the size of the full moon. A spectrum from one had been obtained. It indicated 'a copper compound of the type known to be used in rocket experiments'. Already 'some nine scientific reasons' (not elaborated) were known to exist as to why the phenomena were not meteors. However, their frequency and unusual vivid-green coloration were themselves probably good enough grounds for suspicion. La Paz had by this point suggested they were either man-made or new natural phenomena. In early 1949 La Paz saw one himself and recorded the colour as green/yellow, with an estimated wavelength of about 5,218 angstrom units. At a meeting on 22 March 1949 'higher military authorities' apparently advised the FBI that a new wave of sightings was imminent (how did they know?) and that the fireballs were considered to be unknown natural phenomena, although they were termed 'unconventional aircraft' in the heading of the report itself!

A rather novel UFO conference was then held at Los Alamos to consider what to do. It was attended by staff members from the

Air Force project, intelligence officers and many scientists, including La Paz and other famous names such as Dr Edward Teller (atom-bomb physicist) and Dr Joseph Kaplan (expert on the physics of the upper atmosphere). As Ruppelt remarks, 'This was one conference where there was no need to discuss whether or not this special type of UFO, the green fireball, existed. Almost everyone at the meeting had seen one.'[12] For two days La Paz tried to convince those present that the phenomenon could not be natural. He cited several aspects, including the flat trajectory and unusual colours. His case was apparently well argued but not probative. The Air Force Geophysical Research Division was given a somewhat belated directive to mount a study project, but it did not begin until a year later.

Land-Air Incorporated (a geological surveying firm) were contracted to set up a round-the-clock watch for a six month period between 1 April and 15 September 1950. This involved two electronically linked cine cameras, each with a clock and the angle of tilt superimposed on the frame as the film was shot. The independently located cameras both tracked the same object; theoretically, this would give valuable information about flight path and velocity. The peak of fireball activity had passed over a year before, but there had been a group of reports of sightings near Vaughn. So the equipment was set up there. On 24 May around ten objects were seen and photographed. Again on 31 August 'much film was expended'. But on neither occasion were the results analysed to produce information about speed and direction. Spectrum gratings for the cameras were available but hardly used, as the military personnel who were trained to use them had been sent to the Korean War. Equipment was available to measure electromagnetic frequency, but this was never used because the irregularity of the events seemed not to justify it. During the six-month period visual observation of green fireballs continued sporadically but the centre of observed activity was shifting about 150 miles to the vicinity of Holloman Air Force Base. The contract was extended to run from 1 October 1950 to 31 March 1951, with the equipment in the new location. The

---

[12] Ruppelt, *Report*, pp. 66–78.

fireballs then stopped appearing at Holloman and no new results were obtained.

After this failure Project Twinkle seems to have dwindled away, although it is hard to say, as only scattered documents have been retrieved. Putting them together is a major task. From what we know it seems likely that the degree of scientific competence, or the resources available, were inadequate, because no correlations between filmed objects and those verbally recorded by eyewitnesses at look-out sites were ever attempted. This basic and potentially important step was not taken because, apparently, the work would have taken several days!

Dr Fred Whipple, an astronomer from Harvard, tried to suggest that moonlight reflected off small, detached clouds was the answer. The reported characteristics make this idea so ludicrous that one wonders if Whipple was serious. But he did study a number of the reports in relation to the strength of the moonlight, finding no correlation. La Paz continued to hold to his belief that the UFOs were neither meteors nor other natural phenomena. The meteor explanation was dealt a fatal blow when the statistics showed that on over half the nights of observation there was cloud cover. Indeed on 10 per cent of the nights it was totally overcast. La Paz urged the Air Force in an August 1950 report that if these 'devices' (as he felt sure they were) were *not* US weapons then 'a systematic investigation of the observations should be made immediately'. The project work continued and internal memos went on expressing concern, so we should presumably assume they were *not* US weapons.

But then what were they? Green fireballs are by no means a thing of the past. British UFO records contain contemporary accounts. In May 1978 a former Royal Air Force pilot, Gerry Mitchell, saw three of them whiz past his car in quick succession near a vast oil-refinery complex in Cheshire. In late 1983 there was a spate of them over the Essex coast (where there are more oil refineries). And one of the strangest stories involves a close encounter with a green/yellow fireball on a beach in Suffolk in 1975. This was right next to the big nuclear power station at Sizewell.[13] The attributes of all the phenomena were identical

[13] B. Butler, J. Randles and D. Street, *Skycrash* (Spearman, 1984), pp. 16–17.

with, or similar to, those which Twinkle had tried, and failed, to identify all those years ago. Twinkle represents the first real attempt to study UFOs scientifically. It is sad that it remains one of so very few such instances available for scrutiny.

The Robertson Panel

We may never know the whole truth about official studies during 1949, 1950 and 1951. To what extent there was government concern as Project Grudge lay dormant and Project Twinkle continued to fail we cannot judge. But the secret services continued to talk in their internal memos about UFOs in alarmist ways, and there are some puzzling references in the documents. In the released FBI memos and documents, after several which discuss Twinkle, there is one dated 8 December 1950 and labelled 'Strictly Confidential'. It came from Army Intelligence in Richmond, Virginia, and advised the FBI that the intelligence unit there had been put on an immediate high alert for any data whatsoever concerning flying saucers. They claimed not to know why. After this the files contain nothing more until a document dated 29 July 1952 which stated that 'The Air Force is attempting to send up jet interceptor planes in order to obtain a better view of these objects. However, recent attempts in this regard have indicated that when the pilot in the jet approaches, the object invariably fades from view.' What happened during the intervening 20 months? How long did the 'high alert' last, and what was it for?

Probably the most interesting development at this time was a sudden reversal of policy (as offered to the public). During 1951, UFOs were considered important again. Edward Ruppelt was approached in September and asked to take over the remnants of Grudge and to make it work (this was the beginning of Project Blue Book). Ruppelt enjoyed his work and knew what needed to be done. He was not a UFO believer but he soon saw how powerful the evidence was. As 1952 brought a massive wave of sightings, including complex radar/visual encounters over Washington DC, Ruppelt made numerous suggestions for scientific experiments which could help demonstrate UFO reality or unreality. The first to be adopted was the gathering together of a panel of top scientists to review the best of the UFO evidence. As he says, 'Although the group of scientists wouldn't be empowered to make the final decision, their recommendations were to go to the President if they decided that UFOs were real. And any recommendations made by the group of names we planned to assemble would carry a lot of weight.'[14] Air Force Intelligence and Pentagon officers opened a book to collect bets on the decision the panel would reach. When Ruppelt put down his money, the odds were five to three in favour of the UFO.

The Air Force were not the only ones interested in creating this panel. Indeed Ruppelt hardly realized the extent to which he was being manipulated into organizing things. The CIA were deeply concerned, for different reasons. As a released 2 December 1952 document shows, 'the reports convince us that there is something going on that must have immediate attention . . . they are not attributable to natural phenomena or known types of aerial vehicles.' Beneath the surface, official support for the existence of alien UFOs was as strong as ever. The CIA hand in the scientific panel can be plainly seen from released files, but at the time they said that their involvement had to be kept from public gaze because it would alert people to the importance of UFOs. So great restraints were put on all those who knew about the plans.

Ruppelt's published comments about the panel's conclusions contain an anomaly.[15] His book was published in 1956, when the panel report was still secret, and he was probably taking a gamble even discussing it in general. Ruppelt was not able to name the six panellists, although we now know who they were, thanks to Dr Hynek who attended some sessions. Ruppelt gives an almost entirely opposite view of the panel's conclusions to the one prised out of secrecy many years later. It seems that the boss of the Air Force's own public-façade UFO project was deliberately fed false information by the Pentagon and the CIA, probably because of his pro-UFO stance.[16]

As a preliminary to the main meeting, an initial three-day forum of scientists working with the Air Force was held during

[14] Ruppelt, *Report*, p. 261.
[15] Ibid., pp. 275–96.
[16] Steiger, *Project Blue Book*.

November 1952. This unanimously recommended that the data
must be seen by a 'higher court'. It seems that this first step was
used as a means to persuade the 'big guns' of science that they
really ought to see what the Air Force had to offer. Apart from
Hynek, five individuals were gathered together for a scheduled
five full days of top-secret conference in Washington DC: Drs
Luis Alvarez, Lloyd Berkner, S. Goudsmit and Thornton Page
(who were respected experts on physics, radar and rocketry), plus
the team leader (the theoretical physicist and relativity specialist)
Dr H. P. Robertson. The make-up of this panel (not a psychologist among them) is probably significant. It shows the areas of
science thought by the US government likely to be relevant to
UFO study.

The panel met between 14 and 18 January 1953, but spent the
whole of the last day revising the final text of the report and the
first four days had only involved sessions of about four hours
each. It was hardly an exhaustive study. Berkner only showed up
for the last two days and Hynek had to miss out on certain CIA-
dominated sessions because he did not have CIA security clearance, unlike the other scientists. The scientists were outnum-
bered by Air Force Intelligence and Secret Service men.

Ruppelt did his best to state the importance of the matter,
spending the first day of the meeting briefing them on the facts
and figures that had been uncovered. Reports selected as 'prime'
cases numbered 1,593 (out of 4,400 received by the Air Force
over the first five years of study). Of prime cases, only 10 per cent
were definitely explained as mistaken identity. There was insufficient data to draw conclusions from many, but a staggering 27
per cent (higher than either Air Force project total to date) were
considered real unknowns. Some disturbing information was
reported by Ruppelt. For instance, 'UFOs were habitually reported from areas around "technically interesting" places, like
atomic energy installations, harbours, and critical manufacturing
areas . . . According to the laws of normal distribution, if UFOs
are not intelligently controlled vehicles, the distribution of reports
should have been similar to the distribution of population in the
United States – it wasn't.'[17] There was also a plea on the agenda

[17] Ruppelt, *Report*, p. 261.

by Hynek for more serious research. He was dissatisfied with the lack of scientific development in the Air Force projects and wanted the matter to be viewed as one for science grants, not defence budgets.

A few cases were discussed in detail (Ruppelt says 50, Hynek says only 22). Much time was spent reviewing the only two pieces of cine film then available (one of these was not made public through the media for some months). These films had been made at Great Falls, Montana, in August 1950, showing two white discs in daylight flight over a water tower,[18] and at Tremonton, Utah, in July 1952, where a naval officer filmed a formation of discs in daylight.[19] They had been subjected to extensive analysis by photographic experts. Both were considered unexplained. The probability is that the panel were right in dismissing the Tremonton film as showing high-flying seagulls. However, the Great Falls film has defied every effort to identify the UFOs. The Robertson panel concluded that two aircraft in the area at the time constituted the only available explanation, even though the witness who took the film claimed to have seen two aircraft elsewhere in the sky minutes later. The official investigation into the case was very detailed, and Ruppelt comments 'we studied the flight paths of the two F-94s [aircraft]. We knew the landing pattern that was being used on the day of the sighting and we knew when the two F-94s landed. The two jets just weren't anywhere close to where the two UFOs had been.'[20] The panel apparently ignored this work after viewing the film twice.

Major Dewey Fournet, an engineer, then described his study of some hundreds of the best reports. Those with sufficient detail had been analysed for their flight characteristics and compared with similar characteristics for the standard explanations, such as aircraft, balloons and meteors. Even those with but a small possibility of being such ordinary phenomena were then discarded. The only remaining candidates for study were the unknowns with totally unconventional flight characteristics. Fournet had prepared a long, critical appraisal and reached the opinion

[18] J. Randles, *UFO Reality* (Robert Hale, 1983), pp. 193–6.
[19] Ibid., pp. 196–8.
[20] Ruppelt, *Report*, pp. 289–302.

that they described craft with intelligent control and advanced design. In his view this meant alien.

The Robertson panel considered all this evidence, but concluded there was no proof. Ruppelt, however, would never have understood any outcome other than one which recommended an upgrading of scientific interest within the Air Force project. This is precisely what the 'doctored' version of the conclusions that were given to him did recommend, but the 'real' recommendations were different. The truth came out years later. The panellists were really being directed by the CIA, who needed their advice on the defence implications of the reports. It was seriously believed that an enemy might wait to invade until a wave of UFO sightings occurred and then sneak in to bomb the USA. The authorities would be seriously hampered in receiving and assessing reports of invading aircraft if there were huge numbers of UFO reports – sorting out which were which would be time-consuming, expensive, and likely to hinder defence efforts. Ruppelt was puzzled about why the panel spent so little time talking science and so much time talking politics. He had no idea that they were not really there to decide if UFOs were a novel phenomenon. The real recommendations spoke of using cartoonists like Walt Disney to make funny UFO films. This would both ridicule witnesses, to stop them reporting, and alleviate fears that UFOs might be potentially hostile. Surveillance on UFO groups was suggested too, because they might bring the truth about the Robertson panel's recommendations into the open and thus jeopardize the effort to downplay the subject. Incredible as it may sound, this still goes on. A CIA memo dated 1976 tells how they 'keep in touch with reporting channels in this area to keep the agency informed of any new developments'.

So was the whole Robertson panel a put-up job by the CIA? It is hard to say. It is more likely that the scientists were themselves misled and not offered much of the most interesting material. Clearly scientific investigation came a poor second in the panel's concern over the question of UFO reports and the defence of the USA.

The CIA and the US government got exactly what they wanted – a justification for playing up the significance of the explained cases and forgetting about, or hiding, the unexplained ones.

Wholesale ridiculing and debunking was about to begin. That it worked is shown by a CIA memo dated 17 December 1953, under a year after the panel met: 'The definite drop in the number of sightings during 1953 over 1952 could be attributed to actions following these [Robertson panel] recommendations.' This is the only CIA memo which refers to the time during and after the panel's report that has been released. There must be others in the files the CIA declines to give the public. Their contents must be rather an embarrassment to quite a few people.

Project Blue Book

Project Grudge became Project Blue Book just before the Robertson panel met. Ruppelt retained leadership of the new study and until the end of 1953 continued to chase up new cases with great skill and enthusiasm. But he did not understand why, with the implementation of decisions taken by the Robertson panel, the official attitude towards UFOs should change yet again. All his efforts to stimulate scientific projects were blocked. He wanted diffraction gratings for cameras to obtain hard data. He was stopped. He urged new procedures to concentrate efforts on the promising cases. He was stopped. He even had to pay his own fares when following up cases his superiors felt were too hot and should be left alone as inconclusive. He wrote: 'This period of "mind changing" bothered me. Here were people deciding that there was nothing to this UFO business right at a time when the reports seemed to be getting better . . . Maybe I was just playing the front man to a big cover-up.'[21] In the spring of 1954, rather disillusioned, he left the Air Force and set about writing his book on ufology. It raises questions about the motives of government policy, for, as he argued, unless rigorous and open scientific study could be applied to the data the public would continue to remain ignorant of what was happening around them. Ruppelt knew what he was talking about, even though some of the secret documents we now have (and there are others we still do not have) were kept from him. UFOs *were* 'serious business', as a late 1950s government memo called them. We do not know if any

[21] Ibid., pp. 296–308.

solid proof was being hidden, but there was a great deal more excellent evidence 'under wraps' than was openly admitted – all for the sake of throwing the public off the scent.

In Ruppelt's early days with Project Blue Book he had sensed the need for proper scientific evaluations and he urged a rapport with the Battelle Memorial Institute, a prestigious scientific research body. A contract was offered them to do a detailed study of all the Air Force reports received before the end of 1952. Their primary task was to compare, parameter for parameter, the unknown cases with those regarded as identified. If UFOs were genuinely novel phenomena then this work would (as near as possible) be able to prove them so. For this reason, when Battelle agreed to accept the contract, intense secrecy surrounded it. It was the sort of venture nobody wanted the media to find out about. Hynek had made it plain to him that even to mention the word Battelle would be a crime that would probably involve instant dismissal from his role as science consultant. And Ruppelt, despite his obvious lack of concern about challenging the Air Force in his book, refrained from referring to it. It seems that even the scientists on the Robertson panel (which met while Battelle were mid way through their contract) had no idea the investigation was happening! On the other hand, the Battelle scientists knew about the Robertson panel, although they did not know its real purpose or about its links with the CIA. Indeed they tried to stop it, because they could not understand how anybody could think of convening a five-day meeting of a few scientists *before* the results of their year-long research study. Of course, Battelle stood no chance of succeeding in this, since the Robertson panel was not meeting for scientific reasons. As recently as January 1984, Dr Thornton Page, one of the panel's members, has publicly commented on that fact.[22]

Blue Book's 'Special Report 14' (as the Battelle study was called) was conducted during 1953 but not made public.[23] There

[22] Letter to *International UFO Reporter*, Jan./Feb. 1984.

[23] J.A. Hynek, *The Hynek UFO Report* (Sphere, 1978), pp. 272–8. This book documents Hynek's time as consultant to Project Blue Book, and discusses many key cases. Steiger, *Project Blue Book*, reprints official papers and a complete list of all cases rated 'unknown'. Microfilm records of all Blue Book files are available from the US government on payment of a fee.

was good reason for this. Of the over 4,000 cases on file only 2,199 were deemed sufficiently detailed to be usable. Each of these reports was tabulated according to all analysable discrete data and a complex process of rating the witnesses was adopted (according to factors such as age, observational experience, 'attitude' towards UFOs, etc.). Based on this, cases were ascribed to one of four categories (excellent (9.7 per cent), good (34.5 per cent), doubtful and poor). The next stage in the work was the grouping of reports into one of ten evaluatory categories (aircraft, astronomical, balloon, birds, clouds etc., light phenomena, psychological, insufficient data, other and unknown). Each case was individually set out in detail on to a worksheet, and a preliminary evaluation offered by one of the team, after due consideration. It was then given blind (without the category assigned to it) to an evaluation panel. The panel could draw upon outside consultants in specialized areas. If the two evaluations (from the Battelle worker and the panel) matched, then this identification was adopted for the case. If they did not, debate continued until a consensus view was reached. In a situation where *either* evaluation of the case was that the case should be an unknown then a full evaluatory meeting was called to discuss the merits of that case, drawing upon all the advice needed. The final statistics were arrived at in an extremely careful and responsible manner. This was much more scientific than the methods used by the US Air Force to identify cases. However, this massive shake-out of the data did not get rid of the phenomenon, as some people had hoped.

One startling result is that it was *not* the poorer cases which generated the most unknowns. The trend was the reverse of this. The better the calibre of witness and amount of collected data the *more* likely the case was to be rated unknown. Of the excellent cases, 33.3 per cent merited this rating, as compared with just 16.6 per cent of those termed poor. All told, 261 cases (out of the 2,199) that were rated either excellent or good in quality of data, achieved the evaluation 'unknown'. This figure is only for US sightings recorded by the public Air Force projects to the end of 1952. What would a global survey in 1984 reveal? This aspect of the study is so important because it counteracts an often-used claim of the sceptics. They say that the unknown cases are simply ones which would become known if they had more data. The results show this contention to be wrong. On its own, this set of figures suggests that if UFOs are not a problem with scientific interest it is difficult to imagine just what would be.

The actual number classified as unknown by Battelle constituted 22 per cent of the reports used. This closely matches the various other figures quoted so far. Amazingly, when in 1955 the Air Force decided to talk about Battelle, in order to discredit some serious UFO books just published, they dreadfully misrepresented the figure. In the release offered the media, 22 per cent were dismissed as 'the few surviving unknowns'. Surely to describe almost a quarter of the total as a few survivors is going a bit far. The new head of Blue Book stated in a secret report that this disclosure of the Battelle results was 'serving well the purpose for which it was intended'.

However, Battelle had been commissioned for another reason, as already mentioned. What happened to its parameter-for-parameter comparison of the unknown cases with the identified ones? This is the statement offered to the public: 'The results of these tests are not conclusive since they neither confirm nor deny that the unknowns are primarily unidentified knowns . . .' Then followed some irrelevant comments about there being no proof of alien technology or visitors from space in the Battelle figures, which the study could not have proven one way or the other – and had never been intended to. After such rigorous investigation, such inconclusive results are surprising. Of course, the true results were not made public. Of six parameters studied (colour, duration of sighting, number of objects seen, brightness, shape and speed) only one (brightness) had a probability level above 1 per cent that the unknowns were the same as the knowns. The probability for duration and number of objects seen was way below 1 per cent. Of course, any one result on its own would not be very significant. Subtle factors might provide freak answers. But if you pool these test results the overall probability that the unknowns are simply known phenomena that have not been identified stands at less than one in a billion. It would seem that whoever drafted the release to the public was ignorant of the rules of probability. It would be fascinating to see a similar piece of research done, to this degree of thoroughness, using a larger and more recent set of data. This should be quite feasible with the development of computer technology. Perhaps some brave scientific institute will think of giving it a try. But the question of most concern here is why this highly significant scientific study was kept away from the scientific community.

The history of Project Blue Book after the Battelle study covers 15 years (1955–69), but it can almost be written off in a few lines. It seemed to be using some interesting methods, since the apparent number of unknowns tumbled to incredibly low levels after the Robertson panel instructions began to bite. Recall what Battelle and Projects Sign and Grudge found. The new Air Force figures for unknowns showed 12.6 per cent for 1951, 19.3 per cent for 1952, 7.5 per cent for 1953, 8.4 per cent for 1954, 4.0 per cent for 1955, and 1.5 per cent for 1956. From then on until 1969, the figure did not rise above 3.3 per cent in any one year.

Readers will no doubt wish to know what change in the phenomenon produced these results. The truth is that the Air Force simply changed their classification system. 'Probable' and 'possible' categories made their debut. For a sighting to get rated a 'possible balloon' seems to have literally depended upon the whim of a Blue Book officer. Certainly it required no luxuries, such as evidence, in support of the solution. When it came to working out the figures, all probables and possibles, along with the phrase 'insufficient data', were simply collapsed into one heap along with the cases genuinely identified. Naturally, the unknowns were artificially decimated. But the public were not told this and the statistics were used as part of the debunking process. UFOs had officially disappeared, and so no scientist was going to want to take an interest in them.

Of course the government's own research went on, and still does. The prize was still envisaged as a great one. There is no other way of interpreting a CIA internal memo from April 1976, released under the Freedom of Information Act. It says that the CIA had 'been receiving UFO related material from many of our science and technology sources who are presently conducting related research. These scientists include some who have been associated with the agency for years and whose credentials remove them from the "nut" variety.' It should not need to be stressed that this modern 'UFO-related material' remains impenetrable, even under the Freedom of Information Act. And in other countries, such as Great Britain, even less opportunity is given to the public to find out about official UFO investigations.

The end of Project Blue Book was in some ways rather like its beginning. There had been more than a decade of open hostility between the private UFO groups (who mostly believed the cover-up existed because some fantastic and horrific truth was known to the authorities) and the Air Force investigators (who probably did not even know there was a cover-up). Certainly the Air Force wanted an excuse to rid themselves of the UFO problem, but they had debunked so well that no scientific body would take an interest. NASA, for example, rejected the chance to take over the project in 1966. Nevertheless, all the efforts of the US government had failed to stem the tide of UFO sightings. Many reliable people went on seeing them and a few individuals went on reporting them. Every so often an impressive case would hit the headlines and give new impetus to the calls for better official study. UFOs landed, stopped motor cars, burned witnesses' skins and did all the usual things. A New Mexico policeman reported a UFO landing and little aliens emerging from it; he could point to holes in the ground and the still-smouldering desert scrub as help arrived (see p. 134). The ever-resilient Allen Hynek, now with almost 20 years of experience and confidence, pressed the Air Force to set up a new scientific panel. Sensing that this might be the chance to give someone else the headache, the Air Force agreed.

In February 1966 a commission led by Dr Brian O'Brien met. We know that cosmologist Dr Carl Sagan was one of its members, though we don't know the other names. They unanimously recommended that scientists should study the UFOs, and proposed that selected universities be offered contracts and paid to spend an average of ten man-days per case on about 100 of the best cases each year. This, they felt, might produce some answers. Each university team ought to include a psychologist, an astronomer and a physical scientist. They suggested also that the Blue Book files should be turned over to Congress and 'relevant public persons' in order to alleviate all suspicion of a cover-up. Needless to say the UFO community welcomed this idea and Project Blue Book liked it too. But naturally the other scientists and government officials involved were probably rather less keen to let out any files. The Blue Book files remained secret.

Nevertheless, pressure was mounting in Congress, with even such respectable figures as Gerald Ford putting his weight behind those who wanted to know more about UFOs. Some action was called for, and the result was one of the biggest fiascos and scandals in ufology's turbulent history.

4

Transferring the Problem: Science in the Ascendant

There is a scientific mystery here that is being ignored.

James E. McDonald, atmospheric physicist,
University of Arizona

It is tempting to speculate about what might have happened had scientists had responsibility for studying the UFO enigma right from the start. Things would probably have been very different. When the opportunity for independent scientific investigation did arise in 1966, enormous problems had to be met which had a major effect on the policies and methods adopted.

A major barrier was the popular image of the UFO and its investigators. Scientists saw the subject as a fool's paradise where silly ideas vied with one another for supremacy. There was no hard evidence for researchers to work on, because of the secrecy which had surrounded government investigations. The attitudes of the various government agencies which had been involved had helped to spread the idea of UFOs as the invention of disordered minds; the opponents of government policy had assumed that this demonstrated both the reality and the alien nature of the UFOs. While the concept seemed entirely logical to them, it was far from obvious to the sceptic. The media tended simply to express the views of one side or the other, so shaping public opinion rather unhelpfully. Young scientists growing up in this atmosphere naturally picked up many misconceptions, so when they finally began to be involved there was a great deal of ground to be covered.

The USA

The Condon Report

The O'Brien Commission's recommendations were forced upon the US Air Force by Congress in the spring of 1966, but in a modified way. During the next few months extensive efforts were made to find the university teams, but nobody was interested (despite a total contract grant of $300,000). A list of 25 institutes (including MIT and the universities of California and North Carolina) had all said 'no' before the University of Colorado was approached. They were told that they were second choice (behind only the National Center for Atmospheric Phenomena Research) and this white lie helped. But even so the university needed much cajoling, as an August 1966 memo from future project co-ordinator, Robert Low (the university business administration officer), shows. It was entitled 'Some Thoughts on the UFO Project'. He wrote to his university bosses:

Our study would be conducted almost exclusively by non-believers who, although they couldn't possibly *prove* a negative result, could and probably would add an impressive body of evidence that there is no reality to the observations. The trick would be, I think, to describe the project so that, to the public, it would appear a totally objective study but, to the scientific community, would present a group of non-believers trying their best to be objective but having an almost zero expectation of finding a saucer.

He went on to propose that stress be laid on the psychology of the witnesses and not 'the old question of the physical reality of the saucer'; thus 'the scientific community would quickly get the message.'

Low's words were hardly well chosen and the 'trick memorandum', as it came to be known, eventually got national media exposure. But when the university gave the go-ahead Low's ideas were set in motion. It was the psychology department who took the crucial decision as to whether to proceed or not. The questionnaire for case investigation was 22 pages long – one page only being devoted to the UFO event and the rest to describing the witnesses. Low administered the study.

Chosen to figurehead the project was Dr Edward Condon, a famous quantum physicist. He had been involved in the atomic-bomb development and so had high security clearance. He had also challenged the government in a toxics-poisoning battle and so had public credibility as far as telling the truth was concerned. However, Condon's views on UFOs were embarrassingly obvious, and heavily biased the work of the project. Those few scientists who did have a track record in the field, such as Hynek, were banned from participation on the grounds that they were not open-minded. Dr Jacques Vallée, a young astrophysicist and computer specialist, who had just co-written an original book about UFOs[1] (the first by a scientist), was left out because this had made him mildly committed. Yet three months after signing the contract undertaking the work, in October 1966, Condon gave a perfect illustration of how open-minded he was when he told a public meeting: 'It is my inclination right now to recommend that the government get out of this business. My attitude right now is that there is nothing to it.' Then he added with a smile, 'But I'm not supposed to reach a conclusion for another year.' Despite several more statements of a similar nature he went on to apply for (and get) an increase in funding, in order to extend the work into the autumn of 1968. Condon's behaviour during this two-year period was a source of much concern to the team of about a dozen scientists gathered by the university for the work. He never investigated a case, spoke to witnesses or pursued the results of those who did. He went around making jokes and telling anecdotes to the media as he 'represented' the study. He even took a bow at a contactee convention, alongside people who claimed to have Venusian lovers! He volubly talked about all the cases nobody with any serious interest or knowledge would have glanced at for more than a second.

Low's attitudes were little different. After four months he wrote a paper describing the main gist of the project as 'nonsense'. Then, in the summer of 1967, he visited Europe for a month at project expense. He refused to meet leading UFO researchers or follow up cases with overseas components. Instead he went to Loch Ness in Scotland. He justified this by saying that

[1] J. and J. Vallée, *Challenge to Science* (Spearman, 1967).

the monster did not exist and neither did UFOs, so it was important to look at how people by the loch were studying a non-existent phenomenon. As you can probably gauge from the above, the Condon project was little more than a joke at the taxpayer's expense. But it was a damaging joke. In view of the background to the study it is possible that Condon and Low had a private contract to ridicule UFOs, along the lines that the authorities needed. Or perhaps they had been deliberately selected for the work because of their likely approach.

The rest of the staff, however, worked hard to study UFOs. They were supposed to have been given full government support and any files from Project Blue Book that they wanted. But in some cases they were denied access or stalled by Air Force officials. On other occasions they discovered a current case through their UFO contacts long before Blue Book staff told them about it. And the Blue Book files, even when available to them, were often found to be inadequate. Consequently, much responsibility fell on the shoulders of the civilian groups APRO (Aerial Phenomena Research Organization) and NICAP (National Investigations Committee on Aerial Phenomena) (both formed more than ten years before). They helped create an early notification system for interesting cases. Yet despite this, as Dr David Saunders, one of the mathematical psychologists involved, said: 'we found ourselves discarding case after case because the evidence that might have made them watertight, and that might have been available if we really investigated, was not already handed to us on a silver platter.'[2]

A decision was taken to produce a 'case book', containing a few hundred of the best cases, which could then be circulated to all other major universities before completion of a report. This was never done, mostly because of inefficiency – the whole project nearly collapsed into chaos.

The 'old' cases chosen for study were a surprising mixture of a few classics and other rather dubious examples. Many cases that any competent investigator would have recommended for restudy

[2] D. Saunders and R. Hawkins, *UFOs? Yes!* (Signet, 1968). Our information on the Condon Project comes largely from this book, the project report, and D. Jacobs, *The UFO Controversy in America* (Signet, 1976), as well as discussions with Allen Hynek and Richard Sigismund, November 1983.

were ignored. The same applied to 'current' cases during the one-year period (1967) when these were pursued. The filter process supposedly used was a mockery, as several reports made it to the final list for what can only have been their 'crank' value or because Condon found them funny. As scientific evidence they were useless. Useless cases were often followed through to the bitter end at the expense of more promising ones. For instance a 'psychic message' was sent in predicting a UFO landing. So a team was dispatched to the site to wait. The informant's previous ramblings about universes populated by bears had no apparent effect on the credibility of the case in Condon's eyes! But it made a nice after-dinner speech. This appears to have been an important 'scientific' consideration during the Condon project.

Eventually, in mid-1967, the Low memo of August 1966 was found by disgruntled project members, who were naturally shocked; but they mostly kept it to themselves and battled on, because they were becoming intrigued by the cases they did study properly. The civilian groups were less happy. They saw their work being ignored; they heard Condon and Low laughing about what to them was a serious scientific issue, and they began to feel that the University of Colorado was just one more puppet in the government whitewash operation. As a means of appeasement (and to make sure some useful cases kept coming in) the memo was shown by the other project members to a few leading UFO experts. The project members wanted the ufologists to realize what they were up against, and assure them that they did not share Low's views. Dr David Saunders, Dr Norman Levine and several others felt that the project had to continue despite the obstacles and that the final report was bound to make clear that the UFO data *were* of scientific interest. There was never any doubt in their minds that the result would be a recommendation to government for further scientific study. The UFO groups were persuaded to go along with them, and (to their credit) they did not attempt to make media capital out of Low's indiscretions. Like the scientists, the ufologists wanted the project to see its term through. But, in January 1968, one of the ufologists (Dr James McDonald, an atmospheric physicist (not part of the programme) sent a long letter about the project's progress to the university. He referred to the memo in passing. Low and Condon exploded with rage and there was a crisis, with hard words spoken on both sides. Saunders and Levine were accused of treachery and theft and dismissed on the spot. Another team member walked out in disgust, claiming that there was 'an almost unanimous lack of confidence in Low's ability to direct the project' and that the majority view of the team (that there was definitely something of interest in the UFO data) was being seriously misrepresented by him and Condon. The project stumbled on to its conclusion a few months later, although very few of the original members except Low and Condon saw it through. Disgusted ufologists made the memo public after the disintegration of the study. The rumpus created reached the US Senate after the story was featured in *Look,* a US magazine. The sacked psychologist, Saunders, published his own view of the project and how it should report, called *UFOs? Yes!* which came out a few weeks before Condon published the final report in November 1968.[3]

Condon handed the report to the National Academy of Sciences. They approved it, though they pointed out in comments to the media that they only approved the methodology, and not the conclusions. The 1,485-page dossier was then made public. 'Advance' copies went to journalists just hours before its official release, a calculated move in keeping with previous US Air Force policy. There was so much technological padding and jargon (complex chapters on the optics of radar, atmospheric diffraction and so forth) that it was anticipated that no journalist would try to read it in time to comment on publication. Condon's most brilliant tactical ploy was to put the conclusions and recommendations right at the front of the book. Any busy journalist, or interested reader, would only need to look at that and decide from it what the report itself said. The conclusion was that there was nothing whatsoever to the UFO mystery. The report maligned the integrity of witnesses, investigators and interested scientists. Abandonment of government interest was recommended, plus discouragement of scientific research. Banning the use of UFO data in education was proposed. Later Condon was quoted as suggest-

[3] The Condon Report was published as E. Condon (ed.), *The Scientific Study of UFOs* (Bantam Press, 1969).

ing that authors of UFO books should be horsewhipped in public! These comments are not surprising in view of the project's history, but they indicate the likelihood of another put-up job. What about the results of the study itself? Relatively little of it discusses UFO data. Only 91 cases are cited, and a third of these are more or less passing references. The remaining 60 or so given in some depth are a poor collection. One would expect a scientific study to work with the best available evidence, but these cases give a wholly false impression of the real strangeness of UFO data. It would be kind to charge Condon and Low with gross incompetence, fuelled by a considerable lack of objectivity.

If you suspect that our description of this project is biased, we suggest that you go to your reference library, find a copy of the Condon Report, and struggle through it. Once you reach the case histories you will find that, despite the poor sample, the percentage left unexplained is a familiar one. We estimate around 22 per cent should be termed 'unknown' (it is hard to tell as the report contains no basic figures whatsoever). You will also confront time and again conclusions to cases in such words as 'a natural phenomenon . . . so rare it has never been reported before or since', or others which talk of 'at least one genuine UFO', 'an extraordinary flying object' as well as 'evidently artificial', and so on. It is difficult to see where Condon's conclusions come from.

(Condon went to his grave still calling ufologists 'kooks' (nutters). Recently, NASA scientist Dr Thornton Page, who had been a member of the 1953 Robertson panel, spoke out about this. Page says that he personally 'started with the conviction that UFOs were "nonsense" . . . but after that . . . came to see that a small fraction of UFO reports were very difficult to explain.'[4] Page found Condon extremely unhelpful when he asked him for some advice on an entry he had written on UFOs for *Encyclopaedia Britannica*: 'he shouted at me . . . then there was a bang, and silence. I am told that he threw the phone on the floor with such violence that it broke.')

The Air Force immediately accepted the Condon Report and quietly closed Project Blue Book. They still refer to the study as a watershed in their UFO interest. It may be that Condon and Low

[4] Letter to *International UFO Reporter*, Jan./Feb. 1984.

did genuinely disbelieve in UFOs, to the extent that they missed the importance of their own data. It may be that the Condon Report was the product of the Air Force, deliberately contrived to get rid of their longstanding 'grudge'. Perhaps it was CIA-inspired in the way that the earlier Robertson panel sessions had been. We do not know the truth. Only time and the Freedom of Information Act may eventually tell.

Post-Condon Scientific Debates

It is arguably true that despite the events which led up to it and its unshakeably negative conclusions the Condon Report is one of the best things ever to have happened in the UFO study. This may seem curious, but in fact several scientists read it carefully and became convinced that UFOs were worthy of serious study. Gradually the number of such scientists increased, until today there are hundreds of committed scientists in many different fields actively pursuing UFO research. Even at the time of the University of Colorado study the American Institute of Aeronautics and Astronautics had formed an 11-man sub-committee, chaired by environmental scientist Dr Joachim Kuettner. It later was to report with a devastating attack on the level of scientific endeavour displayed by the Condon project. Some months later, on 29 July 1968, a symposium on UFOs was held in the US House of Representatives. This involved a number of interested scientists, including Hynek and McDonald. The young cosmologist Carl Sagan joined them. There was universal pessimism about the outcome of the nearly concluded Condon project. The recently released Low memorandum had not helped.

The following year (1969) with the Condon Report having been published and the US Air Force waiting for the right moment to announce its decision to renounce UFO study, the American Association for the Advancement of Science decided to hold its winter seminar in Boston and include UFOs as a key item on the programme. Once again this shows the widespread disquiet about the work that the University of Colorado had done. Condon was predictably furious and tried to stop the AAAS from going ahead. The AAAS pointed out that scientists were supposed to be open-minded, and emotive reactions like those Condon displayed could not be used as reasonable grounds for cancellation. But Condon wrote a seven-page letter to his friend, vice-president Spirow Agnew, requesting that the White House step in. Agnew rightly declined.[5] The meeting took place between 26 and 29 December 1969. At the same time the Air Force attempted to renew Condon's credibility. 'Coincidentally' they released the news to the press that Project Blue Book was being dropped and that official UFO study was ending. Hynek had been told this long before, and says the closure had been put in hand the best part of a year earlier. The announcement was made just before the AAAS meeting. But the AAAS fought back, holding its own press conference before the meeting, chaired by Dr Thornton Page, who had supported the sceptics on the 1953 Robertson panel – until he began studying the UFO data!

The AAAS conference was probably the fairest hearing UFOs have ever received from scientists. Sceptics such as Dr William Hartmann (who had analysed the photographic cases in the Condon project) presented papers. Long-associated believers, such as Hynek and McDonald, presented their evidence. (McDonald had decided to reinvestigate some of the cases that Condon had found in the Air Force files but he was sadly to die soon afterwards in tragic circumstances.) There were also those who were uncommitted, such as Sagan. Topics ranged freely from psychological to physical aspects. Page and Sagan then edited all the papers into book form. This remains a major document in UFO research.[6]

Probably the most important thing to emerge from the symposium was a declaration signed by 13 scientists (of *all* persuasions and including Hartmann, Hynek, McDonald, Page and Sagan) requesting the US Air Force not to destroy the files of their UFO projects and to hand them over to a scientific institute

[5] See Jacobs, *UFO Controversy*.

[6] T. Page and C. Sagan (eds), *UFOs: A Scientific Debate* (Cornell University Press, 1972). See also J.A. Hynek, 'Commentary on the AAAS Symposium', *FSR*, vol. 16, no. 2, 1970. Extended versions of the papers from the conference were published in: J.A. Hynek, 'Twenty-one Years of UFO Reports', *FSR*, vol. 16, nos. 1, 2, 1970; J. McDonald, 'UFOs over Lakenheath, 1956', *FSR*, vol. 16, no. 2, 1970.

or university where they could be used for serious research. This seems a reasonable plea and must have carried some weight. It duplicates a similar one made to the British Ministry of Defence in 1978. The US Air Force denied the request and no files were released.

Hynek was now free of his government bonds and decided the time was right to set down his 20 years experience as ufology's most knowledgeable scientist. When his book appeared in 1972 it was a further milestone in UFO history.[7] Achieving no progress towards scientific analysis *within* the Air Force, Hynek had long worked covertly *outside* it. A private enclave of interested scientists had been gathered together to provide a UFO 'think-tank'. Known as the 'invisible college', which formed the title of a book based on its work by member Dr Jacques Vallée, it was the spring-board from which could be launched a real UFO science.[8] Hynek, Vallée and others, including Dr David Saunders (the sacked member of the Condon team) and Dr Richard Sigismund (an accepted Condon member who had refused to work with the project once he saw the direction it was taking) all set about creating CUFOS (the Center for UFO Studies). This was the first UFO group built by, and around, scientists. Founded in 1973, it set up a world-wide data base, known as UFOCAT, maintained on computer by Saunders. This invaluable tool has over the years produced numerous print-outs which tabulate data according to case type or other criteria and constitute important research material.

CUFOS has also published various in-depth research reports and catalogues and for quite a time had a toll-free 'hot-line' phone number which could be used by the public, police departments and airports. They also paid for astronomer Allan Hendry to act as full-time investigator for the Center. Hendry took his work very seriously and would never rest until a case was explained, if it possibly could be. He produced a book which is

[7] J.A. Hynek, *The UFO Experience* (Regnery Press, 1972).

[8] J. Vallée, *The Invisible College* (Dutton, 1975); published in the UK as *UFOs: The Psychic Solution* (Granada, 1977). Hynek and Vallée edited the results of the think-tank meetings and published them in *The Edge of Reality* (Regnery Press, 1975).

rightly regarded as one of the modern classics of the field.[9] But
CUFOS had to rely upon funding from people interested in
UFOs, exactly as all the other civilian groups do. No grants were
available from anywhere. Eventually the money began to run out
and they could not afford either Hendry or the hot line. They had
to close down their office and transfer the extensive files to the
upper stories of Hynek's large house in Evanston, Illinois.
CUFOS survives but it has learnt how tough life is for those in the
UFO investigation business.

Following the lead of CUFOS, amateur groups throughout the
world tried to improve their standards. Investigators had to
become accredited, specialization in certain aspects of ufology
became common and scientifically refereed journals were now
the aim. The number of interested young scientists grew. CUFOS
held a conference in Chicago in 1976, and such conferences
became a regular feature of the more dedicated international
groups. (They had to be dedicated because no scientific UFO
conference has ever made a profit.) BUFORA (the British UFO
Research Association) has sponsored three 'international con-
gresses', in 1979, 1981 and 1983. At these an International
Committee for UFO Research was created to forge common
methodologies. People from all the major research-orientated
nations are involved.

Other groups have also followed the CUFOS lead in producing
serious 'special reports', which are ufology's nearest equivalent to
scientific papers. Steuart Campbell in Great Britain compiled a
detailed study on a landing with physical traces and assault on the
witness.[10] Mark Rodeghier in the USA summarized 'vehicle-
interference' case reports and analysed them, using the UFOCAT
data base.[11] In Australia, a wide variety of papers have been
produced on specific types of UFO event, e.g. entity cases. All
these point the way forward for the subject's development.

It is already becoming easier for serious UFO books to be
published. Some, such as the compilation of articles by psychologists, sociologists and physiologists edited by NASA scientist Dr

[9] A. Hendry, The UFO Handbook (Sphere, 1980).
[10] 'Case History no. 1, Livingston, Scotland' (BUFORA, 1982).
[11] CUFOS, 1981.

Richard Haines, are so technical that they look like university textbooks.[12] A small indication of the progress of ufology in the wake of the Condon Report is the fact that mainstream scientific journals now accept articles on the subject. *New Scientist,* published in Great Britain, had before 1983 only published one UFO piece (a sceptical appraisal by James Oberg, who works for NASA as a UFO-watcher, which won a competition). In 1983 there were serious research articles by us and by Paul Devereux and a team of geophysical scientists with whom he is working, each discussing different features of the subject.[13] While this hardly means that ufology has been accepted, it does imply progress.

France

GEPAN

In the spring of 1974 the French Minister of Defence, M. Robert Galley, gave a remarkable interview on national radio which was not internationally reported. He categorically asserted that UFOs are real and that the French government is studying them. He even said that if people could but see the extent and quality of the evidence (including radar trackings and jet chases) then they would be disturbed.[14] Galley was a close friend of President Pompidou, who was apparently not happy with this revelation. He told the Defence Minister that the government had enough trouble on its hands without bringing the UFO problem before public gaze. Nevertheless, as nobody outside France seems to have realized the importance of the interview, it raised fewer problems than it might have. It may be significant that France is not part of the NATO alliance. While the US Air Force policies are probably closely linked with the British MOD, and with much

[12] R. Haines (ed.), *UFO Phenomena and the Behavioural Scientist* (Scarecrow Press, 1979).
[13] J. Randles and P. Warrington, 'The Neglected Science of UFOs', *New Scientist,* 10 Feb. 1983; P. Devereux and P. McCartney, *New Scientist,* 29 Sept. 1983.
[14] The speech is translated in full by G. Creighton in J. Bourret, *The Crack in the Universe* (Spearman, 1977).

of the Western world, France is one of the few developed countries which might be expected to have an independent stance on UFOs. That it does indeed seem to take them seriously ought to make us think.

Galley revealed in his interview that the government was passing UFO data for evaluation to the CNES (the French equivalent of NASA) in Toulouse. Dr Claude Poher was in charge of the study there. By 1 May 1977 his work was sufficiently impressive to lead to the French putting it on a much more official basis. The government offered a substantial grant to fund a new division of several staff at the CNES under Poher's control. This division was given the name GEPAN (which stands for Study Group into Unidentified Atmospheric Phenomena). The scientists and engineers were mostly ignorant and uncommitted about UFOs, but the upper echelons at GEPAN were not. Dr Pierre Guérin, an astronomer associated with the project, wrote about a year after its start that 'an intelligence controls the UFOs. And it is not ours.' Later in his article Guérin said that the governments of the earth knew the truth about UFOs (that they came from an intelligence which coexisted with us on the planet and may actually own us!) but that they did not have the faintest clue how to present such a truth and maintain world order.[15] Guérin was no stranger to UFO research (although his articles had been originally penned under a pseudonym). He did not write for every UFO magazine, nor on a range of topics. But his few reports in the international UFO journal *FSR* were always interesting, as indeed where those of his 'boss' at GEPAN, Claude Poher. Poher had frequently published results in FSR before the establishment of GEPAN.

The world-wide UFO community had good reason to welcome GEPAN. Many felt it marked a new phase of open communication in official policy. It was created just as Spielberg's film *Close Encounters of the Third Kind* (based on Hynek's book) was being released. It is no coincidence that the leading ufologist heading the US UFO project in the film is French. British

[15] P. Guérin, 'Thirty Years after Kenneth Arnold', *FSR*, vol. 25, no. 1, 1979. Guérin's views have yet to be proved or disproved; we simply report them here.

government sources (members of the House of Lords) have even told us that this is part of a 'conditioning process' to ease through a gradual revelation that friendly 'aliens' live among us. They say that the pleasant imagery of Spielberg's later film *ET* is no accident. This may well be just a joke at our expense, but we understand from American researchers that exactly the same story has been 'leaked' by sources there.

GEPAN was, unlike the Air Force projects in the USA, very co-operative as far as ufologists were concerned. In a February 1979 document GEPAN outlines how the study is operated. There are field workers, including an early-warning team who can be rapidly sent to the site of any incident. Back at base there are scientists in various disciplines to study the evidence collected. Psychologists are on call to evaluate witnesses and laboratory back-up is available to assess hard evidence. The *gendarmerie* act as an initial filter to pass on well-put-together reports on interesting cases. Those with merit are then looked at on site by the scientists. There are also sub-groups within GEPAN who specialize in radar cases and physical-trace cases. A 'scientific council' meets from time to time to discuss results and future programmes. The case files are undoubtedly the best in the world.

The results of this work are surely spectacular enough to have warranted mention in the scientific press. For example, of 354 filtered reports received during 1978 no fewer than 53 per cent referred to close encounters. Of these 25 per cent were rated 'unexplained' and a further 34 per cent 'potentially unknown but lacking probative data'. These results (which, to quote GEPAN, 'after analysis by our experts ... pose a real question' are staggering, but have not been publicized. Nor has their finding that the more detailed the reports and the less explainable the phenomenon, the higher the percentage of witnesses rated as having 'high credibility'. Indeed they quote figures (again for 1978) showing 23 per cent of the unexplained cases having witnesses with 'high credibility' and just ten per cent where the credibility is rated below average.

GEPAN was not secretive in the US Air Force sense, just cautious. These early results prompted the scientific council (GEPAN's governing body) to remark, when it met to consider them, that 'great vigilance regarding the distribution and publication of these studies and results' was essential.[16] GEPAN received increased funding after this. It stated in 1979, 'we estimate that the witnesses we have met have really seen the things which they report to us.' The logical conclusion from this is that, as GEPAN says, 'the study of the cause of these phenomena is potentially capable of bringing forth new knowledge.' In private some of the group (Poher and Guérin) were going even further than these very direct published conclusions. This seems to have worried the French government, for Poher left to sail round the world, and stopped writing about UFOs. A new, young astronomer (Dr Alain Esterle) took charge. He was much more restrained and did not contribute to the UFO literature. He also ensured that fewer of the internal reports of GEPAN's work were leaked. But in May 1981 he attended a UFO congress in Great Britain, where he said privately that the work of GEPAN was proving that UFOs were alien.

GEPAN has published a steady stream of 'Technical Notes', often 70- or 80-page booklets complete with graphs, charts, maps and photographs. Some of these are theoretical or statistical. Others relate case investigations in great depth. One in our possession, for instance, is dated 8 March 1982 and analyses a close encounter on 26 January 1981. An orange, cigar-shaped object with three 'portholes' on its side made a rendezvous with a farmer's car and hung low overhead. The car's engine failed and its electrical circuits were damaged. It is similar to many events reported from all over the world, but here there was immediate and extensive scientific investigation. GEPAN's conclusion is that the investigation 'does not permit us any acceptable solution to explain the collection of data; not an explanation in physical terms and not one in psychological terms.' In fact it was 'in the proper sense, an unidentified aerial phenomenon according to GEPAN'.[17] Such cases must have influenced their thinking, contributing to the increasing tendency to say nothing about their work. Each published document is now individually numbered,

[16] *Le GEPAN et l'étude du phénomène OVNI* (GEPAN and the study of UFO phenomena), (GEPAN, Toulouse, 1979).
[17] GEPAN Technical Notes 11, Toulouse, 1982.

illustrating how few go outside GEPAN. Our copy of the description of the above case was obtained in mid-1983 but is only number 34.

By the summer of 1982 the change of attitude in GEPAN had been detected by French UFO investigators. Fernand Lagarde, editor of a respected UFO magazine there, *Lumiers dans la nuit,* said, 'The collaboration is strictly one way only.' He complained about stone-wall tactics by the scientists and even that witnesses had been told by GEPAN not to talk to civilian groups.[18]

In February 1983 Jenny Randles visited France and found ufologist circles rife with rumours that GEPAN was about to be closed down as an economy measure. The view of French researchers was that the team had not found anything important and was just a front for something secret, rather like Project Blue Book. They seemed ignorant of the kind of things Poher and Guérin had published in England and could not believe what Esterle had said on his visit.[19]

The French economy in 1983 was indeed in difficulties and the Mitterand government was looking for areas of spending to cut. It timed an announcement about GEPAN over the weekend of an Anglo/French UFO conference in Boulogne, the first time that ufologists from both countries had got together. It was a significant venture, but it had the edge taken off it by the news about GEPAN. On the day researchers crossed the channel back to Great Britain (21 February) the *Sunday Times* reported the 'demise' of the official French project (although it had never mentioned its creation or any of its work before!). The *Sunday Times* article, entitled 'Flying Saucers Sought No More' was a light-hearted romp at the expense of UFO researchers. It was also totally misleading. It called the alleged decision to scrap GEPAN 'an amusing display of scepticism about the existence of extraterrestrial life' and termed the group 'an expensive folly'. It furthermore spoke of it having achieved nothing, other than taking two years to expose a notorious abduction hoax. (The hoax in question had actually been seen through by UFO re-

[18] F. Lagarde, 'A Warning to us All', *FSR*, vol. 28, no. 1, 1982.
[19] An example of the Poher research published is Poher and Vallée, 'Basic patterns in UFO observation', *FSR*, vol. 21, nos. 3, 4, 1975.

searchers very quickly and it is doubtful that GEPAN ever took it seriously.) Needless to say there was not the slightest whisper of any of the published GEPAN results as given in this chapter.

It should be added that GEPAN was *not* closed down, although the *Sunday Times* did not get around to explaining this to its readers. In fact the scientists opposed the move strongly and the authorities drew back.

A few months after the *Sunday Times* had written off GEPAN, Alain Esterle turned up in the British press (and was even mentioned on the national news). GEPAN had apparently found a case where there was incontrovertible evidence. A farmer had seen a UFO land and the soil and plants at the landing site had undergone strange biological changes. While detailed information on this case is hard to obtain from GEPAN, we understand that they sent samples to several independent laboratories, and that all the test results were identical. Everybody was astonished. We await more information on this case with great interest, but will it be forthcoming? There is reason to doubt that we will find out more, for soon after this news a 'reorganization' within GEPAN was announced. Esterle was replaced by an engineer. We are told that he is under instructions not to talk about future progress. However, after six years of research the fact that the French government decide that a mechanical scientist is the best person to head the project certainly suggests they do not think UFOs are hallucinations!

Guérin has recently issued a new statement, in which he argues that there has been a cover-up and suggests the reasons for it.

It is not the scientists – naturally sceptical as they are – who had induced the political and military leaders to refuse to take 'UFO stories' seriously. It is these authorities themselves who are concealing from us what they know . . . and [they] have put it into the minds of the scientists to deny the existence of the UFOs, or at any rate, into the minds of a great majority of them who are not sufficiently interested in the matter to search through the records for themselves.[20]

If you are still unconvinced, get hold of those records and those documents. And then make up your own mind.

[20] P. Guérin, *FSR*, vol. 28, no. 6, 1983.

5

The Failure of Ufologists

What has ufology done wrong? Why has it failed to make its case with sufficient impact?

In July 1981 Dr J. Allen Hynek (former consultant to the US Air Force, professor of astronomy and undoubtedly the most respected and most important proponent ufology has ever had) summarized many of the problems when he made a plea for a new professional body created from *within* the subject to regulate its own behaviour: 'the besetting sin of ufology today . . . is that it presents to the outside world a most fantastic hodge-podge of unprofessional actions, statements, manœuvres, intrigues and balderdash. The latter often takes the form of fast-buck artists who publish an amazing amount of undigested tripe.' As he says further:

ufology is today what chemistry was when it was alchemy . . . a grand assortment of superstitions, beliefs, wishful thinking, etc. But eventually the science, and the profession of chemistry, evolved out of the alchemical mess. Ufology must become a profession, and the start should be made soon, for unless this happens we face another several decades of buffoonery, ridicule and idle prattle about sightings, and useless bickering and unproductive competition among the non-professional dabblers in ufology.[1]

Strong words – but of very great importance. We would echo them most sincerely. It is unquestionably true that UFO enthusiasts are themselves to blame for the fact that they are not taken

[1] 'Ufology as a Profession: A Manifesto', *CUFOS Newsletter,* September 1981.

more seriously. They may (and do) twitter on about scientists
who are biased and who ignore their data, or (if they are feeling
especially paranoid) pin the blame on to the government for
wanting to destroy their credibility. It is remarkably tempting to
respond in this way. Gordon Creighton, scholar, diplomat and
editor of *Flying Saucer Review* (a publication which once had a
good reputation for the way it treated the subject), has even
written a number of articles endeavouring to justify his rather
strange belief that UFO books are being systematically removed
from library shelves as part of a plan to reduce public interest!
The real truth of the matter is much less glamorous. The fact is
that ufology, as a whole, consists of people whose motivations for
involvement are not pure enough, whose methods are not ethical
enough and whose standards of performance are not good
enough for their work to be taken more seriously. To be sure,
there are excellent ufologists, a small hard core of maybe 200
individuals world-wide. They are deeply concerned to improve
standards, but they function in isolation and rarely get the chance
to work together.

Every major UFO organization in the world is, as Hynek puts
it, a 'hodge-podge'. UFO work is entirely voluntary. No funds
come from respected institutions or governments to support it.
Yet to study UFOs properly does require expenditure. Often this
must be produced directly from the pockets of the active investigators, who may be willing to sacrifice personal comforts for a few
new scraps of knowledge. Yet this has its limits: many a ufologist
has had to give up his or her expensive involvement despite
continued interest. An organization starved of funds has virtually
to accept anyone who comes along willing to pay the membership
fee. This produces a curious blend, where a national body of, say,
500 members (usual for a country the size of Great Britain) has
perhaps just 30 or 40 serious workers who recognize the failings
of the subject and would want to correct them. The other 460
members comprise a spectrum ranging from a few pseudo-
religious fanatics (who think God rides a UFO and who await the
day of revelation), through a nice sprinkling of schoolboys,
genuine but very naïve witnesses, and people who have selected ufology as a good way to make new friends, to that ufological
parasite, the armchair expert. This breed of ufologist reads a fair

bit (rather selectively) but never thinks really seriously about UFOs. Often he has his own pet theory (which may be that UFOs are members of the twenty-fifth-century time travellers' tourist board, or that ET is alive and well and currently phoning home from Hemel Hempstead). The armchair expert cannot even begin to justify these ideas from the data. Nor would he want to. His friends love to hear him chat away and he gets the occasional write-up in the local newspaper for his troubles. UFOs to him are exciting, ego-boosting and great fun. Whether they actually exist or not, and if so what they really are, are questions divorced from his reality.

Serious ufologists know this problem and may wish to be free of it, but gaining freedom often entails severe action which may be difficult to justify. The money these people provide does at least fund some research (although most groups have the strange belief that research comprises the publication of a glossy magazine with as many pages as possible). Since the magazine is the one thing sure to attract the armchair ufologist, giving him a more up-to-date source of information than the average book, the hard core always regard it as mandatory policy. They must attract back those armchair experts when the next year's subscriptions become due. The dedicated, serious ufologists end up running social clubs and magazines for the primary benefit of the non-dedicated, less-than-serious ufologists.

To be fair, this picture is rather over-gloomy. The hard core ensure that their groups undertake some useful activities (e.g. investigation or the publishing of a few research reports). But there seems to be great adherence to the strength-in-numbers myth. The few serious enthusiasts are scared of removing themselves from the general UFO scene and creating their own small, international body. The thinking behind this hesitation is that a team of a few ufologists, no matter how serious, would not be able to compete with one that has hundreds or thousands of members, even were such a group to be entirely aimless and lethargic in its approach to the real issues. The big group would attract the reports of sightings and the attention, which the serious ufologists still need access to in order to conduct their research.

That such a fear has some grounding is shown by an approach

made to Jenny Randles by one journalist from a television
company. In soliciting information about UFOs he asked for
details from BUFORA (the British UFO Research Association).
Jenny acts as BUFORA's Director of Investigations and it is
probably the best respected of the national British societies. It
has around 400 members and suffers in the ways already described, although it has tried very hard to overcome these, having
strict standards for investigation and being a chief party to the
creation of the 'code of practice' mentioned in chapter 1. The
journalist had, however, already spoken with the Aetherius
Society. This is a London-based movement whose ideas include
the belief that Jesus is a spiritual being living on Venus who
regularly chats to high priests, some of whom hold services in a
converted garage in a member's back garden. Certainly the
Aetherius Society does neither research nor investigation into
UFOs. It has no need because it knows what UFOs are. It has
considerable attraction and thousands of members. On this criterion alone (that it had more members) the journalist chose to
take their word, rather than BUFORA's, saying that it was
endorsed by more people so must be more representative.

To list what ufologists (even serious-minded ones) have done
wrong over the past decades would take an embarrassingly long
time. A few 'benevolent sceptics', as they like to call themselves,
have tried to do this in books with titles such as *UFOs Explained*
(actually a ludicrous and misleading title, as is one of the favour-
ites of the armchair experts, *Flying Saucers From Mars*[2]). Such a
catalogue of error would positively benefit those people willing to
sit down and think through their mistakes, but the sad truth is
(and this is one of the worst errors in itself) that the ufologists
ignore the sceptics. Books written by Phillip Klass, Donald
Menzel, James Oberg, Ian Ridpath or Robert Shaeffer[3] suffer
from lack of availability. Going against the trend of public desire
(to believe in UFOs), they sell in limited numbers and rarely

[2] By C. Allingham (Methuen, 1954).
[3] See P. Klass, *UFOs: The Public Deceived* (Prometheus Books, 1983); J.
Oberg, *UFOs and Outer Space Mysteries* (1982); I. Ridpath, *Messages from
Space* (Fontana, 1979); R. Shaeffer, *The UFO Verdict* (Prometheus Books,
1983).

make paperback editions. This is all the excuse most ufologists need for never tracking them down. Even if they did come across one they would probably dismiss it as unimportant. Very few working ufologists bother to look at the arguments of their detractors, which at times (although certainly not always) are cogent and informed. It may not be irrelevant that by failing to read these books UFO enthusiasts can avoid pondering the unstable ground upon which their beliefs rest and, more importantly perhaps, can hide from the numerous preconceptions which to them may appear logical but to anyone else look like self-delusion.

Stanton Friedman, a nuclear scientist with an interest in UFOs, is an undeniably sincere and hard-working investigator, yet his beliefs demonstrate the dangers. The point is important since many outsiders tend to presume, as Friedman does, that UFOs must be spaceships or at the least alien intrusions of some sort. In fact the evidence for this view is a very long way from being 'overwhelming'. Most journalists, for example, when they approach serious UFO workers, are obviously bemused to find that it is possible to accept that the evidence supports the probable reality of UFOs but does not support the probable reality of alien spaceships. This to them seems logically contradictory, for surely either UFOs do exist or they do not; and if they do, then the only reasonable explanation seems to be those aforementioned aliens. Now, UFOs *might* be alien intrusions. There remains a slight possibility that they could be. But it is perfectly possible to look at the evidence in several other ways, none of which imply an alien origin. Some may even imply the non-existence of a real UFO enigma.

The sequence of inductive reasoning about UFOs is followed in quite the wrong way by most ufologists. First, they should ask, do these reports indicate that any phenomena are being observed? Second, if so, what practical possible explanations, in keeping with current science, can be suggested? Third (and only third), if puzzling reports still exist after exhausting the first two steps, what possibilities, which are out of keeping with current science, can be suggested? The alien-intrusions hypothesis about UFOs is only one of the options (and not necessarily the most likely) which comes into play during this third stage. But UFO enthusiasts leap over the first two stages as if they did not exist and push to one side all the other options. Before they ask the two really fundamental questions about the subject, 'do UFOs really exist?' and, if so, 'what are they?', they have their answer – they are spaceships. In the end, of course, they may be proved right, but to assume this is not the scientific approach to a subject as interesting and as baffling as the UFO phenomenon.

Ufologists should refrain from making dogmatic statements about the nature of their subject (which they are certainly not in a position to prove, although they may have interesting data that tentatively suggest them). Instead they should unite in the simple attempt to prove that a real phenomenon exists. With this they should then whet the appetite of scientists. At this stage that is enough. To attempt anything else simply courts disaster.

6

Science and Scepticism

*The scientific establishment has held its nose as though
carrying a decaying rat to the city dump.*

Dr J. Allen Hynek, astronomer,
Northwestern University, Illinois

The whole question of the existence and explanation of UFOs has
a public image that equates it with fringe religions and cults. You
will find books on the subject labelled 'occult' and filed alongside
those which discuss spoon bending, lucky charms and reading tea
leaves. (The reasons for this have been examined in previous
chapters; it is largely the fault of gullible UFO enthusiasts and the
newspapers and publishers who pander to the human desire for
adventure and mystery by their sensational accounts of sightings
and 'abductions'.) On the other hand, books which speculate on
the existence of extraterrestrial life will be placed in the 'science'
category and will merit reviews in serious science journals. Yet if
truth be told, we know *less* about the reality (or otherwise) of
alien life forms on some distant hypothetical world than we do
about the existence of genuine UFO phenomena.

Speculation about alien life forms seems to be a sensible
extension of current scientific speculation, whereas UFOs are a
threat to the common scientific world-view because they represent an apparent anomaly. They do not 'fit in' with current
scientific knowledge or theory. But surely it is wrong to dismiss
them because of this – we may learn more from looking at things
that do *not* fit, than by ignoring them and building only on what
we know.

This rejection of phenomena or new ideas is not unique; it has happened many times in the history of science. Einstein's ideas of relativity, Darwin's evolutionary concepts or Wegner's Theory of Continental Drift were each so controversial as to require time to be accepted. But that did not make them wrong.

The study of certain phenomena, such as UFOs, is harder to justify than it need be for sociological reasons. We might compare ufology with the research that is done into lucid dreaming. This occurs when the dreamer retains full awareness that he is dreaming and can, in some cases, control the dream imagery. This is uncommon. Dreams themselves are an entirely subjective experience: we only know that other people have them because they tell us that they do. There is no objective evidence for their occurrence and we have no photographs of dreams.

If logic were the only criterion for scientific research, lucid-dream study would be hard to justify. But it is not. The research exists quite happily within the scientific community, as does investigation into other subjective or obscure fields. The reason is simple. No controversial theory is attached to the problem. Were the popular view to be that dreams are messages from one's dead relatives, and lucid dreams examples of possession by their souls, then it would not be quite so easy for the psychologists seeking to justify this line of work! And yet, one hopes that scientists would recognize the reality of the basic phenomenon and the inadequacy of the popular explanation, and so instigate research in order to find a better one.

Ball lightning is perhaps the closest modern parallel to the UFO problem. It is a rare form of electrical discharge, often (but not exclusively) associated with thunderstorms. As its name implies, it is usually spherical and floats about in the atmosphere, tending to discharge with an explosion or retort. It has been observed for centuries but is relatively rare and has been ignored by scientists. The problem is that no current theory of lightning formation predicts it, which does not prove it to be impossible but does mean that *if* it exists theories of atmospheric electricity require modification. The modification of theories is not in itself a problem. Scientists do it all the time, but they are reluctant to do so without weighty evidence. Normally they will not (cannot, given the scientific method) consider a rare anomaly that has not been predicted. They will listen with limited sympathy until such time as solid evidence is built up by the advocates of the need for change.

The documentary evidence for ball lightning has been poor. There are few photographs and no known cine film. But its credibility has slowly been established by persistent scientists and a rising number of credible observations. Direct observation by scientists themselves, reported within the scientific literature, has done more than decades of claims by ordinary people. Some researchers still deny it but they are now in the minority. Various hypotheses, within the context of current scientific knowledge, are being developed to try to explain it.

The UFO phenomenon in its relationship with science closely parallels this position but it has the added burden of a highly sensational and emotive image. It is reasonable to argue that if the *News of the World* or the *National Enquirer* had regularly offered the public stories about 'killer creatures in a stormy sky' ball lightning would still be the laughing-stock of scientists.

UFO researchers must make it clear they are simply trying to prove that a scientific mystery exists and not to vindicate any particular theory of its origin. Far too many people presume that if one tries to argue that UFO events are real then one is also proclaiming the existence of little green men. Of course, such a possibility exists, which is why we have not refrained from saying so or offering evidence that *seems* to suggest that some governments think so. But, of course, they might have got it wrong. One *can* believe in UFOs and disbelieve in alien spaceships.

John Hind, an Irish ufologist, summed up this problem when he said:

One is left wondering what exactly it is that we are supposed to prove. It seems to me that, when thousands of people every year are reporting literally fantastic experiences we have a very promising area for study. Whether our study tells us something about the physical universe, extra-human intelligence or the human condition is secondary in importance.[1]

Ufologists find themselves in the position of geologists who, because they are incapable of showing that the planet's fossil

---

[1] J. Hind, 'The Myth of the UFO', *UFO Research Review,* vol. 3, no. 2, 1978.

record is consistent with biblical history and 'the flood', could well be told by a Christian majority that fossils therefore cannot exist. They are mistaking what must presumably be millions of 'coincidentally' shaped bits of rock. Of course this does not occur. Fossils exist and we all accept the fact, looking to the geologist to tell us what they are. Where then is the difference with UFOs? The fact is that ufologists themselves have problems coming to terms with their own enigma. Geologists generally have a consensus opinion about fossil formation. But there is much honest disagreement about the fundamentals of the UFO phenomenon. Some researchers insist that the solution lies mainly in the social or psychological fields. UFO events are somehow explicable as a human phenomenon. The magazine *Magonia* is a champion of this view and ufologists such as Dr Jacques Vallée key proponents. The *Magonia*-style ufologists (who call themselves 'the new ufology') tend to deny the physical aspects of the mystery. They thus incur the wrath of the other major school (sometimes given the name 'nuts and bolts ufology'). Formerly this kind of researcher was automatically assumed to believe that UFOs were spaceships. But there has been a major upsurge in theories which grant the UFO a real, physical basis but do *not* invest it with intelligence or mechanical construction. However, the divergence is still there, and adds to the difficulty of persuading scientists – either psychologists or physicists – that this is something they should be studying. A phenomenon which does not neatly fall into a particular branch of study is likely to lose out, as scientists are trained along rigid disciplinary lines, and tend to think (and have their funds provided) within certain categories.

It is important to recognize that ufology has a psychosocial and a physical component. The approach to the subject had been rather like scientists trying to understand the human brain. Physiologists look at it in physical, biochemical terms and discuss electrical impulses. In this way they can explain a great deal, such as the nature of migraine headaches or the origin of tumours. But physiologists are lost when it comes to explaining how one human being falls in love with another, how he or she conjures up a creative masterpiece, or why two people with the same size of brain have entirely different intelligence quotients. These are problems for the psychologist to grapple with. Only when it was appreciated that there were really two problems, not one, did either science find it could start generating credible theories. Physiologists can search for all-embracing theories about the workings of the brain because they know that subjective human traits do not need to be encompassed.

Ufology as science is therefore an artificial concept. It is rather like 'brainology' – which is also non-existent. The total understanding of the UFO enigma will require advances in several scientific fields. Almost certainly each will deal with different data, just as brain physiologists and brain psychologists have unique fields of operation. Acceptance of this fact is crucial, if we are ever to have scientific study of UFOs. But that study will *not* be a new science as such, not in the same way that atomic physics grew into a discipline of its own when we began to unlock the secrets of the basis of matter. Instead we will probably broach new avenues or extend a few old ones in several current scientific disciplines (see chapter 12), and see more co-operation between scientific disciplines.

Thomas Kuhn, the historian of science, wrote, 'No part of the aim of normal science is to call forth new sorts of phenomena, indeed those that will not fit the box are often not seen at all.'[2] Scientific concepts are all-important. Allen Hynek likes to remind us that there will be a twenty-first century science, even though twentieth-century scientists often forget this. Seen in this light, UFOs, while strange, are by no means impossible. All scientists ought to pin such a reminder on their office walls.

In 1781 when Sir William Herschel observed a fuzzy disc in the heavens nobody thought it could be a new planet. Scientific theory suggested that Saturn was the outermost in our solar system and the discovery of another one would just upset the harmony. So Herschel assumed that the fuzzy disc was a comet. It took a lot of checking and self-persuasion, and then a great deal of persuasion of others, before the discovery of what we now call the planet Uranus came to be accepted. Uranus is actually on the threshold of naked-eye visibility and had been telescopically observed several times before Herschel 'found' it. But nobody

---

[2] T.S. Kuhn, *The Structure of Scientific Revolutions* (University of Chicago Press, 1970).

was expecting a planet and so nobody 'saw' it.

Two psychologists (Bruner and Postman) once performed an illuminating experiment. They showed people a group of playing cards for the shortest possible exposure time to allow correct identification of the cards. But they seeded 'anomaly' cards into the usual pack, such as a *red* six of spades or a *black* four of hearts. At first everybody interpreted these cards wrongly but logically. The black four was seen as a spade instead of a heart. Then, as the exposure time was increased, people began to hesitate. They would comment that something seemed 'funny' about the anomaly card but could not explain what. Finally, at a very specific longer exposure time, the anomalous card was recognized for what it was. However, there were some people (even at 40 times the standard exposure time for correct identification) who still failed to see the anomaly. They were very distressed by it. One exclaimed, 'I don't know what suit it is! I don't even know if it's a red! I'm not sure what a spade should look like . . .' This experiment has many lessons for ufology. It shows, for instance, how a witness can see a light, interpret it as a UFO and become emotionally distressed because at one level he realizes he is dealing with a misperception. But it might work the other way as well. A witness may see a genuine UFO and desperately try to explain it away to himself, becoming acutely disturbed because he knows what he is seeing is not in line with the normality that he thinks ought to be there.

Scientists are human beings. They must sometimes behave in this way. UFOs are a challenge to their world-view and so, as serious anomalies, may generate unusual responses in those forced into confrontation with them. Vallée gives an interesting example of this response taken to an extreme.[3] A group of scientists observed a UFO and tracked it with a theodolite. One might expect that the excitement caused by being unable to explain what they saw would make them study UFOs carefully. Sadly it did not. Instead they destroyed the evidence and dropped the whole matter.

Philosopher William James correctly reminds us that 'our

---

[3] J. Vallée, *The Invisible College* (Dutton, 1975); published in the UK as *UFOs: The Psychic Solution* (Granada, 1977).

science is but a drop, our ignorance a sea.' However, many ufologists have yet to learn to stay within scientific confines while speculating. Theories must be accompanied by *testable* predictions before scientists will listen. Fortunately, the sea of ignorance about UFOs is at last showing ripples of scientific interest, and this is enormously encouraging.

PART 2 · CURRENT INVESTIGATION

7

The Problems of Investigation

The central problem for UFO research is in the standard of investigation of the cases which comprise the data base. It has to be said that nothing can undermine the foundations of the subject as effectively as poor investigation of UFO events. Conversely, thorough investigations, whatever their conclusions (UFO or IFO), can only support the work of researchers who labour over unravelling this perplexing subject. But it is very difficult to achieve a high overall standard. As we have seen, the great majority of people involved in the subject and its investigation are not trained in the various disciplines associated with investigative techniques. Indeed the only reason for the involvement of some people is that they want to see a UFO, and many of these are very young or inexperienced enthusiasts. Clearly this situation is far from satisfactory. However, the serious researcher can of course take steps to minimize the problems.

Recently more and more serious researchers have been refusing to accept data from sources of dubious reliability, preferring to ignore material rather than introduce inaccuracies into their work. Also in recent years some organizations have tightened their criteria for accepting 'investigators'. BUFORA has introduced a scheme whereby only their members of proven competence can be regarded as investigators. It has also developed a training scheme for investigators. Many British researchers have collaborated in the adoption, in 1982, of a code of practice (see appendix). It is hoped that this code, which we were instrumental in instigating, will be adopted by all investigators. Time will tell whether these and other attempts will bring about a rise in the quality of investigations.

Interpretation of the enigma relies totally on accurate investigations. Clearly, any interpretation based on erroneous data must be faulty, and this fact has led to the downfall of many. We believe that the most common interpretation of UFO events, that UFOs represent a visitation by an extraterrestrial technology, is based upon simplistic and erroneous assumptions. We also believe that the opposite view, that UFOs do not exist, is equally wrong. In our experience many sceptics and debunkers are equally guilty of simplistic and erroneous interpretations, e.g. the oft-cited claim that 'there is no evidence for visitation by extra-terrestrials; therefore UFOs do not exist.'

With very few exceptions, those actively involved in UFO research in Great Britain are working in their own time and financing their own research. No matter how professional the approach under these circumstances, the results must suffer. Lack of time can either mean that a project will take considerably longer than it might otherwise, or it may be rushed and con-densed. Both situations invite error. Financial insecurity is the single greatest problem which holds back progress on a number of fronts. The authors have frequently made the point that research projects need not be expensive, and there are many which would benefit from modest amounts of funding for small-scale equip-ment or other needs. If both time and money were readily available, it is doubtful that lack of motivation would present a problem. A further consideration which needs also to be taken into account is the integrity of the participants.

At an early stage in our involvement we saw that in some ways the enigma was self-perpetuating; this is partly because people are selective in their interpretations of reports. For example, where the reported 'object' is unlike an aeroplane, no checks would be made to determine whether an aeroplane might have been the stimulus. While it might seem laborious to check out all possible sources of stimuli, the examples of misidentifications quoted in this book and elsewhere (e.g. *The UFO Handbook*) make it abundantly clear that the integrity and accuracy of the investigator is a factor which needs careful consideration.

A good example of misidentification involved two women, one

aged 65 and her daughter-in-law, aged 30. The site was a home in Hastings, England and the event took place late one October evening in 1981. At about 8.55 p.m. the older woman was watching television when she felt compelled to look out of the window. She was amazed to see a large yellow object in the sky and went out to obtain a better view. She described it as being like 'two blobs of golden jelly, wobbling and pulsating'. It also seemed to take on the appearance of a cross. The woman telephoned her son and daughter-in-law to alert them to the spectacle; although they lived close by, they were unable to see the mysterious object. However, her daughter-in-law made the short journey to join her. At first, the object was not to be seen, but after five or ten minutes it reappeared and they watched it together for half an hour. The object took on various forms during this time. It was said to be 'forming its own camouflage by emitting a cloud'. The women claimed that they saw the vapour coming from inside the object. While they watched, on five occasions aeroplanes approached it, two of which they said were military jets which had gone to investigate. Each time an aeroplane approached the object disappeared behind its cloud. The object also appeared as a vertical cigar shape, two giant golden discs (like dinner-plates) and a crescent. Later it was seen as a bright red disc on the horizon. They were astonished by the speed with which it had moved. They both wished that it would return, and it did, dramatically. It returned 'very close' and was said to be over a nearby house. At this point the younger woman said she was able to see more detail and described rotating lights near the bottom of it and two solid, near-vertical sides above. The object again disappeared and they knew that this time it was final, but were grateful that it had answered their previous telepathic request to return. The object disappeared just before 10.00 p.m.

After this the older woman telephoned the police because she felt that 'someone in authority ought to be told.' Two policemen duly arrived and took details and said that they would call back if their senior officer felt the incident should be pursued. The fact that they did not call back was taken by the women to mean that an official cover-up was in operation. The following day the older woman claimed that she saw strange characters at the top of her television screen. There were dashes and the letters z and c. She thought that this was connected with what she had seen the previous evening, a message perhaps. In addition, both women had suffered localized headaches over one eye; these recurred for the following three weeks. Perhaps the most significant effect alleged by the older woman occurred on the Thursday following the original event, which had occurred on a Sunday evening. At about midday the woman had felt tired and cold. She lay on her bed and suffered what she described as a black-out for the next 14 hours. The next thing she remembers was waking up at 2.30 a.m. At first she thought she had suffered a stroke. A doctor was called and he could find no evidence of a stroke or any other cause. The woman had not suffered from any such black-outs before and felt strongly that it was an effect of the UFO. She wondered what had happened to her during the 14 hours and hinted strongly at the possibility of a time-loss such as she had read about in a recent Sunday newspaper article about some sensational cases involving alien beings.

The investigator, Philip Taylor, said that the witnesses constantly inferred that the UFO was without doubt an alien spaceship and 'they', the aliens controlling it, were mentioned many times. The event was described as a 'miracle' and it was said that the aliens were good as opposed to evil. They also felt that there must be a reason why they in particular had been chosen for this contact. Furthermore it was said that they thought that the aliens were protecting them and that they now felt more confident about the world in general. When asked about the headaches and blackouts the older woman said that these effects were not deliberately harmful. Both women repeatedly described the object as beautiful.

Following a report of this sighting in local newspapers the women received a typical variety of phone calls and letters. These included members of a local religious sect, a local headmaster and a local councillor who all said they had seen it. The councillor said she had been 'terrified'. Commenting on the newspaper article involving their report the women said that the 'Royal Observatory at Herstmonceux pretended it was the Moon.' The consistent attitude taken by the witnesses was that 'the authorities' knew exactly what was going on, and that only by publicizing reports such as theirs could the truth be generally known. In

November 1984 one of the women wrote to Jenny Randles and related the events described above, assuming that Jenny did not know of them. She pleaded for someone to take seriously what she insisted on calling 'the miracle' in her back garden.

In this case we have an apparently spectacular and inexplicable event witnessed by two people who agree on the salient details of the event and who clearly believe they saw an alien spacecraft. The witnesses appeared very sincere and undoubtedly genuine in their beliefs. Philip Taylor's unambiguous conclusion was that the witnesses had been watching the moon shortly before it set. The sky had been covered by broken cloud and this had affected its appearance. At the time of the event the moon was approximately at its first quarter at that latitude and set that particular day at 10.02 p.m. There is no doubt that the two women seriously misidentified the moon and regarded it as a UFO. Needless to say they denied having watched the moon and indeed testify that they saw it over their shoulders. This would have been impossible from the point where they observed the event.

Philip Taylor, by profession an astronomer at the Royal Observatory, produced an excellent report which should be used as a model by other investigators. Despite the fact that the 'UFO' had been identified, he still produced a thorough report. This, and the case it details, illustrate a multitude of points relevant to many UFO events. To begin with, many investigators would not have bothered to submit a full report for an identified event, particularly one involving such a mundane stimulus as the moon. Second, it does not require us to point out the escalation from simple misidentification to the extremes described. To the seasoned researcher this aspect should not be surprising. Virtually all UFO reports contain some elaboration of the basic details. We have frequently drawn attention to the considerable amount of information available about eyewitness testimony and investigative techniques so as to minimize the inaccuracies which can be incidentally or deliberately introduced by eyewitnesses. Clearly eyewitness testimony can be affected enormously by the beliefs of the witnesses – their own interpretations of what they see. But see p. 165 for a discussion of the usual overall accuracy of eyewitness descriptions. One book in particular is worth mentioning because of its direct relevance to the UFO enigma – *The Psychology of*

Anomalous Experience by Professor Graham Reed.[1] It contains a wealth of information on many aspects such as the 'time-gap experience', 'hypnagogic and hypnopompic imagery' and, perhaps of most relevance, a section of the anomalies of judgement and belief. It is interesting to speculate what might have been the outcome of a case such as that of the two women had the investigator not realized what was actually responsible. The true facts would probably not have come to light in time to prevent a further escalation of the event towards the bizarre. The case would at least have been notched up as another 'unidentified' with all the hallmarks of a 'nuts-and-bolts' UFO. As Philip Taylor pointed out, the witnesses constantly used the term UFO to mean an alien spacecraft and not to indicate something unidentified.

Third, a further chapter might have been opened if the woman's claim of a time-lapse experience had been taken to be more significant. There is a very real possibility that she might have been subjected to regression hypnosis in an attempt to gain access to a memory of that period. Experience and research have shown a considerable number of problems arising from the use of regression hypnosis in UFO investigation. The possibility of extracting some kind of UFO incident is highly likely – even where no 'real' incident exists. A more detailed discussion of hypnosis is included in chapter 10. The problems associated with its use in such circumstances are such that many researchers would prefer not to apply the technique at all, rather than to cloud the issue with controversial conclusions. Herein lies something of a dilemma. While many researchers do not regard hypnosis as a reliable technique for use in investigation, it would be both interesting and valuable to know more about why hypnosis produces such consistent and remarkable (if unreliable) stories in time-lapse cases. As we will see later, even people with no experience of UFO events can be hypnotized and regressed to an imaginary UFO experience with surprising results.[2]

In the example quoted above the witnesses referred to an article in the *Sunday Mirror* which had detailed the experience of a policeman in West Yorkshire, England, who had seemingly

[1] Hutchinson University Library, 1972.
[2] *Journal of UFO Studies*, vol. 1, no. 1, published by CUFOS, 1982.

suffered a fifteen-minute time loss. Part of the investigation into this case involved the use of hypnosis on the policeman in an attempt to help him recall that period. Subsequently it emerged from the regression sessions that he had been abducted and subjected to a pseudomedical examination by an alien on board a 'UFO'. The effect that this had upon the women from Hastings is clear: they felt that the older woman's period of 'black-out' might conceal an abduction by aliens. The subject is self-perpetuating, and this is a perfect example of the process at work.

The case also highlights another dilemma: whether articles such as that in the *Sunday Mirror* should be encouraged (i.e. assisted) by people involved in the subject. It would be impossible to prevent UFO incidents being followed up by the media, and indeed there is a body of opinion which contends that the popular media are suitable channels through which to present news about UFOs for the large interested proportion of the general public. The opinion has also been expressed that payments obtained from supplying the media with details of and articles about UFO events might be used to finance research. However, there is a fine line between publishing accurate and objective material and satisfying the desire of the public and the media for the more bizarre and 'exotic' aspects of the subject. After all, 'Two women watch UFO for an hour' is far better media fodder than 'Two women watch moon for an hour'.

Despite the fact that there are many cases where witnesses have totally misinterpreted a mundane situation, there are still cases where the object observed remains unidentified despite exhaustive investigation. It would not be unreasonable to argue that some or all such cases are simply those to which we have yet to fit the appropriate mundane situation. But there are cases where this is unlikely. Whereas some consider 'unidentified' to imply that the UFOs are spaceships, others interpret the situation rather differently. We believe that there *are* unidentified flying objects, but they are not necessarily spaceships. Our research shows that there are two different types of UFO event. In some cases the witnesses objectively observe a phenomenon, while in others they subjectively experience an event. In the case of the more 'objective' group the witnesses observe something and can make quantifiable judgements of various details. In our opinion there is an as yet unexplained type of transient atmospheric phenomenon which we have termed UAP (unidentified atmospheric phenomenon). Cases involving UAPs are discussed in chapter 9.

In the other group of UFO cases the witnesses would be better described as percipients. In such cases they are more subjective in their descriptions and rather than being observers they 'participate' in a UFO experience. The case of the two Hastings women is typical, and here the unidentified component is not whatever the UFO was – in this instance the moon – but rather, the 'unidentified' mechanism or belief system which caused them completely to misinterpret a familiar object.

Plate 1 Science meets the UFOs! This is one of a sequence of four photographs which are much celebrated within ufology. They were taken by Almiro Barauna, a freelance photographer aboard the Brazilian Navy training vessel, *Almirante Saldanha*. The ship had a crew of sailors and scientists on a research mission to the desolate crags of Trindade Island, 800 miles off the South American coast, as part of International Geophysical Year. Just after noon on 16 January 1958 this lens-shaped object allegedly approached them, hovered over the island and then departed. Its fuzzy outline is supposedly due to a greenish vapour or mist seen around its perimeter. Computer enhancement has apparently verified that the images show a real, large object some distance from the camera. But the case remains controversial because none of the scientists on board have ever come forward to support the story. (*Fortean Picture Library*)

Plate 2 Popular myth has it that the first 'flying saucer' was spotted in 1947. In fact, strange things in the sky have been seen throughout history. If any modern-day UFO phenomena do turn out to be natural atmospheric events (or UAPs) then it is logical to expect that they have always been around, though perceived differently according to the expectations of the time. This Samuel Coccius illustration from the sixteenth century 'Basel Broadsheet' depicts a local Swiss 'sighting' on 7 August 1566. Are these black globes medieval UAPs? (*Fortean Picture Library*)

Plate 3 The immediate forerunner of the 'flying saucer' was the 'foo fighter'. These balls of fire were seen by several pilots, on both sides of the conflict, during the second world war. Contemporary opinion was that they were German secret weaponry, perhaps a means to foil radar detection. This is a good example of the way the 'UFO' is viewed according to the social climate of its day. Four decades later some would doubtless suggest that aliens had sent mini-probes to monitor the war. Or we might conclude that they are some form of UAP. Sceptics will probably look for an answer in terms of canopy reflections in the pilot's line of sight. (*Fortean Picture Library*)

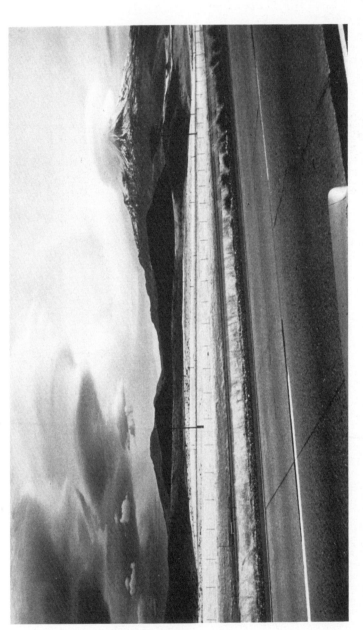

Plate 4 UFO investigators must always be prepared for human error. It is surprising what some people will report as alien craft – even humble clouds! Those not used to seeing lenticular clouds piled over mountain ranges, such as these in California, can easily be fooled into speculating about giant 'mother ships' drifting across the sky. This does not only occur in exotic locations. Jenny Randles investigated one case which turned out to be a lenticular cloud over Sunderland! (*Rene Dahinden/Fortean Picture Library*)

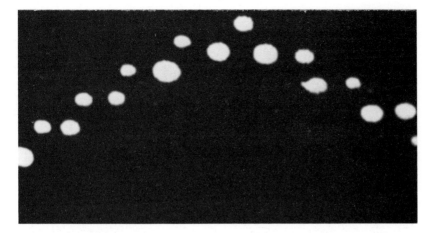

Plate 5 UFO formations tend to be viewed with suspicion by seasoned investigators, since most occurrences have been explained. V-shaped light formations have eventually been related to aircraft refuelling high in the sky, flocks of birds reflecting ground lights and drifting parachute flares during military operations. These lights were photographed by Carl Hart Jr on 30 August 1951, over Lubbock, Texas, during a wave of similar local sightings which became known as the 'Lubbock Lights'. In this case no definitive explanation was reached. (*Fortean Picture Library*)

Plate 6 One of the first questions a UFO investigator should ask on seeing a 'UFO' photograph is 'Did you see anything odd when you snapped the shutter?' Surprisingly often the answer is 'no'. Wilfred Power took this picture of a giraffe at Plymouth zoo in Devon during August 1972. The disc-like UFO was not noticed by anyone until the print was developed. Did an alien craft zip overhead too fast to be detected? Or is the more likely alternative (a processing fault on the film) to blame? Experienced ufologists will (sadly) tell you that ninety-five per cent of all UFO photographs provide no evidence for UFO reality at all. (*Plymouth UFO Research Group/Fortean Picture Library*)

Plate 7 When an apparently genuine photograph of a UFO turns up it is rightly given full investigation. This case is doubly interesting because it shows something which is very unlikely to be a UAP. It looks, and apparently behaved, like a structured, powered disc, and was observed by two witnesses in broad daylight. Farmer Paul Trent and his wife obtained two shots (of which this is one) from their home near McMinnville, Oregon, on 11 May 1950. The pictures have been subjected to a vast amount of analysis since, including computer enhancement. All tests were passed with flying colours. This case remains one of the very few where witness testimony and photographic evidence both strongly support the reality of large craft of unknown origin in the sky. Even the Condon scientists failed to resolve this one after much effort, and deemed it unexplained. (*Fortean Picture Library*)

Plate 8 The aftermath of a collision between a UFO (or UAP) and Deputy Sheriff Val Johnson's police car near Warren, Minnesota, on 27 August 1979. The case has been fully investigated, but no satisfactory explanation discovered. See pages 93–8. (*International UFO Reporter*)

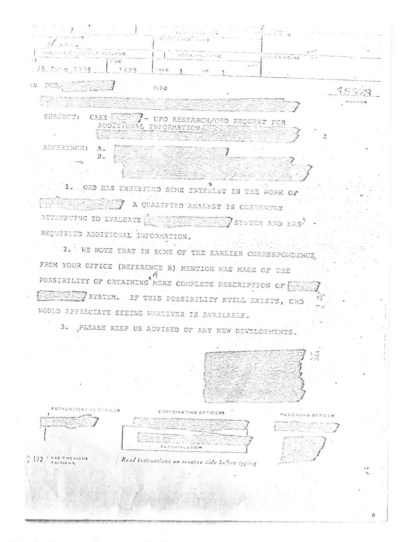

Plate 9 Since the Freedom of Information Act became law in the USA private citizens have had the right to obtain documents from the security services, provided this does not infringe national security. Countless UFO documents (including some whose previous existence had been denied) have been extracted from bodies such as the NSA, FBI and CIA. Others have been refused on security grounds in cases taken as far as the Supreme Court. This June 1976 CIA memo postdates the official end of government interest in UFOs by seven years! The level of censorship it illustrates is not untypical, and is mild in comparison with some others. It evidently relates to research by the Office of Research and Development (a CIA scientific sub-group) into UFOs, with specific attention to 'propulsion systems'. Other CIA papers also refer to research being conducted over the past decade by scientists under security agency control. Yet *none* of this material has been made available, despite requests. Most scientists do not realize that serious scientific research is going on under strict secrecy. Officially, the US government continue to take the line that UFOs (a) do not exist and (b) are of no interest to them.

Plate 10 Site photographs taken by Peter Hough of the Manchester UFO Research Association at the location of the Abram, Lancashire, incident of 13 August 1982. The top one depicts the view the witnesses had across playing fields behind their homes, as the cigar-shaped object travelled from the colliery, from left to right towards Crank Woods and the alloy plant. The lower one shows the second location of the main witnesses, beside Abram Alloys and the old pit shaft, looking into the woods along Plank Lane. The ball-like UAP made a close approach down this path. The witnesses' car was parked in the same position as Peter Hough's car in this picture. (*Peter Hough*)

8

UFO Types: Some Examples

Throughout this book various incidents have been related to illustrate certain aspects of the subject and as examples of specific types of experience. It is useful to explore some cases in more detail to show the range of problems with which investigators are faced. These accounts are not comprehensive and are not intended to put forward all the relevant available information. Certainly the UFO phenomenon does not depend on a few isolated cases. The real strength of the evidence is not that a witness may claim to have been abducted by the occupants of an alien spaceship in 1954, which by careful detective work may be shown to be dubious. The strength lies in the fact that hundreds of people all over the world, year in, year out, reliably observe things in the sky that they cannot understand. To explain many as prosaic events and infer that all the others are the same is unjust. One factor frequently overlooked by debunkers is that skilled and experienced investigators regularly identify the phenomena involved in some 90 per cent of raw reports. When considering these cases it should be realized that we are not presenting them as unexplainable but as cases which to the best of our knowledge at the time of writing are unexplained.

Strange Objects in the Sky

Type: UAP
Date: 13 August 1982
Time: 9.30–10.30 p.m. BST
Place: Abram, Greater Manchester, England

Investigators: Peter Hough and Jenny Randles (Manchester
UFO Research Association – MUFORA) and Arthur Tomlin-
son (Direct Investigation Group of Aerial Phenomena)

The popular image of a ufologist is of someone investigating the
truth of an abduction by aliens. The following is a far more
common form of investigation.

During the late evening of 13 August 1982 a man was called
from the front room of their home by his wife, who had seen
something unusual in the sky to the rear of the property. When
they went out into the back garden they both saw a large, light-
grey-coloured, cigar-like object moving across the sky from the
south-west to the south-east. The rear of the object was described
as 'teat shaped' by the woman; it glowed and left an orange trail.
Alongside the house is a playing field and the couple moved into
it to gain a better view. One of their neighbours was already there
with his nephew watching the object.

Their attention was caught by two small lights which were
apparently moving around in the distance near a local colliery.
The mine is about three-quarters of a mile away. Then another
small light appeared from the direction of Horwich (to the north).
This light moved very fast and at low altitude. It joined the other
two lights 'flying' around the colliery. The latter object or light
seemed to be shaped like an ice-cream cone, was light grey in
colour, had two orange lights at the rear, a white one at the
leading edge and white light spreading as a fan beneath. After
watching these for a few minutes the witnesses returned their
attention to the cigar-shaped object and found that it was now
moving slowly sideways towards them. On it there seemed to be a
horizontal row of square holes from which issued bright white
light. The glow from the rear had ceased but the light from the
square holes was alternately bright and dim. One witness likened
them to portholes. The first two lights from the colliery area
began to move up towards the object. Then, shortly after they
had moved, the cone-shaped object moved upwards too, and
then with a burst of speed overtook the other two. Then it either
flew behind the cigar-shaped object or it flew inside it; either way
it was not seen again. The two other lights remained in view close
by the large object.

The principal witnesses decided that a better view could be gained from a site down a local lane; this journey took about five minutes by car. During the journey the witnesses lost sight of the objects. Once in the lane they parked the car under a bright light from the yard of a local factory, Abram Alloys, and spotted the lights and object again. The time was approximately 10.00 p.m. The cigar-like object was now over Crankwood and moving to the north-east. The two lights stopped over the Plank Lane area to the east. One light made as if to move off towards the large object but changed course and began to move towards the witnesses along a shallow valley. The large object by this time was about to disappear from view behind some trees but not before the woman saw it perform a strange manoeuvre – it moved from the horizontal to the vertical and back; this it did repeatedly, all the time maintaining its outward motion relative to them.

The light in the shallow valley was now approaching them quickly and they decided it was time they drove off. As they were about to move the woman watched the light approaching them, but her husband's attention was caught by what appeared to be the two headlights of a car coming around a bend in the lane about 300 yards away. As he hurriedly reversed the car to turn around, the woman looked along the lane and rather than seeing the two 'headlights' saw one orange-coloured ball about three feet in diameter. It was moving towards them. As they drove off down the lane he was able to glimpse the orange sphere in the driving mirror. When they reached some houses at the end of the lane they stopped the car and, feeling more secure, got out, but no lights were to be seen. On the way home, they found the car's indicators were not working. When the couple reached home a news programme on the television was just finishing and they judged the time to be 10.25 p.m.

In addition to the neighbour and his nephew in the playing field, another witness saw the initial events from a nearby house. He described how two lights had 'flown' around an object 'much bigger than an airliner' and how the lights flew behind or into the larger object. His description of the main cigar-like object tallies almost exactly with those of the other four witnesses.

Shortly after the main witnesses' return home their ten-year-old son came home from playing with a friend and quite independently described how he and his friend had seen something strange in the sky over Crankwood. He said it seemed to have coloured lights and 'sparks'; they thought the time had been about 10 p.m. There were several other possible witnesses to the events, although of course there is no way of proving they saw the same things. A number of unusual things were apparently seen in the general area at about the same time. For example a couple from St Helens, a few miles west, saw an orange, cigar-like object with what they interpreted as 'portholes'. The husband in this instance is a qualified engineer keenly interested in aviation, and he was confident it was not an aeroplane. This couple say the event they witnessed occurred on the same date as the above account, though it was not reported until some time later. They say they were ignorant of the main sighting.

Two days after the incident the Abram couple noticed that the lights on their car were not working. It had not been used since their return from the lane on the 13th. Investigation showed that wires to two of the car's fuses had charred and were now brittle: the two fuses had blown. Although the evening had been dark the couple could not remember if they had used the car lights during their return journey. The lamps at the factory and the street lights close to the end of the lane meant there was only a short distance of lane where full headlights might have been necessary. They cannot recall whether the lights worked normally or if they were not used. As a consequence it is impossible to say when the fuses actually blew, though the possibility remains that the fault occurred during the incident.

The husband, now retired, was a mining surveyor with the National Coal Board and is an expert on the local geology. While apparently ignorant of any theory linking the UFOs with piezoelectric phenomena, he pointed out the position of several faults in the area. Investigations linked the position of the lights to the proximity of the Pennington fault, the largest in the area. Enquiries at Abram Alloys uncovered the fact that it had been built at the top of an old mine. The shaft is now covered, but right next to the spot where the couple had parked their car. The vicinity is notoriously unstable and there have been several small-scale earth tremors in recent years. This, plus the fact that a rich quartz vein was found nearby, may well support the Devereux hypothesis of 'earthlights' (see chapter 9). During the course of the investigation it emerged that the husband had, over a number of years, experienced psychic-type experiences, including precognition and seeing ghosts. These had continued after the UFO sighting. Whatever one's view of them, it must be remembered that there are independent witnesses to support the fact that something strange did occur in the area on that evening. Taking all the accounts into consideration we must conclude that some form of UAP was observed.

Collision of car with UFO

Type: close encounter of the second kind[1]
Date: 27 August 1979
Time: 1.40 a.m. local
Place: near Warren, Minnesota, USA
Investigators: Allan Hendry (CUFOS) and others

'As a police officer I work with logic, truth and facts. In this case the facts do not necessarily represent a logical explanation. That's a bit frightening.' So said Deputy Sheriff Val Johnson following an incident in which his patrol car apparently collided with a UFO. The incident was reported in detail in the *International UFO Reporter*,[2] the source from which this account is taken.

Val Johnson is the only witness to the event which occurred in a rural area of flat land with few houses and buildings. The roads there are laid on a rectangular grid pattern, with an uninterrupted view from one to another. As Johnson was driving west from a small town called Stephen he caught sight of a light near some trees which he knew to be two-and-a-half miles away near a road junction towards which he was driving. At that junction he turned left (south) on to highway 220 and headed for the light, which as

---

[1] A close encounter of the first kind (CE1) is the close approach of a UFO which interacts with the witness or the environment. A close encounter of the second kind (CE2) involves similar interaction but leaves permanent, scientifically testable evidence (effects on witness or environment). See p. 136 for CE3 and CE4.

[2] *International UFO Reporter*, vol. 4, nos. 3/4 and 5, 1979.

far as he could tell had been stationary. He accelerated to
65 m.p.h. As he drew closer he could see that the light did not
appear to be illuminating the surrounding area. After he had
driven about a mile south along highway 220 the light seemed to
'greatly accelerate' towards him. It covered the remaining half to
one mile in an instant. Deputy Johnson heard no sound from the
light, and it appeared as a blinding glare. He lost consciousness at
this point but recalls the sound of breaking glass.

When he regained consciousness the patrol car was at right
angles across the other side of the road, and facing east. His head
was resting against the steering wheel and his eyes hurt. He
radioed for assistance at once; that call was timed at 2.19 a.m. At
2.21 another deputy was dispatched to assist him. When Johnson's
colleague Greg Winskowski arrived he noticed a red bump on
Johnson's forehead. It was assumed that this had occurred when
Johnson hit his head on the steering wheel and that this had
knocked him out. He was shivering, no doubt from shock, and an
ambulance which had been called to the incident took him to
hospital at Warren. He was examined by a doctor at 4.00 a.m.
Apparently by this time the red bump on his forehead was not
conspicuous and the doctor was not informed that Johnson had
been unconscious; therefore he concentrated on the eye pain.
This the doctor concluded was due to 'mild welding burns'; the
direct light of the doctor's instruments caused considerable discomfort – hurting so much that he did not make a thorough
examination. He treated the irritation to the eyes and bandaged
them. At 5.00 a.m., after tape-recording a statement, Johnson
was allowed home to rest.

During this time the patrol car was being moved back to the
base garage. The obvious damage was catalogued: one headlight
was smashed, a small circular dent was found in the bonnet, the
windscreen was shattered, a red light on top of the car was
punctured and dislodged from its housing and two radio antennae
were bent backwards. During the course of this examination, and
while Johnson was recording his statement at the sheriff's office,
it was noted that the dashboard clock and Johnson's wrist-watch
were running 14 minutes slow. They had both been set correctly
at 7.00 p.m. the previous evening and timings logged by Johnson
before the 'collision' prove that they had been running correctly
up until the incident.

At 11.00 a.m. that morning Johnson and his senior officer drove to see another doctor, an eye specialist. When the bandages were removed it was found that the irritation had cleared up, and there was no discomfort from direct light. It was established that the irritation and discomfort had had sufficient time between the two examinations to heal.

The initial communication about the incident was telephoned to CUFOS on its toll-free facility. As soon as details of the incident were known to Hendry, checks were made to explore the possibility of the events being anything to do with any known aircraft movements. No movements were known which might explain the events; this of course is not to say that aircraft may not have been involved. The following day Hendry flew to Warren to commence his investigation. By this time the sheriff and his men had conducted a search of the road for shattered headlight glass; this was located and therefore identified the spot at which the 'collision' took place, adjacent to milepost 68 on highway 220. The patrol car had travelled another 855 feet before the tyre skid marks on the road indicate the point at which the brakes locked the wheels, bringing the car to a halt 99 feet further along the road. Prior to Hendry's arrival the sheriff had conducted a survey of the whole area using a Geiger counter; no readings higher than the usual background count were recorded. Hendry searched the area near the trees where the 'UFO' had first been seen but could find nothing which might indicate the presence of anything unusual. Checks were also made to see if any aircraft landing marks could be found, but they too proved negative. Radar plots of the area during the night in question were also investigated. However, nothing emerged to explain the events.

Hendry made arrangements with several agencies to study the various areas of damage on the patrol car.

Windscreen

The screen remained intact but there were four distinct places where localized fracturing had occurred. One was on the inside face of the inner glass ply and the other three were on the outside face of the outer ply. It was concluded that the four fracture points represented different points of impact and that the time lapse between them was a few milliseconds. The laminate was not punctured or torn. It was also concluded that all the damage to the screen was due to mechanical forces and not to thermal stress. Meridan French, the windscreen expert from the Ford Motor Company, made tracings of the fracture damage which gave some indication of the nature of the damage. However, after several days of work he could only say that the 'cracks were due to mechanical forces of unknown source.'

Antennae and light lenses

The two radio antennae had been bent towards the rear of the car through angles of about 65 and 90 degrees; these bends occur at different heights above ground level. Using a Bausch and Lamb stereo optical microscope engineers examined the surface of the 65-degree bend in the roof-mounted antenna. From their report we learn that:

deposits of insect debris and road way matter covered the forward facing surfaces with a noticeably cleaner surface in the area located at the bend. The bend had occurred smoothly with no cracking of the metal at either the outside bend or any other location. No impact marks resulting from collisions with 'pieces' of any kind (except insects) were evident.

Both the mounts by which the antennae were fixed to the car incorporate a spring device which would absorb any stress if the antennae were to be struck and forced to bend in any direction. On release the antennae would return to their normal position. It is odd that the antennae bent and that the spring mounting did not apparently absorb the stress.

The engineers from the materials-testing laboratory of Honeywell Incorporated at Minneapolis also examined the headlight glass. 'The pieces of headlight lens glass recovered from the road showed brittle fractures typical of glass breaking from collision with flying particles. Numerous insect deposits coated the glass.' There was a small hole in one of the red light covers mounted on top of the car; examination showed this to be due to collision damage from a particle. Tests for radioactivity, magnetic anomalies and metal hardness were also conducted on the damaged car. The results of these indicated no unusual effects.

The conclusions of these investigations were that the damage to the headlight and red light and to the dented bonnet were the results of a collision at high speed with (probably) roadside stones. The antennae were not bent by stones hitting them, nor was heat a factor in their damage. The report did suggest that the bending may have resulted from a high velocity air blast or electrostatic (or similar) force.

Wristwatch and dashboard clock

The two timepieces had suffered a delay of 14 minutes and this had apparently happened during the incident. It was felt that because Johnson's wristwatch was not anti-magnetic a magnetic anomaly might have caused the effect. In an attempt to determine if this had been the case a magnetometer was used to map the magnetic field of the patrol car and a similar car for comparison. There was no significant deviation, which suggests that there had not been a 'crippling magnetic field' acting on the timepieces. Both watch and clock functioned normally after the incident.

The explanation of what Deputy Sheriff Johnson encountered that night has still to be found. The case, and others like it, suggest that there may not be a single explanation; rather, a number of factors combined to confound simplistic interpretation.

This event is odd enough. The following account appeared in the same issue of the *International UFO Reporter,* describing an event which took place near Vermillion, South Dakota, USA, on 29 August 1979 at 2.00 a.m.

Russ Johnson (no relation to Val Johnson), was driving alone, again on a lonely road (Highway 50), two days after the deputy's experience to the hour and 400 miles to the south. Again the sky was clear and the weather good. This Johnson also described seeing a light like a headlight just ahead of him on the highway for about 2 seconds. Then in the space of another 2 seconds the light rushed at him and suddenly engulfed his car. 'I thought I was in a light bulb.' Closing his eyes against the blinding light, he slammed on the brakes and hoped for the best. Just like Deputy Johnson his car skidded to a stop and spun sideways across the road facing east. He then opened his eyes ... watch the light source rush silently westbound rise in angle slightly ... and vanish abruptly. The witness acknowledged that what looked like a vapour trail could easily have been only a retinal after-image.

The case is *so* similar to the deputy's that it must be asked if this wasn't sheer mimicry. Yet it took place hours before even the local press went to print with word of Deputy Johnson's experience. It wasn't until the following day, Thursday, that someone in South Dakota could have heard about it . . . and Russ Johnson contends that he did *not* know about it at the time. Besides, he is not claiming that he or his car suffered injury and, no, his timepieces weren't affected!

A third almost identical case was reported in *UFO Research Australia* vol. 5, no. 5, 1984, which occurred in Tasmania on 20 August 1979.

The Very Strange Helicopter

Type: close encounter of the fourth kind
Date: 19 August 1979
Time: 9 p.m. BST
Place: East Didsbury, Greater Manchester, England
Investigators: Norman Collinson, Harry Harris and Mike Sacks
    (MUFORA)

The primary witness in this case is a woman aged 36 at the time of the experience. We'll call her Linda. She is a mother and house-wife, with two children (Andrea, then 15, and Marcus, then 5). She was known to Harry Harris through a mutual friend and reported her story two years after it had happened. She had told nobody except family and close friends.

The family live in a south Manchester house beside a meander-ing stretch of the River Mersey. A busy motorway crosses the river near a line of pylons, and a large oval area of land is wedged between the river bends. At about 8 p.m. on a warm, sunny evening Linda and her children left the house to walk along a path that curves along the river bank, to pick wild flowers. Her hus-band, Trevor, who is an engineer, was at work on a nightshift. They reached a point where the river curves away from the motor-way at, they estimate, around 9 p.m. Dusk was later than normal because it had been a very clear day, but it was growing dark.

Linda saw an object in the sky which she first thought to be the moon. It looked like a golden ball of fire just above some trees. It crossed the river ahead of them and moved east, to disappear beside a steep embankment. The children had apparently seen it too, and they all wondered if it had been an aircraft on fire and about to crash. So in haste they scrambled up the grass- and bramble-covered slope, which rises about 20 feet at a fairly steep angle. This took a few minutes, but on reaching the top they had an open view to the east and south over very flat land. The object was still visible – in the sky, but very low down. From their new vantage point they all had a good view of it. They saw it now as a pulsating light, and the children say they saw their mother staring at this as if transfixed.

Linda's description of the object as seen from the bank-top is that it was similar to a gondola, with a dome-like top and curved girder-like underside. It appeared to float like a balloon and bob up and down as a helicopter can. They considered this possibility but decided that it would have to be a very strange helicopter indeed. A red light rotated around the rim of the dome and an extremely bright, magnesium-like white light poured out of the rest of the object. Linda said it was so bright it hurt her eyes. Andrea later likened the object to a rocking chair, with the girder structure similar to the middle of a metal bridge. Marcus describes the object in similar terms. When he got home he begged his father to take him back into the field so he could see the 'crashed boat' again.

Linda became terrified at the sight of the object and they all fled, even though the UFO was now seen to be moving off in the wake of an aircraft which was heading towards Manchester Airport (about four miles away to the south). In the confusion Linda fell and twisted her ankle, and the children had to help her home. Trevor had returned from work, and he immediately commented on Linda's limp: 'Who did that – a spaceman?' He swears he was joking!

When we heard this story two years later, it was impossible to check the details, but Peter Warrington points out that around 9 p.m. on an August evening Manchester International Airport is very busy with holiday traffic. His opinion of the sighting is that it is quite possible the three witnesses mistook a light plane or a helicopter. We have both visited the site in August and have confirmed the number of aircraft that do pass over, at low altitude. In addition, we saw that the National Grid electricity-distribution pylons stand clearly visible from the location of the main sighting. Their lattice girders show a marked similarity to the witnesses' descriptions and sketches.

However, the witnesses all vehemently deny that they saw an ordinary aircraft and it is rather difficult to imagine how they could all have invested a pylon with the ability to fly. It must be remembered that these events occurred on their doorstep and that they walk this path so often that they are familiar with the air traffic that passes overhead.

The question of whether there was any 'missing time' is interesting. Only when asked about this did Linda remember that Trevor was not due home until 10 p.m., but allowing ten minutes (maximum) for the sighting and a similar time to hobble home they estimate it could not have been after 9.20 p.m. when they did return. But Trevor was there.

On the strength of this, regressive hypnosis was undertaken by a qualified psychiatrist, Dr Joseph Jaffe. Only Linda and Andrea were hypnotized (Marcus being judged too young). But the little boy does claim spontaneous memory of seeing 'people' inside the craft with 'heads shaped like raindrops'. Andrea vividly recalled the experience under hypnosis, but stuck to her conscious version – where they all ran away. When challenged about the time lapse she was puzzled, admitted it existed, but said all she could recall was 'nothing . . . it's dark blue . . . there are white circles.' The dark-blue/black colour features in Linda's story too. And, of course, the sky would be this colour as the day became night. The mother had a much fuller 'memory' under hypnosis and described standing paralysed beside the landed craft. A six-foot-tall figure in a dark one-piece suit talks to her mind and urges her to go towards the object. Then she feels herself floating and next remembers being inside a brightly lit room on an orange bed or table. The alien has a yellow puppet-like face with slanting eyes and she recalls the name 'Algenyon' but does not know what this means.

Linda responded with enormous fear during the hypnosis. But

is it conceivable this landing could have happened where it did? The field is in open view of dozens of houses, none of whose occupants apparently saw anything!

We have a typical 'close encounter of the fourth kind' (CE4) paradox here (see chapter 10). Did they see a helicopter and fantasize the rest? If so, why were their perceptions so distorted? And why does Linda's hypnosis memory so closely match those of other witnesses in similar CE4 situations? All we can do is suggest some points that may help. First, on the question of timing: the estimate of the missing period is, to say the least, uncertain. When Jenny Randles questioned Trevor carefully he admitted he might have arrived home as early as 9.30 p.m., as he occasionally did. This could make the time lapse disappear. On the other hand, both Linda and Andrea developed a strange weal or wound on their knees after the event. Neither knew where it came from, but the two were clearly similar. They did not know that US researcher Budd Hopkins had noted exactly this feature on several of his abduction witnesses after their encounter! Finally, to add to the confusion, there is the problem that Linda (as with almost all CE4 witnesses) is a 'psychic repeater' – she frequently has vivid dreams and imaginative experiences which sometimes possess a predictive flavour. Just before the UFO encounter a strange ghostly figure was seen by her wandering in their garden. It vanished mysteriously. Whatever it means this is all too familiar to the seasoned investigator of CE4 cases. There is a very specific pattern which all tend to follow, and this encounter is a typical example.

Five Holes in the Ground

Type: close encounter of the second kind
Date: 9–11 June 1981
Place: 'Le Guery' (pseudonym), France
Investigator: GEPAN

There are relatively few instances where physical traces have been left on the ground in the wake of a UFO landing. Even so, Ted Phillips, a US researcher, has collected a file of several hundred. Frequently these involve fairly insubstantial data that provide little or no evidence that anything unusual has to have been responsible. It is rare indeed that a detailed on-site investigation is conducted by scientists.

By far the most detailed analysis of a trace report has come into our possession through GEPAN, the French government team (see chapter 4). This report has never been translated into English or been published in the UFO literature. The 25,000-word investigation, with full results, maps and photographs, more than compensates for a significant drawback to the case, one so severe that we have gone on record in the past as suggesting that no case of this type should be considered. The problem is that, while the traces themselves are of great scientific interest, no UFO was seen causing them. They were merely discovered. That said, this is a phenomenon in need of study. Because of the way it was reported and its characteristics it falls into the UFO category. Its features are in most senses identical with less well-studied reports where a UFO was alleged to be responsible.

The saga began in the late afternoon of 12 June, when a farm-worker ploughing a maize crop saw something strange on the ground in front of him. Stopping to investigate, he found a circular patch, later measured as about 21 yards in diameter, where the soil was cracked and broken. Several of the young plants were missing and others in the zone were desiccated and showed signs of charring. There were also five holes in the ground. He told the chief farm-hand, who was not himself too interested but who did advise his boss, the farmer M. Emmanuel. After some hesitation, and having visited the field himself, M. Emmanuel reported the matter to the local police four days later. They recognized that this was something GEPAN should know of at once and brought the scientists to the spot the same day – sending a telex, followed by a fuller police investigation report. Its heading was 'Damage Caused by Unknown Object', already perhaps a presumption, as nobody had seen an object causing the effects.

This initial police report described the holes as about one-and-a-half to two inches in diameter, and about eight inches deep. They sat in a slight depression around which there was 'a specific odour which cannot be defined'. When GEPAN arrived this was no longer present.

Apart from the damage to the crop and ground which the farmer could not explain, it was the very precise alignment of the five holes in a trapezium formation which led the police to feel that GEPAN were the obvious people to study the case. Three scientists spent 48 hours on-site doing a full investigation. This included extensive interviews with the police and all those who had seen the phenomenon, plus a complete biological study of the traces. The ground in general was dry, but not cracked, it having rained a week before. The soil in the area is typically very fertile. The maize elsewhere had reached a height of about one foot eight inches and was growing well. First visual impressions of the site were of a grey patch of soil with the aligned formation of holes clearly visible inside it. It had not suffered burning, in the usual sense.

After confirming the police measurements the scientists conducted tests to determine the magnetic-field intensity and possible ionization at the site. The Hall-effect magnetometer found no significant magnetic anomaly, and radiation levels were found to be in keeping with background levels.

Detailed studies of the angles and depths and other features of the holes were made. No apparent geometrical relationship was noted in these figures. The holes seemed to be independent of one another. The pressures necessary to create holes to these depths were evaluated by several processes.

A full examination of the chemical properties of the soil at the site and in the surrounding area revealed more interesting information. There was no change in the structural basis of the soil but the relative humidity did significantly alter, being about two per cent lower in the affected zone. Mineral salts were present at the surface, creating the discoloration. This led GEPAN to conclude that no chemical or disease had led to soil changes but that a surface disturbance of a physical/chemical nature was responsible. A temperature above 100°C was considered necessary for the effects.

Next a detailed botanical study was made, checking plant heights and degree of desiccation in the leaves along two axes (X and Y). X represents the shortest direction of the zone of damage and Y the longer of the two. They were taken at right angles to one another over the irregular oval zone of surface effects.

Reliable analysis methods were used and graphs plotted. The results of these were very significant. There was a definite relationship between both height of plant and degree of dessication, varying with distance from the central point of the damage. The closer to the centre the greater the apparent effects that had produced desiccation and stunted growth over the six days since the supposed event (when the unaffected maize elsewhere was growing at a general rate of about four inches per day). In addition, effects were between two and three times more severe along the Y axis. From these results GEPAN concluded that 'the zone of damage has been subjected to a localized thermal and/or intense electro-magnetic effect.'

Examination of the principal discoverer of the traces, M. Guy, narrowed the date of the cause to either 9, 10 or 11 June. He suggested that much rain fell on the 9th and that a storm might have struck. Weather data were consulted and confirmed the rain and a totally overcast sky but not the storm. However, it was sufficient to warrant examination of one possible cause for the damage to the field. Had it been struck by ball lightning? GEPAN found, to their surprise, that almost no research had been conducted into the potential ground traces that might be left by ball lightning. Also, scientists who they consulted could not even suggest what kind of atmospheric conditions were conducive to its formation. One local woman did relate how on the night of either the 10th or 11th (when a storm was meteorologically improbable) she had heard a strange noise which had caused the dogs on her farm to bark for a few minutes. She had not gone outside to investigate and the noise and barking had ceased in a few moments. Whether this was likely to be relevant was not evaluated by GEPAN.

In conclusion the scientists could only note that some sort of thermal or electromagnetic force had struck the maize crop in this small area. A ball of lightning descending from the sky was certainly feasible, but since so little was known about its interaction with the ground this could not be proved to be more likely than the more hypothetical suggestion of a stranger UFO (or UAP) event. And certain factors, such as the aligned holes, were difficult to explain in terms of ball lightning. Whatever the solution, the GEPAN study points to the scientific value of studying alleged UFO traces. If ball lightning does prove to be the culprit in this and other cases, it is obviously an atmospheric phenomenon which we need to learn more about.

The Car that Died

Type: close encounter of the second kind
Date: 6 November 1967
Time: 1.30 a.m. GMT
Place: River Avon, Hampshire, England
Investigator: Tony Pace (BUFORA)

Reports that UFOs can cause interference to vehicles, especially engine, lights and radio malfunctions, are remarkably common.[3] Indeed, in terms of pure science, these cases offer one of the most important puzzles to be unravelled. The scene at the start of the film *Close Encounters of the Third Kind,* where a truck driver meets a UFO on a lonely road, typifies the phenomenon very well. But it may not be appreciated that this drama is based very firmly on actual events. The case which follows is one of a hundred or so 'car stops', as they are often called, reported and investigated in Great Britain alone. It is one of the most significant, and was used as a model for the film scene.

Carl Farlow was driving a Leyland Comet diesel truck on a night delivery run down the A338 in Hampshire. He was between Avon and Sopley, heading for Christchurch with a load of cookers. It had rained earlier but was now fine and dry; the night was cool. The truck approached a crossroads, at which the right turning led to a bridge over the River Avon. The river flows in parallel with the road at this point. Suddenly he noticed his headlights dim and after a couple of seconds they faded altogether. He pulled up rapidly, but his engine was still running. At this point he noticed a large, oval object to his right, moving slowly from over the river across the road in front of him. It was at the height of a telegraph pole and by comparing it with the bridge he gauged it to be as much as 80 feet long. It was a deep

---

[3] G. Falla, *Vehicle Interference Project* (BUFORA, 1979); M. Rodeghier, *CUFOS Report,* 1981.

purplish-red colour and emitted a continuous humming noise, which Carl could hear through the open window of his cab. By now the object was hovering above the road – wider than the road and so covering the grass at each side too. As Carl sat rooted to his seat in terror he began to smell a pungent burning odour – as he describes it this sounds like ozone. After a few seconds the object began to move off to his left, accelerating as it did so. It shot away, rising a little as it moved off very rapidly indeed.

It was only at this point that Carl realized another vehicle had been involved in the encounter. This was a Jaguar that had been heading towards him but had stopped, pulled up on the grass verge. As they had been approaching from the other direction, the occupants, a veterinary surgeon and a young woman, had seen the UFO from the other side. Carl was still in his seat, gripping the steering wheel, when the car driver came over to him. The vet told him that as the UFO had come across his car had lost both engine power and lights, and his companion had become hysterical. Having confirmed that they had all seen the same thing, the car driver suggested they call the police. He knew there was a telephone-box nearby (beneath where the UFO had been, in fact). The light in the call-box was not working, although neither man had noticed if it had been functioning before the UFO's arrival. The vet tried to use his hand-torch to illuminate the phone. He always carried this with him and had used it earlier that night. But it was not working now either. Within a few minutes of the phone-call a local police patrol car and officers from the regional headquarters had arrived on the scene. In the light these vehicles cast, Carl Farlow says the scrubland over which the UFO had hovered looked brown and burnt. He thought that the tarmac road surface seemed to have melted at this spot. Both men were taken to Christchurch police station where they were independently interviewed and asked to sign official statements. This went on until 4.30 a.m. The woman, suffering from severe shock, was taken to a local hospital and kept in overnight for observation. She refused to talk to investigators later. The police arranged for the two men to stay in a hotel for the rest of the night, and then they were taken to the police station at Bournemouth. Here they were interviewed by an officer from the Ministry of Defence.

Carl needed to collect some personal effects that afternoon, and on being driven to Ringwood, he had to pass the exact spot where he had seen the UFO. He found a remarkable scene. A bulldozer was levelling the ground where the grass had been burnt. Two men were taking measurements on the road with what looked like a theodolite and a Geiger counter. Someone else was putting a fresh coat of paint on the telephone-box. About a week later, on a delivery run to Bournemouth past this spot, Carl says he found the road surface freshly covered with new tarmac over an area of about 200 feet.

Thirty-six hours after the incident, Carl was allowed to collect his lorry from the police compound at Christchurch. The engineer in charge told him that all the electrical systems were burnt out. An army truck had to give him a tow in order to start the lorry. Eventually he reached the head office of his haulage firm in Shropshire. The lorry was taken in for repair and required £400-worth of replacements, including a new dynamo, starter motor, regulator, ammeter, batteries and bulbs.

This extraordinary story is by no means unique. Virtually all its features have been found many times in cases all over the world. Occasionally the engine is only partially impeded or the lights only partly dimmed, but generally this type of case is one of the most consistent in the UFO records. Any scientist who studies a few dozen of the more detailed investigation reports will be hard pressed to conclude anything other than that a most impressive and mystifying phenomenon was genuinely being observed.

Multiple stops of this kind are common. For example, almost exactly ten years before, on 3 November 1957, several cars and trucks at Levelland, Texas, USA, suffered independent failure between midnight and 1.00 a.m. as a deep-red, oval object overflew. This occurred during a major wave of sightings in the USA. The 1967 case happened amidst one of the biggest waves of UFO sightings Great Britain had ever known, which led to questions in Parliament. Not until 1977 did a new flood of events take place. As might be anticipated, this also included car stops. On 6 June 1977 a motor cycle and a Jaguar car in Durham were both impeded by a large oval object overhead (see p. 180).

Another British mini-wave came in November 1980. On that occasion, police officer Alan Godfrey, in Todmorden, West

Yorkshire, had his car engine stopped and his radio distorted by a large, oval UFO that hovered over the road and evaporated rainwater from the surface of the tarmac.

It seems that every spate of UFO sightings includes car stops following the standard format. Wet-weather conditions seem to be a common factor. It could be that at times when UFOs are common for some other reason, the presence of the rain, atmospheric moisture or a frontal system, triggers a UAP which causes car stops. In this case the fact that a diesel engine did not fail, although the truck's lights did, when a nearby petrol engine and its lights both malfunctioned, is not without significance. The ozone smell (another very frequently described feature of such cases, as are electrostatic tingling sensations) points to intense ionization in the vicinity of the phenomenon. Indeed researchers suggest that the interference to electrical circuits and battery torches is only explicable if the ionic flow is somehow temporarily blocked.

These particular cases provide a very rich field of study for the scientist. Probably the intelligent behaviour attributed to the UFO is an error, possibly arising from the phenomenon's attraction to the metal bodies of motor cars – lonely, moving outposts on quiet country roads. But if this is a UAP, as seems likely, it is an impressive one which deserves full scientific investigation.

A Repeater Witness

Type: close encounter of the first kind, instrumentally detected; photograph
Dates: 26 February 1980; 5 May 1982
Times: 7.40 a.m. GMT; 11.00 a.m. BST
Place: Milton Keynes, Buckinghamshire, England
Investigators: Ken Phillips and Peter Warrington (BUFORA)
Psychological study by Dr Alexander Keul, Salzburg University

One of the strangest aspects of the UFO close encounter is the existence of 'repeater witnesses' – people who undergo not just one but several unusual UFO experiences, defying the laws of chance if these were simply unusual physical events which are seen when somebody just happens to be in the right place at the right time. That such repeaters tend to experience close encounters of a highly subjective nature is one of the key reasons why researchers feel the exotic UFO may be different from the relatively straightforward UAP. As noted elsewhere in this volume, CE4 percipients are frequently repeaters, not just in the sense that they have more than one alien contact but also in the clearly relevant fact that they see ordinary UFOs (without experiencing contact) and also have a definite track record of other types of paranormal experience (especially seeing ghosts and having predictive dreams or visions).

We have here to present one of the most remarkable repeater cases ever investigated. It has a number of features which make it difficult to accept but we are quite satisfied that the witness and investigators are sincere. The primary witness is Anne Phillips, aged 40 at the time of the first event, and a well-educated housewife, of Irish descent but brought up in north London. She is a trained upholsterer with a good eye for design. Her interest in UFOs is minimal and she holds to no specific theory about them. However, she cannot be said to be unfamiliar with UFO data. Her husband, Ken, is one of the most experienced and best-respected ufologists in Great Britain. He was one of Jenny Randles' predecessors in the role of Director of Investigations for BUFORA, a post he held in 1974 when he and Anne married. Currently he is BUFORA's Director of Investigational Training and his hundreds of investigation reports over the years have always been conducted to a very high standard. To make matters even more problematic, at the time of the first experience in February 1980, BUFORA's current Chairman (Arnold West) was a house guest. For a UFO to home in on the Phillips household on that day might seem a little difficult to swallow!

It was a very cold, winter morning, the temperature well below freezing. There was dense fog, with visibility under a third of a mile. Ken had just set off for work and Anne, in bed, was woken by a noise. She first thought it must be Arnold, but he had gone out. However, she was awake enough to get up and look through the window of their semi-detached home. This affords a view northwards, over the roofs of some older houses on the estate, across flat land to the horizon several miles away. Of course none of this was visible, beyond the closest houses, because of the severe weather conditions. Yet in the sky, at an elevation of about 15 degrees (and so above the roof-tops) there was a red ball. This was not unlike the setting sun when seen through mist – a dark, dull red. It was very small, like the point in the centre of an old TV screen, but it expanded as she watched. Considering the visibility, this presumably means that it did literally expand, rather than move towards her. It eventually appeared very large, so that its size was not unlike that of the sun. Her first thought was that it was indeed the sun, but then she realized she was facing in the wrong direction. There was no sound, and the air was very still and quiet.

After a couple of minutes' puzzled observation, during which the ball stayed as it was, Anne recalled a polaroid camera they had bought two months before. She fetched it from another room, returning to find the object still there. She fiddled with the controls and then, observing the UFO through the viewfinder, took one shot. As she did this the object vanished. She did not see how. A few seconds later the photograph developed. It probably displays a degree of shake. However, against the pale-cream background of the foggy sky appeared a distinct but faint trail of red light. This ran from the lower centre to the bottom of the frame, giving the impression that the object had suddenly dropped as she took the picture. But, as the print completed its development, the trail vanished. All that remains, apart from the monotone background, is a faint smudge the colour of dried blood at the bottom of the picture. It appears diffuse and insubstantial.

This odd effect on polaroid development has been noticed on a number of occasions when this type of camera has been used by a witness. One claimed that a UFO he snapped was on the print as it began to develop and then disappeared as development was completed. Actually this is possible. What probably occurs is that the camera, having no exposure or shutter-speed control, cannot compensate for the gross difference in exposure between the light sky and the much darker (but also substantially smaller) UFO. However, in the early stages of developing this is partially corrected when the print is in effect underdeveloped. By the time full development occurs the overexposure of the image makes the

UFO much less prominent, if not invisible. In the Anne Phillips photograph this problem severely affects the quality of the result and removes from view the apparent trail caused by the inferred descent of the UFO. Unfortunately, without a negative, no meaningful analysis is possible and no underdeveloped print can be produced to retrieve lost detail.

All this is intriguing. The story and the photograph were studied by us soon after the incident, thanks to Ken. However, little could be learned considering the poor quality of the image. For this reason (plus the inherent credibility problems), the case was not discussed or published within the UFO movement. Then, just over two years later, it all happened again in what amounts to an action replay!

The site was identical – the same bedroom and the same window. Anne was alone in the house making the bed when something made her look out of the window and she saw an almost duplicate phenomenon (although slightly larger this time). Her first reaction was to say to herself, 'Oh God – not another one!' The previous event had precipitated dream images of a mildly disturbing nature, so she tried to ignore this repeat performance. But, in Anne's own words, 'I tried to ignore it, but it didn't seem to want to be ignored.' So she found herself going for the same camera and returning to face the same window, even though she now realizes she could have photographed it from a different angle from Ken's office.

The weather on this occasion was completely different. It was a mild, early May morning, although the sky was fairly consistently overcast with greyish/cream cloud. The dull red object was in the same location in the sky. Carefully focusing the camera, she took one shot, but realized too late that the flash bar was attached. The reflection of this from the window startled her and contributed to the overexposure of the picture once again. Incredibly, the object behaved exactly as it had on the first sighting, although this time she feels she saw it drop at the instant she pressed the camera shutter.

The picture is very similar to the first one, the cream background being dominant. But nearer the centre is a bar-like object of the same colour as the smudge in the previous photograph. This seems to be a ball-like object distorted by camera shake. At the bottom right corner of the frame is a much larger patch, again of the same colour. Suggestions as to what this might be have not clarified matters. If it is the edging of the window frame, there is no obvious reason why it should appear to be that colour (the frame is dark brown). She says there was nothing else in the sky at the time.

Comparison photos taken with the camera at the same place show no sign of any camera defect or red coloration to the film. Other shots on both films producing the two UFO shots were normal.[4]

After the second sighting Anne put the photograph away and did not tell Ken about it, hoping she might forget the whole thing. But several days later, when nothing more had happened but she could not forget, she told him all about it. The dream images which upset her after the second event were similar to those after the first, and recurrent; they involved her floating or hovering over a vast, open land with desolate plains. The landscape was unfamiliar to her and she says it gave her a very depressed feeling 'like one of those days when you look out at the sky and it is all grey, colourless and miserable with rain drizzling down.'

One more significant aspect of the case mentioned spontaneously by Anne is that on both occasions (but particularly the second) the area outside the window was unusually deserted. It was, she said, 'very strange. Normally there is movement at this time of day, but it was complete desertion – no cars, people, children playing, sound – nothing.' This is a very common feature in UFO close encounters, especially in repeater-witness cases. It represents a kind of sensory isolation. Jenny Randles has coined the term 'Oz-factor' to describe it and believes it is an important clue to the reality level of such experiences.[5]

Of course, Anne's dreams and the Oz-factor have similarities. She had also had a precognitive dream of President Kennedy's assassination, which she told others about beforehand and which

[4] The photographs are impossible to reproduce effectively in black and white, but are available in BUFORA case files.

[5] See J. Randles, *UFO Reality* (Robert Hale, 1983); Randles, *The Pennine UFO Mystery* (Granada, 1983); Randles, 'Not the ETH', Magonia, October 1984.

featured the same sense of loss and emotional vacuum.

Ken Phillips, who has obviously been keen to interpret the events, has consulted earth-mysteries researcher Paul Devereux, who favours a geophysical explanation for UFO phenomena. He suggests that a nearby fault might generate UAPs, and it is true that many light phenomena have been seen in and around Milton Keynes in the past. Yet on both occasions (despite extensive attempts) no other witnesses to Anne's UFO were discovered.

This seems anomalous in the second occurrence particularly (mid morning on a spring day in a fairly large housing estate). However, Oz-factor states are commonly associated with what appear to be quasi-conscious experiences. They can be seen by small groups of witnesses (often by one witness alone) and yet not seen by nearby crowds in a shopping street or at a bus-stop. In a previous book[6] we defined what we called a 'sphere of influence' which seems to surround some UFO events, inside which you must be in order to experience them.

On a more psychological level, Dr Alex Keul (noted for his in-depth psychosocial profiles of close-encounter witnesses) has taken special interest in this case, undertaking a full psychiatric study of Anne and conducting Rorschach (or ink-blot) and anam-nesis tests on her. He pronounces her psychologically normal but notes that her mother died several months after the second incident, leaving a deep emotional gap in Anne's life. He suggests that the UFO (the shape of which mirrored the mother symbol), coupled with the feelings of isolation and depression, were a precognitive recognition of this imminent death, by her subcon-scious mind. Obviously Ken's interest in ufology meant that UFOs were much in mind in that household, so such a recog-nition might have been externalized in her experience as a UFO. This idea seems far-fetched; it raises far more questions than it successfully answers at the moment. But the evidence certainly suggests a psychological component in the experience. The re-lationship between the human mind and the external world needs further investigation.

[6] J. Randles and P. Warrington, *UFOs: A British Viewpoint* (Robert Hale, 1979), pp. 200–1.

Mid-air Encounter

Type: daylight observation, medium definition
Date: 21 June 1982
Time: 11.15 a.m. GMT
Place: 45 nautical miles south-east of Brindisi, Italy
Investigators: Phillip Taylor (BUFORA) and Peter Warrington

This incident serves to demonstrate two aspects which are frequently found, though seldom within one event. On the one hand
it is in many ways typical of a type of event which, while not
necessarily spectacular, is very puzzling. On the other, it illustrates the way the media interpret the unusual in whatever way is
most convenient at the time. The reader may recall that in June
1982 the Princess of Wales was expecting the birth of her first
child. In a number of newspapers in Great Britain, this UFO was
referred to as 'an omen of the imminent Royal birth'. The object
seen has not yet been identified but it is not likely to have been an
omen!

The witnesses involved, two pilots and two passengers, were
flying in a Dan-Air Boeing 737 aircraft between London (Gatwick) and the island of Corfu. The flight had been quite unevent-
ful until the aircraft reached southern Italy. The route was via
airways Blue 9 and Amber 14, the junction of the two being at
Brindisi. The aircraft had flown south from Dubrovnik to Brindisi
on the 'heel' of Italy and then turned south-east towards Corfu.
The exact position of the incident is known to be 45 nautical miles
on a bearing of 125° (magnetic) from Brindisi, i.e. on the centre-
line of the airway.

The aircraft was descending from 27,000 feet to 19,000 feet and
passing through 23,000 feet when the object was first seen by the
captain, who drew it to the attention of his first officer and two
passengers who were visiting the flight deck at the time. Initially
the object was ahead and slightly to the left of the aircraft, and at
approximately the same altitude. As the aircraft came closer to
the object it became clear that it was neither climbing nor
descending relative to their altitude; as far as the witnesses could
detect this, the object was stationary. It appeared to be an

oblate spheroid (round with flattened ends), and black and shiny. Although its angular size (i.e. the size of the angle subtended by the object at the observer's eye) was relatively small, it was clear from the duration of the sighting and the apparent very slow speed of the object as it was passed by the aircraft, that at first the object was an estimated five miles ahead, and as the aircraft passed to its right 'it was no more than two miles away' according to the captain. The shiny surface of the object reflected the light of the sun, since at the time the sky was clear of cloud. The sighting was described as lasting between 30 and 60 seconds. Needless to say, none of the witnesses was able to identify the object.

At the time, the flight was subject to Italian air-traffic control but was just about to be passed on to Greek air-traffic control. No report of the event was made at that time, partly because there was no civilian radar coverage of that area, and partly because of language difficulties. The crew did consider making a general radio broadcast to other aircraft but it was understood that there were none within 30 miles. The event was subsequently reported on the crew's return to Gatwick later that day.

Additional relevant details are that at the time of the event the aircraft was descending at approximately 1,500 feet per minute and the airspeed was 280 knots (which equates to a speed across the ground of about 340–60 knots). The outside air temperature was thought to be about −20°C. No unusual indications were observed on any of the aircraft's instruments. The weather radar on the aircraft was in 'standby mode' at the time and not in use. After landing at Corfu, the aircraft departed about an hour later for its return to Gatwick. Although a similar route was flown nothing unusual was seen.

Clearly, if one accepts the details of the incident as reported, the number of possible explanations are somewhat limited. Perhaps the first and most obvious potential explanation is that it was a weather balloon, though if this were the case then the witnesses' descriptions would be unusually inaccurate. However, details of weather-balloon releases in the area were sought. In fact an Italian Air Force base at Brindisi released weather balloons on a regular basis. The details of balloon releases may be found in an Italian notice to airmen dated 13 January 1982, which states that balloons were released from Brindisi at 5 a.m., 11 a.m., 5 p.m. and 11 p.m. GMT. The maximum weight of the balloon is 10 lb, its length at launch is about 12 yards and its rate of ascent, 1,000 feet per minute. Because of the expansion of the balloon as it rises, the length of the entire piece of equipment would increase by approximately six feet every minute.

It was not possible to obtain details of weather conditions at sea-level. However, details were obtained of the wind direction and speed: at 18,000 feet it was 280° at 30 knots and at 30,000 feet 280° at 40 knots. The incident in question took place at 11.15 a.m. GMT, 45 nautical miles to the south-east of Brindisi. For obvious reasons of safety, one must presume that the launch of the balloon took place at approximately the correct time (11 a.m. GMT). This being the case, the balloon could have reached 23,000 feet by the time of the event at 11.15; however it could not have reached a position 45 miles from its point of release. Clearly, if it had, its altitude would have been greater than 23,000 feet. In fact the balloon would not survive a climb higher than about 45,000 feet; it would burst and its instrument package fall to earth. No balloon released earlier would still have been in the sky at the time of the incident without having been reported as seriously malfunctioning.

It is safe to conclude that whatever the crew and two passengers saw, it was not a weather balloon. Although other possible explanations have been considered, to date none seem likely. For example, on the days surrounding 21 June 1982, a NATO exercise was taking place to the west of Italy. However, no aerial activity involving the area of the incident was planned.

This case is not included with any inference that what was seen might be some form of 'exotic UFO', but rather as an illustration of an unusual event, witnessed by people who were in a familiar environment, and who reported the event in a 'matter of fact' and sincere manner.

Between them, the specific cases outlined in this chapter typify the elements of the UFO mystery.

9

Unidentified Atmospheric Phenomena: Possible Explanations

In the previous chapter we illustrated the wide variety of UFO events. In this chapter and the next we hope to demonstrate the implications of these and other cases for a variety of disciplines.

We have already mentioned that UFO events can be very loosely divided into two categories: the objective and the subjective. It should be emphasized that the two categories are as much used for convenience as they are a mode of description. There are some cases which fit into both categories. This is not contradictory: it simply represents an additional perplexing aspect. A large proportion of the 'objective' variety of events which remain unidentified relate to observations of relatively small, self-luminous, spherical or near-spherical objects frequently seen at close quarters. The reader will gain an impression of such events from the following selection of cases:

Date: 25 August 1965
Place: Florida, USA

Two women were seated outside on aluminium chairs, the husband of one standing close by. One woman swatted a fly and was still holding the swatter when a ball of 'lightning', the size of a basket ball, appeared in front of her. She did not see it, though the others did, but she did see the swatter 'edged with fire' and dropped it. The ball, falling to the floor, exploded 'like a shotgun blast'. The incident was over in seconds. No heat was felt from the ball which was described as the colour and brightness of an arc-welding flash, the edges having a fuzzy appearance. There were no marks on the patio floor where the swatter had fallen. The explosion was heard by a neighbour 15 feet away and it was subsequently found that another neighbour's electric cooker had shorted out at the same time.[1]

Date: 28 January 1975
Time: 9.30 p.m.
Place: Hebdon Bridge, West Yorkshire, England

A railwayman waiting at a bus-stop saw an amber ball of light appear in the sky. The object, the size of a penny held at arm's length, moved slowly, hovered and then turned sharply through 90° and disappeared.[2]

Date: 15 June 1975
Place: Stretford, Greater Manchester, England

Two young women saw a pin-point source of white light moving near some trees. They were puzzled and moved to a better vantage point. It appeared to be like a table-tennis ball with spikes all around it and a cone on the top. The women were joined by a third observer and they watched the object move around for about two minutes. Then there was a flash and it disappeared.[3]

Date: 18 November 1975
Time: 5.10 p.m.
Place: Barnsley, South Yorkshire, England

Four people walking near their home saw a vivid-blue ball of light zigzagging across the sky. One witness said he heard a high-pitched humming noise which drew his attention to it. The light disappeared for several seconds at a time, reapparing in unexpected locations, though maintaining its general course. At one point it split into two parts which diverged at 90°; these disappeared,

[1] *Science,* vol. 151, 1966, p. 34.
[2] J. Randles, *The Pennine UFO Mystery* (Granada, 1983), p. 33.
[3] J. Randles and P. Warrington, *UFOs: A British Viewpoint* (Robert Hale, 1979), pp. 73–4.

reappeared, then collided with a flash before continuing across the sky and disappearing from view. The duration of the sighting was estimated as three minutes.[4]

Date: 24 February 1979
Time: 2.45 a.m.
Place: Bryn, Near Wigan, Lancashire, England

A taxi-driver and his passenger saw an orange ball of light to the north. It was stationary at first but then moved westwards and disappeared.[5]

Date: December 1979
Time: unknown
Place: Halewood, Merseyside, England

A man walking home across an open field saw a white light heading towards him. As the object approached it looked like a white fluorescent 'balloon' about seven feet in diameter. It silently swept along just above the ground. As it neared him it shot upwards at an angle and disappeared in a few seconds. When the object was at its closest, the hair on the back of the man's head began to tingle. When he arrived home his arms were covered with 'goose bumps'. His hair stood out from his scalp for two days, according to him and his family.[6]

Date: 3 August 1982
Time: about 4.00 p.m.
Place: Cambridge University, Cambridge, England

Immediately after one of several lightning strikes to nearby buildings a ball of light was seen by several people. To some about the size of a grapefruit, it was seen by others to be about the apparent size of the moon. It was blue-white in colour and very bright. It was visible for about four to five seconds before suddenly vanishing.[7]

[4] *FSR*, vol. 22, no. 4, 1976.
[5] Randles, *Pennine UFO Mystery*, pp. 64–9.
[6] *Northern Ufology*, vol. 75, Aug. 1980.
[7] Letter from Sir Brian Pippard in *Nature*, vol. 298, 16 Aug. 1980.

There are many similar cases, not only in the UFO literature but in sources like *The Handbook of Unexplained Natural Phenomena* edited by W. Corliss, who has searched many other sources for interesting accounts of the unusual. There can be no doubt about the existence of this type of phenomenon; the area of doubt lies in the need for a way of explaining its origins and characteristics and its effects on witnesses who come within close proximity.

In a previous book we set out findings which demonstrated that the level of (objective or subjective) UFO event witnessed was dependent on the distance between the observer and the 'UFO'.[8] At the outer edge of this range only slight effects on the witness may occur, so slight that they might not be reported. In these circumstances the witness reports only an 'objective' type of event. However, as proximity increases, so do the 'subjective' aspects and in these the 'close-encounter' experiences are most frequently described. Since that work was published, several other versions of the idea have been put forward, some no doubt concurrent with our emerging ideas.

It would be easy to assume that many cases of the type described above were ball-lightning events. However, the similarities are not sufficient: to consider these events as ball lightning it would be necessary to extend many of the accepted parameters.[9]

Generally speaking, the shape of our proposed UAP is similar

[8] Randles and Warrington, *British Viewpoint*.

[9] We have included here the incident at Cambridge precisely because Sir Brian Pippard made no mention of ball lightning in his letter reporting the event in *Nature* (although in context this is probably what he was talking about). From the earliest days of interest in electrical phenomena there have been objections to the genuine acceptance of ball lightning. It has been claimed by some to be the retinal after-image from the usual lightning discharge, and others say it is simply being reported by unreliable witnesses. See 'Problems of Atmospheric and Space Electricity' in S.O. Coroniti (ed.), *Proceedings of the Third International Conference on Atmospheric and Space Electricity* (Elsevier, 1965); 'The Nature of Ball Lightning' in S. Singer, *The Nature of Ball Lightning* (Plenum Press, 1971); *Lightning*, vol. 1, ed. R.H. Golde (Academic Press, 1977), J.D. Barry, *Ball Lightning and Bead Lightning* (Plenum Press, 1980), contains not only a thorough discussion but also a very comprehensive bibliography. Our description of the characteristics of ball lightning is based on this work.

to that of ball lightning, varying from the sphere to a range of spheroids. The size of these UAPs seems to exceed the 16 inches often quoted as the upper limit for ball lightning. We suggest a UAP diameter of three to six feet is typical. The colour is most frequently red-orange but, as with ball lightning, can range through to blue-white. A change of colour throughout the life-time of the UAP is not uncommon. Whereas Barry ascribes some structure to the ball-lightning shape,[10] it is more difficult to determine in the UAP. Often 'structure' *is* described by a wit-ness, although this detail may be added by the mind confused by the blinding brilliance of the object.

The motion of the UAP is similar to that of ball lightning; it is not unheard-of for the UAP to follow non-conductive linear structures like fences or roads. This aspect might be coincidental but it is one of the patterns which have led some to speculate about the UAP displaying some control over its movements. The sound of ball lightning is sometimes said to be a 'crackling' but many are silent. The UAP on the other hand is sometimes said to hum at a variety of pitches. The odour, when apparent, is similar in both UAP and ball-lightning events: it is described as like ozone or sulphur. It does seem that direct contact with both types of event can cause damage to objects and various degrees of burn. In the main, witnesses tend not to make direct contact with the proposed UAP; however, some instances of burns on people do occur in the UFO literature. There are a number of other effects, if one counts physiological considerations and changes in behavioural pattern as relevant. These will be discussed later.

The lifetime of ball lightning is said to be in the order of seconds. Frequently quoted figures are one to two seconds and in some cases three to five seconds, which indicates that several minutes is not possible. We suggest that the proposed UAP has a typically observed lifetime of one to two minutes, which might represent an actual lifetime of three to four minutes, possibly longer. If this extended lifetime is correct, then it would suggest a more stable phenomenon. The decay of the UAP is less spec-tacular than that of ball lightning, though not necessarily any less energetic. Ball lightning is rarely observed without accompanying

[10] Ibid.

natural lightning and thunderstorms, but the UAP is probably not
dependent on such conditions.

Barry reports that about ten per cent of observers report an
affinity of ball lightning to enclosures;[11] this figure approximates
to that of the UAP also. We note that there are a number of cases
where ball lightning (or similar phenomena) has been observed
in enclosures representing a 'Faraday cage', such as an aircraft in
flight. One such event occurred on board a Soviet airliner over-
flying the Black Sea on 15 January 1984.

Since this particular type of UFO was recognized, there have
been attempts to suggest an explanation. We suggested in 1979
that the events were natural phenomena, though the mechanisms
were unclear. It was known that other natural luminosities occurred, such as 'earthquake lights', and we proposed that UAPs
could have similar qualities. From time to time cases arise which
serve to highlight the possibility of some observations emerging
from rather unusual causes. For example, in an anecdote in a
television documentary about owls a gamekeeper told how one
evening he was walking along a path close to some woodland. His
attention was drawn to a small luminosity which was apparently
flying to and fro some distance away across a field. He watched
and was puzzled by the movements, which seemed regular. He
was quite unable to recognize what might have been responsible
until the following day when he happened to walk near the place
where the luminosity had been seen. To his surprise he found the
carcass of an owl which was infested with a luminescent micro-
organism. The gamekeeper, recognizing the species of owl and
knowing its flight movements, concluded that he had seen that
particular bird the previous evening shortly before it died.

Infested owls apart, there have been other attempts to explain
this particular type of UFO event. Hilary Evans set out one
theory. To quote from his conclusions:

a hypothesis such as this will seem so far-out as to deserve dismissal
along with Cosmic Brothers or UFO bases in the Welsh Triangle.
Certainly it is the most far fetched hypothesis I personally have put to
paper. Yet I have done so only because the array of evidence seems to

[11] Ibid.

me to demand nothing less. For too long we have been trying to explain the unidentified in terms of the known, and it hasn't got us very far. I suggest that it is time we put aside our preconceptions, add up the evidence, and follow its implications wherever they lead us.

Speaking about reports similar to those of UAPs Evans says:

These reports only seem to make sense when we postulate the existence of some kind of creature or entity, inhabiting our atmosphere; possessing physical properties – albeit very different ones from those of any known earth creature; and endowed with a degree of intelligence, or controlled by someone/something possessing intelligence, which extends to the use of ESP.[12]

To be fair, it should be remembered that in many of the cases which Evans considered the witnesses involved claimed that there was a response or affinity by the 'UFO' to the human witness. As might be expected, reaction to the hypothesis was mixed but it is nevertheless a brave attempt to come to grips with a very strange phenomenon. However, UAPs are not usually vested with life.

The other attempts at an explanation may be considered similar in their overall concept, though it must be pointed out that there are marked differences in the suggested sources of these proposed luminosities. Steuart Campbell, an experienced and respected UFO researcher, has proposed a mechanism for UFO events of the type which we have been discussing. His article suggests that the UFO form is a direct consequence of a condensed and rotating magnetic field. He postulates a mechanism which produces a rotating mass of air, the rotary motion causing ionization, and in turn a luminosity. This would visually resemble the classic 'flying-saucer' shape. Campbell further suggests that as the ions come into contact with the surrounding air, a contraction would take place, resulting in an intensified electromagnetic field. The result of this would be an expulsion of molecules from within the luminosity, thereby forming an object lighter than air which could be free-floating and therefore under the influence of the prevailing environmental conditions. In this way the luminosity could float about and appear in a variety of energy-depen-

---

[12] H. Evans, 'BOLs Balls of Light', *Probe Report*, vol. 3, no. 1, July 1982. See also H. Evans, *The Evidence for UFOs* (Aquarian Press, 1983).

dent shapes. He suggests that the metallic appearance of 'UFOs' might be a refractive effect arising from the 'shell' of such a luminosity.[13]

An often-quoted event which might be interpreted in terms of Campbell's theory was described in our previous book, *UFOs: A British Viewpoint,* and we give the outline again here. The report came from Bridgend in South Wales in the mid 1960s, and told of a sighting by a couple from their back garden. They heard a noise like a distant jet, and then saw a white patch of sparkling mist appear low on the horizon, near a building site. The noise stopped as a reddish light materialized by the side of the mist, and joined up with it. The light then started to blink. The mist glowed and pulsated, dividing into two sections. These sections began to spin around and around. The smaller of the two then moved on top of the larger one, making a shape rather like a squashed bowler hat. Lights of many colours then came on on the bottom of the object which began to 'solidify' into a metallic-looking disc-shape with a dome on top and a reddish glow beneath. After this the object spun around for a few minutes, and the noise like a jet engine began again. Then the object became mist-like in appearance, and coloured lights appeared once again, some now blinking. Suddenly the whole thing disappeared.

This remarkable sighting seems to be a perfect display of the mechanism which Campbell's article describes. As with other theories attempting to explain aspects of the UFO enigma by invoking natural processes, this proposal has received various responses depending on the outlook of the reviewer. We would not be surprised if the type of mechanism described were to be responsible for at least some of the currently unidentified events in the literature.

Two other proposals which have been offered to explain UAP events are broadly similar, though each has its individual aspects. They are the ideas of Paul Devereux and Michael Persinger. Their models are based on geophysical stresses giving rise to luminosities in the atmosphere. They were not the first people to make such suggestions: Lagarde published an article[14] at least a

[13] S. Campbell, *Journal of Transient Aerial Phenomena*, vol. 1, no. 3, 1980.
[14] *FSR*, vol. 14, no. 4, 1968.

decade before, in which a link was suggested between a series of UFOs seen in France in 1954 and their proximity to geological faults.

Devereux set out his theory in his book *Earthlights*.[15] He proposed that the luminosities seen and reported as UFOs are what he terms a 'terrestrial discharge phenomenon' which arises by means of various physical effects from the stressed areas associated with geological faulting. Devereux discussed the range of UFO-type events and concludes that there is a natural cause, even for the humanoid figures or entities often reported. These 'proto-entities' as he calls them are suggested to be 'merely a different development of the same phenomenon – a rare further stage of it'. The book received rather mixed reviews. When it first appeared there was a feeling that the central core of his proposals – that the UFO form was a natural event driven by geophysical forces – was potentially accurate, at least in the confines of the limited studies undertaken. However, for many people the issue was clouded unnecessarily by his proposal that a connection exists between prehistoric stone circles and the UFO enigma. The book was attacked on a number of fronts and vehemently defended by its author. Matters were not helped by the fact that overlays were omitted from a number of maps in the first edition through a production error and consequently some 'close correlations' were not illustrated.

The proposals put forward in *Earthlights* are very similar to those suggested by M. A. Persinger and G. F. Lafrenière in a number of publications.[16] The essential aspects of their theory are that natural geophysical processes which occur in unusual space/time configurations give rise to an electromagnetic luminosity which is responsible not only for the UFO forms but also for some physical and biological consequences. The theory presented suggests that whereas geophysical stresses on a large scale give

[15] P. Devereux, *Earthlights* (Turnstone Press, 1982).

[16] M.A. Persinger and G.F. Lafrenière, *Space-time Transients and Unusual Events* (Nelson Hall, 1977); 'Transient Geophysical Bases for ostensible UFO related Phenomena and Associated Verbal Behaviour', *Perceptual and Motor Skills*, vol. 43, pp. 215–22; 'Geophysical variables and behaviour. IX. Expected Clinical Consequences of Close Proximity to UFO related Luminosities', *Perceptual and Motor Skills*, vol. 56 (1983), pp. 259–65.

rise to earthquake light phenomena, on a smaller and more localized scale, the same processes are responsible for the UFO-related luminosities. In common with the *Earthlights* theory this smaller-scale occurrence does not involve the same fracturing and related seismic activity. Persinger quotes a figure for the 'small area' (12–120 square yards). Within such areas he suggests that electromagnetic forces – EM columns – could be sufficiently intense to produce luminosities. These might last from a few seconds to a few minutes. The dimensions of the EM columns are thought to be about 20–200 yards, their size being dependant on the available energy. It might be that several columns could occur within a localized area. Persinger admits that it is difficult to explain the means by which the luminosity is maintained as a cohesive mass. He suggests that the movement of the luminous body could be determined by both topographical structures and geophysical factors not apparent from the surface.

The reader will recognize that these proposals, or aspects of them, are generally in keeping with the theories put forward by Devereux and Campbell. They currently form the most plausible suggested explanations for the UAP phenomenon, although of course much work remains to be done and differences reconciled. Randles has applied the geophysical stress theory to cases in northern England.[17] It looks potentially valid.

To date, the only experimental results to support the production of luminosities from geophysical stresses have come from the work of Dr Brian Brady of the US Bureau of Mines in Denver, Colorado, and that of a small team working with Paul Devereux in Great Britain. Both have apparently produced laboratory-scale versions of some kind of luminosity using rock-core-crushing equipment. However, there is still some doubt about the nature of these luminosities, the lifetimes of which are fractions of a second. We are not currently aware of any published reports from either group. The number of studies specifically designed to test for the expected correlation has been small.

Persinger himself wrote an article in which he attempted to demonstrate a correlation between records of UFO events from the archives of Charles Fort, and his tectonic-strain theory. He

---

[17] Randles, *Pennine UFO Mystery*, pp. 227–34.

checked records of UFO events prior to 1947, and compared them with records of UK earth tremors over the same period – finding significant correlation.[18] Although there are many problems in applying such a retrospective test, most of these arise from the huge number of variables in both the reported events and the records of them. However, Persinger has had some success in minimizing the problems. (An article did appear in *Nature* proposing a mechanism for the larger-scale phenomenon of 'earthquake lights'; however, it suggested vaporization of porewater as the principal source of the charge.[19])

Persinger describes the effects which might lead to the familiar close-encounter scenario. It is suggested that direct or extremely close contact with the UFO luminosities can be fatal; then, at a range dependant upon magnitude of radiative output, a variety of effects occur. These are the result of current induction within the percipient's brain.

Similar findings to those of Persinger were illustrated by us several years ago. Although at that time we had not formalized a mechanism to explain such effects, the foundations of the concept were established. The actual effects suffered by the witness can be divided into two categories: those arising from current induction; and those arising from psychological factors after the experience, which occur as a part of the process of the witness attempting to come to terms with the direct effects. These direct and indirect effects are considered in the following chapter.

We believe that there are several different phenomena responsible for UAP events. All are probably natural atmospheric processes of one kind or another. One or more of the ideas discussed above may provide the basis for establishing a testable theory or theories of UAP origin.

[18] M.A. Persinger, 'Predicting Contemporary UFO Reports in Great Britain from Charles Fort's Data', *Fortean Times*, no. 41, 1982/1983.

[19] Lockner, Johnson and Byerlee, 'A mechanism to explain the generation of earthquake lights', *Nature*, vol. 302, 1983.

10

Alien Contacts:
Over the Edge of Reality

*The subconscious memory, according to the work of
neurophysiologists such as Penfield, has a record of virtually
every piece of information ever encountered by the individual
. . . surely the raw data must be available for any kind of
fantasy to be created – and created convincingly.*

Malcolm Scott, clinical psychologist, England
(private correspondence with Jenny Randles)

In the previous chapter we showed that a range of physical
phenomena have been observed, often obscured by being reported
as UFOs. However, there are also reports of UFOs which don't
seem to be explicable in these terms. They are frequently interpreted as alien contacts or the manifestation of a technology so
advanced that it appears magical. The scientists Hynek and
Vallée suggested that this area of the subject lay at what they
called 'the edge of reality'.[1]

The purpose of this chapter is to review the research that has
been conducted into the most bizarre cases. Unfortunately researchers themselves have not been sure whether to treat the
descriptions offered by their witnesses as reflections of the physical world or as those of an inner world of consciousness. The
work done reflects this uncertainty, and indeed some researchers
have suggested that UFO close encounters stalk the borderland
between these two worlds and so, as objective/subjective para-
doxes, are of greater scientific importance than if they were

[1] J.A. Hynek and J. Vallée, *The Edge of Reality* (Regnery Press, 1975).

'merely' particular forms of hallucination or encounters with strange denizens of the real universe.

Nevertheless, we must also consider alternative explanations for events such as that at Brockworth (see p. 3), or the following case.

In summer 1901 a young child came home in Bournebrook, in the West Midlands of England, at about 2 p.m. It was a sunny afternoon. He (now an old man) told the tale many years later. Apparently he found a hut-like object in the garden, with a door in one side. As he approached, two strange beings came out of the door, and one of them moved slightly towards him and seemed to wave him back. Both beings were between three and four feet tall, and wore tight-fitting, greyish-green uniforms with dark caps on their heads which had wires coming out of them. After a moment both returned to the 'hut', and a bright light came on underneath it, between it and the ground. Then it suddenly left, with a whooshing noise and a flashing reddish glow. It moved very fast, and then vanished.

This example poses a typical problem. A single witness relates, apparently sincerely, a most 'unlikely' event. There is no physical evidence to support his story, or any other way of corroborating it. But does that fact alone mean that he *must* be wrong?

There will be situations (and many of them) where an 'alien craft' is constructed by the mind of the witness from a very ordinary stimulus. Allan Hendry made some sobering points about the American love of advertising using lights strung beneath a slowly flying aircraft. Seen from certain angles the illusion of a peculiar shape is created. It can be highly persuasive and many usually skilled observers have been fooled by this into reporting UFOs.[2] This psychological quirk for connecting up loosely connected (or unconnected) lights is one we all possess. It reminds one of the game of 'join the dots' – linking them up until something familiar is recognized. But this does not only happen with advertising planes, although they are indeed a very irritating source of IFOs for the ufologist. Ordinary aircraft, helicopters, balloons, and even stars have all been mistaken in this way. They have combined or been distorted in the minds of many a witness

[2] A. Hendry, *The UFO Handbook* (Sphere, 1980).

to create the belief that they have seen a genuine UFO (often of disc or cigar shape).[3] This is a perennial major problem, and one reason why those who claim that all UFOs are potential IFOs have a case to be answered. The vagaries of human imagination are so many and varied that it is difficult to be certain of the exotic nature of any nocturnal UFO sighting. Peculiar craft seen in daytime don't present quite so many problems, but even here there are a number of proven misidentifications that show how objects such as weather balloons (which are often round and silvery) can find themselves transformed into spaceships from another planet.[4]

Dr Richard Haines, a NASA scientist specializing in optics, has been particularly interested in how a UFO shape can be produced in the mind of a witness when a UFO is not there.[5] At his lectures he hands out blank sheets of paper and asks his audience to sketch their concept of a UFO. He then requests basic information of them, such as whether they are believers or disbelievers in UFOs as alien craft, and how much they have read about the subject. He has built up a vast file of tens of thousands of sketches. We both completed the Haines experiment and our conceptions of UFOs were apparently quite normal. Haines has found that there is a very distinct general idea of UFOs common to most people (with minor variations).

It is easy to imagine how a witness who suddenly sees something strange in the sky can persuade himself that this something is a UFO, and the expectation he has of what a UFO would be like begins to affect what he is observing. The ambiguous stimulus (which may not be a true UFO) takes on the form of his conceived UFO and this reinforces his belief that what he is watching really is unusual. It is also normal for a person to try to rationalize away what he is observing: it's a plane, no, maybe a helicopter, or is it a balloon? But nowadays UFO stories are so widespread that people find it easy to think that they may have seen one. No doubt the same sort of mental process would occur even if the stimulus actually was a true UFO, so its acceptance does not mean that no real UFOs exist. But in the early days of

[3] J. Randles, *UFO Reality* (Robert Hale, 1983), pp. 39–44.

[4] J. Randles, *UFO Study* (Robert Hale, 1981).

[5] R. Haines, *Observing UFOs* (Nelson-Hall, 1980).

interest in UFOs there was no such widespread conception of what a UFO should look like and it is true that reported UFO shapes seem to have been more varied then. Often they appeared in formations, akin to the one first reported by Kenneth Arnold (see p. 1).

A key factor in the 'misinterpretation' hypothesis is the relationship between UFOs and science fiction. In early post-war days any alien spacecraft was imagined as possessing a rocket-like shape. And the early UFO sightings often did describe rocket-shaped objects. The switch to the saucer idea to represent spacecraft came very early and persisted in science fiction and film imagery even when the 1960s brought real (earthly) rocket-shaped spacecraft.

Which came first – the saucer sightings or the science fiction representations? Bafflingly, they often seem to have been more or less contemporary with one another. However, at least some of the now-common UFO imagery appeared first in the wave of sci-fi films produced at the height of the UFO craze during the early 1950s. *The Day the Earth Stood Still* predicted the first reliable car-stop cases, with its feature of an alien device stalling all machinery. Many films featured a witness being 'abducted' and then restrained and examined (see, for example, the way the light aircraft is 'beamed aboard' the UFO in *This Island Earth*). Just as in the nineteenth century, when science fiction stories about 'airships' coincided with supposedly real sightings of them, there seems to be a connection between the 'imaginative' conception of the UFO phenomenon and its 'real' manifestation.

This is one reason why some researchers favour a solution on the threshold of objectivity and subjectivity. Ian Watson (a science-fiction writer who has investigated UFOs) and Dr Lyall Watson (a research zoologist) have independently concluded that it could be that in some strange way we actually create reality as we go along.[6] Some people simply imagine UFOs. But it may be

[6] I. Watson, *Miracle Visitors* (Gollancz, 1978); L. Watson, *Life Tide* (Hodder and Stoughton, 1979). (The two Watsons are not related.) Dr Rupert Sheldrake, a biologist, put forward a controversial theory in *A New Science of Life* (Blond and Briggs, 1981) which suggests that reality is conditioned by habit. Naturally, his ideas have been rejected by some authorities of the scientific Establishment, but others have called for further research.

that when enough people accept these imaginings as true, a sort of quasi-reality may occur. Psychologist Dr Carl Jung suggested in his book about UFO dreams that the disc shape might correlate with a mandala – an image deeply etched in the human unconscious. But he couldn't reconcile this idea with the possibility of UFO reality.[7] Of course, what might be happening is that Jung's mandala shape is being stamped upon existent reality, which is thus altered in the experience of the witnesses.

Consider the following case. A couple left their son's home in a village near Shrewsbury, England, at about 11.35 p.m. on the night of 21 October 1983. Their intention was to drive home to a village near Northwich, Cheshire, a journey which would take about an hour and a quarter. Soon after leaving Shrewsbury they saw an object apparently swoop over the road in front of them and then travel alongside the car above the hedge beside the road. There followed a protracted, harrowing, close encounter with this UFO, lasting from about midnight until 12.50 a.m., when it vanished near Cuddington in Cheshire. The UFO had moved from side to side. It had beamed light into the car, but it cast no shadow. It so severely upset the woman that she suffered hypertension and felt very ill. Both people were, of course, highly relieved to get home. They described the classic UFO shape with assorted lights – red, green and amber.

There is no obvious explanation for the experience. Although one can never discount the possibility of unreliability of witnesses, these two seem wholly sincere. The husband, a retired engineer, thought very deeply about it before he decided they should call Jodrell Bank radio astronomy observatory and report what had happened. From here it came to us and MUFORA undertook an investigation within two days of the incident. Jenny Randles immediately asked the couple: 'Did you see the moon?' Both said that the sky had seemed bright, as on a moonlit night, and yet neither had seen the moon. She knew that on that night there had been an almost full moon shining brightly in a frosty, clear sky. It would have been very difficult for them to have missed the moon.

This kind of case presents researchers with a problem. To

---

[7] C. Jung, *Flying Saucers* (Routledge and Kegan Paul, 1977).

suggest that they saw the moon through trees and thought it was a UFO following their car does seem ludicrous, but it fits the facts. Yet the gulf between the appearance of the moon and the 'UFO' they described is so wide that it indicates another factor in the equation which we might put as: moon + state X = UFO close encounter. State X could be a psychological process whereby certain stimuli are 'turned into' UFOs by the mind. In other cases the stimulus is not the moon but an aeroplane, or helicopter. If this idea is right, the UFO problem is different. No longer are we asking what UFOs are; for we know that they are sometimes the moon, sometimes Venus, or whatever. But we still have an important question: we are really trying to understand this elusive state X. A feeling of dissociation (known as the 'Oz factor') is often reported by witnesses to UFO close encounters,[8] sometimes as a vague suspension of time or sensory isolation. In the case just cited the witnesses felt it most strange that they were alone on a road which was usually busy. There was no other traffic at all. Everything was so very quiet. They also heard a humming/buzzing noise and smelt a peculiar odour. These are two very common features of state X. In investigating state X the value of IFOs is enormous. For there are many IFO cases and many apparent UFOs which can be traced to seemingly ridiculous stimuli. The real UFO close encounter may not take place in the outer world of our atmosphere, but in the inner world of the witnesses's mind.

But how do we reconcile this idea with the multiple-witness descriptions from various locations, the UFOs that make holes in the ground and those which can be photographed? Many of these may turn out to be UAPs, but they too can be the stimulus for a state X experience, just as any ordinary phenomenon like the moon, an aircraft or a balloon can. The idea of the existence of state X has been mooted as an alternative explanation to the physical reality of alien spacecraft. That it has some support from the evidence will be made clear as we look at more research. But the question of the residual photographs which show an apparent craft (no matter how few) cannot be lightly eliminated. Many sceptics would prefer to deny the validity of all such photographs

[8] J. Randles, *The Pennine UFO Mystery* (Granada, 1983).

(e.g. those taken at McMinnville, Oregon, USA, in 1950, the ones at Trindade Island, off the coast of Brazil, in 1957, or a few dozen others). To brand these as fakes is the easiest solution, for they do not show identifiable phenomena. Yet there is evidence that supports their reality (including the results of computer enhancement). How do we deal with them? Although they could just be extremely clever fakes, it would be premature to assume this. It has been suggested that in a state X situation the changing of reality extends to the allowance of temporary photographic support, but this is a wild idea which raises many thorny problems – scientists would take a lot of convincing! It is more likely that the objects are experimental craft flown by a very terrestial source.

It is well known that the Germans were developing new aircraft of a saucer shape towards the end of the Second World War. That such a craft was successfully test-flown in February 1945 is also on record. That the 'ghost rocket' sightings in Scandinavia during 1946 were widely regarded as Russian continuations of such experiments is also true. So, it is not unreasonable to suppose that some machine which looks like a flying saucer might have been developed after the war by either the allies or the Soviets or both. Indeed the aircraft manufacturers Avro did publicly show their UFO-like design but the project was dropped.

It is difficult to imagine why – or how – the existence of these devices would be kept secret for so very long. Somebody must build them, if they are of our own making. Would they really be test-flown in areas where they would be seen? Perhaps so, because the belief in UFOs (as spaceships) may allow perfect camouflage. The experimental craft would be reported as alien and nobody would take their presence seriously, except those with a wholly false view of what they really were. A UFO landing in Socorro, New Mexico, in April 1964 involved a device that looked very like the lunar landing module later used by NASA. A policeman, Lonnie Zamora, was chasing a speeding car when he noticed what he took to be an upturned car near an old shack. He stopped to investigate. He found it was an egg-shaped vehicle; with it were two small 'men' in white 'jump-suits'. They got into the object, which then took off, a fiery exhaust scorching the ground as it did so. By the time more police arrived in response to

Zamora's radio call the object was out of sight, but the impressions of a heavy object remained in the still-smouldering scrubland. Ground Saucer Watch, a US investigation group, argue that this case was a test for a space vehicle, even though this is strenuously denied in official circles. Some ufologists say that the UFO/spaceship theory was actively promoted at the time of this case because it suited the government.

In December 1980 two major events happened at the same 'real' time (9 p.m. on 29th in Huffmann, Texas, USA, and 3 a.m. on 30th in Rendlesham Forest, England[9]). Both involved small triangular craft spewing fire. Both were seen by many witnesses; the Huffmann case seems to have concerned an object that malfunctioned and gave radiation burns to three civilian witnesses. When the craft left it did so in retinue with many Chinook helicopters, presumably owned by the US government. The coincident Rendlesham Forest case occurred within a few hundred yards of a US military base and was witnessed by several US military personnel and civilians. It too apparently left traces of radiation. The cases could be coincidental but that does not seem very likely. Either UFOs and the US government were involved in several meetings that night or the US government was testing some kind of secret device. The latter explanation is at least as plausible as the alien UFO theory, although it seems to be stretching the facts too far to believe it could account for all close encounters, particularly those which took place before 1945. Our technology did not advance that fast.

The key aspect of these exotic UFOs are the reports of contact between humans and aliens, variously termed close encounters of the third and fourth kind (CE3 and CE4). Are any of these aliens 'real'? Several studies have been made into the average number of witnesses of UFO events, as one obvious means of investigating witness subjectivity. Work by Vicente-Juan Ballester Olmos and Jacques Vallée (on Spanish data),[10] Fred Merritt and Allan Hendry (on US data) and Jenny Randles (on British data) gives a

---

[9] The Huffmann incident is described in B. Pratt and J. Scheussler, *Fire in the Road* (Prentice-Hall, 1985). The Rendlesham case has been the subject of great controversy (see pp. 157–60).

[10] J.-V. Ballester Olmos and J. Vallée, *FSR* (Special Issue 4, 1971.)

consistent pattern for the average number of witnesses to a typical UFO: between 2.3 and 2.6 witnesses per case (the upper figure is more appropriate when one takes only UAP and ordinary UFO events, i.e. those which do not specifically involve aliens). The typical UFO experience is not a single-witness phenomenon, which does suggest that it is not a simple case of individual imagination. But the average is still lower than one might expect – the number of eye-witnesses to another rare aerial event, an air disaster, would be considerably greater, largely because many such crashes occur at or near airports where there are hundreds of potential witnesses. But this would not account for the entire difference: there does seem to be some form of 'witness selectivity' at work. This may not imply intelligent design on the part of UFOs; it may simply tell us something about the mechanics of a natural phenomenon (that it occurs particularly in areas of low population density).

But how many people witness each CE3 or CE4 incident? (A CE3 case involves observation of an animate alien entity in association with a UFO. A CE4 goes one step beyond and includes contact between that entity and the witness.) Sadly, comprehensive study of witness numbers per case for these events alone has not yet been done. But Jenny Randles has done some preliminary work on a sample of 80 CE4 cases.[11] She divides CE4 events into sub-groups, of which the three main ones are relevant here. Type A refers to contacts where there is a straightforward interaction between witness and entity (with conscious recall). There may, or may not, be a loss of time or memory distortion but some memory of the alien component to the experience is held by the witness. Type C includes cases where no such recall exists, but memory is stimulated later by artificial means (usually regression hypnosis). UFO events which are worth investigating in this way are spotted because of various common factors, such as periods of missing time in the story, vivid dreams (with alien imagery) after the encounter and conflicting or multiple memories about certain aspects of the experience. Researcher Budd

[11] J. Randles, *FSR*, vol. 26, no. 5, 1980.

Hopkins has outlined several more (including physiological clues).[12]

Jenny Randles has recently conducted another survey of all British type A and type C cases on record. Type A cases (those with spontaneous recall) were far more common (34 as opposed to just 10 type C). Twenty of the 34 were single-witness events and the average witness number per case was 1.6, well below the figure for the ordinary UFO (or UAP) event. However, only four out of the ten type C cases were single-witness, and the average number of witnesses per case here was not substantially different from the ordinary UFO figure, standing at 2.1. This implies that (as expected) encounters with aliens are more likely to be subjective than the average UFO event, and that those *not* involving time or memory loss are the most likely to be subjective. But the truly fantastic cases, where there is time and memory loss (and hypnosis triggers off a revived memory of onboard contact or abduction by aliens) are *not* very different in terms of likely subjectivity from an ordinary UFO or UAP sighting. Naturally, with such a small sample these suggestions should be regarded as highly speculative. But data from other type C cases show that multiple witnesses *are* common. The idea is offered as a testable hypothesis – something that ufology needs.

This might suggest that the contacts retrieved by hypnosis are substantially different from consciously recalled CE4s. Contrary to expectation, consciously recalled cases seem *more* likely to be subjective (because *more* of these are single-witness incidents). But this view is misleading because of other differences between Type A and Type C cases, for example that the type A, 'remembered' cases involved 42 per cent of entities being described as

[12] B. Hopkins, *Missing Time* (Marek, 1983). 'Multiple memories' are cases where the witness has two or more memories covering one period of time. Type B CE4s are more like 'waking dreams' and probably not relevant to the main study of UFOs. Commonly known as 'bedroom visitors', such experiences tend to happen while the witness is asleep or nearly so (including hypnagogic/hypnopompic images). They are almost totally subjective, having a witness per case ratio close to one). The subject is fascinating, but more for the psychologist than the ufologist at least in our present state of knowledge. See K. Basterfield, *UFO Research Australia*, vol. 5, no. 5, 1984. For type D cases, see p. 150.

'small' by human standards and only 21 per cent described as 'large'. Yet those type C cases where the memory was artificially stimulated contained very few 'small' entities and 60 per cent regarded as 'large' by human standards. This might suggest that it is only the time loss or memory loss per se that should be considered reliable testimony. The stimulated memory of what happens *during* this period may be artificially produced, with little or no substance, by the hypnosis technique. In cases where several witnesses saw a type C event, hypnosis brings out stories which are usually broadly similar though they can vary in details.

This question has been stressed for two important reasons. First, because some CE4 cases (especially type B) do seem to be a form of sensory illusion akin to hallucination, thus leaving the possibility open that the others may be too. But second, as we have seen, there are many type A and type C contacts which are not single-witness events. (Two of the type C cases in the British sample had no less than five witnesses each.) Multiple-witness hallucinations are extremely rare and most scientists would need strong evidence to believe in consistent five-person hallucinations. And so, we do seem to have at least a suggestion that there may be more to these alien UFOs than mere hallucination. This is certainly the view that many scientists who have delved into the problem have come to. Dr Aphrodite Clamar, a medical psychologist drafted into UFO work on a professional basis with no prior interest, conducted hypnotic retrieval experiments on a dozen separate witnesses to CE4 type C cases. She concluded: 'I cannot say whether the experience was "real" or not; that is, I do not know . . . I am persuaded, however, that all of the subjects do, in fact, believe that something strange and unknown did occur. It happened for them; it happened to them. Who of us is to say that it did not?' Dr Clamar called it 'a problem requiring further exploration'. So it is.

It is, of course, very difficult to know if this curious phenomenon of the UFO close encounter (especially the CE4) is identical with, related to, or entirely separate from, the core UFO (or UAP) phenomenon as already discussed. But the UFO close encounter is so different in its charcteristics and so clearly cries out for a psychological approach, as opposed to a physical one, that it is probably sensible to regard it as an individual problem, separate from the world of UAPs and UFOs, at least in the present stages of our understanding.

A great deal of attention in CE4 research has been focused on the baffling question of 'time lapse', as prevalent in type C cases. This, in turn, has meant that the practice of hypnosis has been gaining more and more ground within ufological circles. Before 1964 nobody dreamt of using hypnosis in UFO research. An American psychiatrist, Dr Benjamin Simon, was the unwitting instigator of a revolution in this respect. He was approached by a couple, Betty and Barney Hill, who recalled a protracted UFO encounter they had had while driving through the night to New Hampshire after a Canadian vacation in September 1961. Subsequent dreams and severe anxiety had plagued them, as had the nagging worry of several hours of missing time. Dr Simon decided hypnosis was the best way to relieve the anxiety and conducted a long series of experiments on both witnesses. He had no interest or belief in UFOs.

What emerged has been told in a best-selling book,[13] and in a television film (*The UFO Incident*). It also made newspaper headlines throughout the world in 1965. Essentially the couple claimed to recall an abduction on to a landed UFO followed by a medical examination by small but friendly aliens with distinctive features (although not too unlike humans). Dr Simon was cautious about their stories, which were very consistent. He suggested that the husband may have been so emotionally close to his wife that he came to regard her subjective experiences as objectively real, and so shared her fantasy. But he accepted that other explanations, including the stories being true, were possible.

This was not the first reported encounter with alien beings. Nor was it the first to involve aliens very like those Betty and Barney Hill claimed to have met. Hundreds of similar stories from all over the world were already on ufologists' files. Indeed, it was not even the first alleged abduction (or on-board UFO experience). Several existed, although they had been given no publicity and it is unlikely the Hills knew about any of them. What the Hill CE4 case did was make ufologists reappraise their data. When a

[13] J. Fuller, *The Interrupted Journey* (Souvenir Press, 1980).

witness came along with a CE3 story and any confusion of
memory (which had often been a common feature) the possibility
that a deeper CE4 encounter might exist was always assumed.
Also, most later witnesses probably had some awareness of the
Hill abduction (or, as years went by, others which achieved
publicity), and so they frequently began to speculate about what
might have happened, wondering if their UFO encounter might
have included an abduction. In some cases at least they probably
hoped that it did. These developments must have both had an
influence on the sudden explosion of CE4 reports which ufologists began to uncover, but that does not necessarily make the
new cases suspect, for the pre-1965 UFO records do show cases
that bear all the signs of being possible CE4s. But because
nobody thought to use hypnosis to stimulate recall they simply
remained enigmatic CE3 cases. It is also possible that witnesses
with type A recall of CE4 abductions would be so frightened of
the ridicule such a fantastic tale might bring on them that they
would not report the incident. Regression-hypnosis experiments
have recently been done on witnesses who claim to have had
strange CE3 experiences prior to 1961. In several such instances
alleged CE4 abductions have been 'recovered'.

It is inescapably true that the Hill CE4 was a watershed in the
study of the UFO phenomenon. Whether the ever-expanding
number of CE4 cases in the 1970s and 1980s is a result of a
combination of witness/investigator fantasy based on this single
report, or whether the agents of the phenomenon (if agents there
be) have changed tactics since 1961, it is hard to say. Or perhaps
it is true that we have merely discovered an anomaly that was
here all the time.

Budd Hopkins, a New York artist, had his interest in UFOs
fired by a personal sighting around the time the Hill abduction
became known. He has since specialized in the search for type C
CE4 cases, using hypnosis (with the help of Dr Aphrodite Clamar)
to probe intensely the missing time period and search for patterns
in the memories which emerge. He is the first person to have
devoted a book to the theoretical questions,[14] although Landsberg

[14] Hopkins, *Missing Time*.

did publish a series of interviews with abductees[15] and veteran ufologists Coral and Jim Lorenzon had earlier written up a collection of CE4 witness stories.[16] There is little overlap in these three books, which between them feature several dozen CE4 encounters, and these are but the most popular of many others.[17]

Much of the work undertaken by Hopkins has been with witnesses who had no clear recall of a UFO event. He looks for multiple memories, missing memories which might imply time-loss, etc., and for wounds and scars which the witness cannot explain. On hypnotic investigation these often apparently turn out to have been received during an abduction and medical examination that was so repressed from the witness's memory that he or she was unaware of it. Hopkins draws on those cases to suggest that there may well be thousands of abductees, happily pursuing a normal life quite unaware of their past encounters with aliens. Jenny Randles undertook research into a 1980 type C experience undergone by policeman Alan Godfrey at Todmorden, West Yorkshire, England. Here the time lapse was only about 15 minutes, and its existence emerged through diligent reconstructive investigation. The witness himself was uncertain enough not to have mentioned it.[18] This, considered alongside contemporary cases where the memory of a UFO witness was seemingly interfered with both during and immediately after a close encounter, certainly seems worth investigating. Jenny Randles felt that the Oz factor might in fact be involved in the time loss, and that CE4 incidents could possibly be at the root of many otherwise apparently 'ordinary' UFO sightings.

In Great Britain lawyer Harry Harris, along with colleagues Mike Sacks and Norman Collinson from MUFORA, have begun to look for hints of CE4 cases and, when they arise (however faint), conduct regression-hypnosis experiments with suitably

---

[15] A. Landsberg, *Direct Encounters* (Coronet, 1982).

[16] C. and J. Lorenzon, *Abducted* (Berkley, 1977).

[17] Books on individual cases include R. Fowler, *The Andreasson Affair* (Prentice-Hall, 1979); Ann Druffel and D. Scott Rogo, *The Tujunga Canyon Contacts* (Prentice-Hall, 1980); D. Haissell, *The Missing Seven Hours* (Paperjacks, 1978); J. Randles and P. Whetnall, *Alien Contact* (Spearman, 1982).

[18] See Randles, *Pennine UFO Mystery*.

qualified doctors and psychiatrists. All sessions are video filmed and a library of many hours involving a dozen or so witnesses already exists. Of course, this approach has its drawbacks. There is appreciable danger of creating a memory by forcing on to the witness the thought that it is desirable that he should remember something (to justify time or expense, merely to please everybody, or even to attract some of the media attention a sensational abduction might achieve). An ordinary UFO sighting is now so routine it is perhaps almost boring to some people. But an abduction by exotic aliens is quite another matter.

To be fair to Harry Harris and his team, some efforts have been made to minimize this danger (although perhaps not as many as one might like). For instance, the psychologists involved often do not know they are searching for a UFO memory, prior to such a memory emerging. There have been cases where the supposed CE4 memory has refused to co-operate as the witness, despite several hypnosis sessions, has done nothing but repeat (usually in more vivid detail) the events he already had conscious knowledge of. This certainly supports (although it does not prove) the view that in those cases where there is success a real hidden memory emerges.

The Harris cases share much with those reported by Hopkins (both in his writings and in discussions with us). They believe a 'cover story' is an important feature: a sort of mental fantasy that masks the real memory and which has to be stripped away by sheer hard psychological work before progress can be made. These cover stores often appear silly. In one Hopkins investigation it involved seeing thousands of rabbits beside a car. In a Harris case the mask was a dolphin in a swimming pool! Hopkins remarks that animals are common cover-story stereotypes, as if they are pleasing substitute images which the mind uses to replace the more disturbing reality on a level of awareness closest to waking consciousness. In this way the danger of the real truth leaking out is minimized.

This presupposes that it is the witness who pushes away the experience, thus creating the time loss as a sort of trauma amnesia. Other researchers feel that the intelligence they infer behind the UFOs is the actual controller of the memory. Workers like Dr James Harder, a US specialist in CE4 cases, suggest that the aliens give a false memory to the witness so that it is less probable he will recognize the existence of a time lapse. A British case, among several which apparently support this view, involved three adults and two children who saw a UFO in June 1978 while driving near Faringdon, Oxfordshire, England. Hypnosis, revealing a fantastic abduction story, was undertaken following strange dreams by one witness and some confusion over a road which they recalled driving along. Upon reflection, and after trying to drive along the route again, they realized this road did not exist.

If this interference with memory really does take place it means that none of us can feel secure in believing that we have never had a UFO close encounter. An investigation by Harry Harris is of interest here. The 'witness', Jenny, was an intelligent insurance broker in her twenties who had vague recollections of recurrent dreams of aliens. From this most insubstantial of starting-points regression hypnosis was conducted, chiefly as a test of what would emerge from a session where there was apparently no CE4 to be uncovered. However, Jenny under hypnosis could not recall any dream that originated the sequence, but when asked to search for any real incident she might be regarding as a dream the floodgates of her mind seemed to open. She saw herself with her husband (then her boyfriend) in a car on a Cheshire lane in June 1980. She went on to describe what could be termed a failed abduction. A UFO came down and blocked the road ahead, pouring out bright light. From it, two tall figures in silver suits emerged and placed their hands on the car. Her husband was asleep and she tried desperately to wake him. She switched off the car engine (but does not know why) and one of the figures tried to get her to come out of the car. She refused completely to do so, and eventually the two entities gave up, returned to the brightly glowing UFO and left.

Was this just a fantasy? Jenny displayed great fear and emotion in describing it, as indeed do all CE4 witnesses (until they describe actually going on board the UFO, when they suddenly become calm). If Jenny's experience was in any sense real, then it means that what any of us may think was only a dream could have been something else.

Underlying all this research, as amazing as it is, remains the fundamental problem of hypnosis. For even those who practise this technique remain unclear as to *exactly* how it works. It appears to involve a weakening of the ego-consciousness of the subject. One of its effects appears to be much greater recall, as shown in its use by police investigators to help witnesses of crimes to remember details. Unfortunately another feature is the enhanced susceptibility of the hypnotized subject to suggestion. Also, because the powers of imagination are stimulated, information from the subconscious (which may be 'real' or 'imaginary') could well up into awareness, thus allowing vivid, but totally imaginative adventures to be recalled as having really occurred. As researchers have come to understand all this, the use of hypnosis in situations where the absolute veracity of hypnotic memory must be counted upon has diminished. For hypnosis simply is not reliable. Nobody would argue that it is not capable of boosting recall and retrieving real information that is in the subconscious but not immediately available. However, depending on many variable circumstances (e.g. the mood of the subject, the way questions are phrased, etc.), fantasy and distortion can intrude into the accounts. All that we can say is that hypnotic regression memories reflect genuine data somewhere between 0 and 100 per cent of the time! The figure varies and is probably somewhere in the middle, for most ordinary people, but it is impossible to calculate. Where does this leave us in attempting to investigate CE4 cases? Quite evidently with nothing but an increased degree of confusion.

Dr Alvin Lawson, a Californian lecturer in English, and William McCall, a medical hypnotist, have conducted experiments to help resolve this problem. They took subjects specially selected for lack of knowledge of UFOs and asked them, under hypnosis, to imagine a UFO abduction. They did this by way of 'lead' questions, e.g. 'You are now being examined – what happens?' They then compared the results with memories of supposedly real abductions they had obtained. The experiments revealed many features common to both, but there were significant differences too. For instance, the imaginary abductees did not believe their hypnotic memories to be real. They answered questions calmly and unemotionally and displayed none of the severe psychological reactions common to virtually every reported CE4 hypnosis session. There was also greater variety in their descriptions of UFOs and aliens.

The work has been criticized for various weaknesses, for example the way subjects were drawn, as volunteers, only from among university students and the very low number of people used in the experiment (eight). However, Lawson and McCall have gone on to examine drug-induced hallucinations and other types of hallucinatory experience. They claim to have found patterns which are common to these and CE4 memories. For example the symbol of a tube or tunnel is a typical hallucinatory feature. Lawson and McCall claim that this can be related to such things as UFO light beams. From this and a general similarity between frequently reported UFO entities (in US cases) and a human foetus, they have come up with the extraordinary hypothesis that the CE4 hypnotic memory is a reliving of the deeply repressed birth trauma. In other words, a subject returns to this first memory of stress and fantasizes an account based on fleeting and incomprehensible images taken into the subconscious during those initial moments of life. Few, if any, psychiatrists or psychologists (whether open-minded or hostile to the UFO enigma) believe that this theory has any merit. There is little evidence to support the belief that a newborn baby is capable of retaining memories of the birth process. And even if this were so the extension from it to the use of such data in a subsequent fantasy is not very easy to comprehend.

Another argument against the Lawson and McCall experiments is that they created the similarities with real abduction stories by asking their key questions, such questions being structured on what we already know from 'real' abduction stories. This seems circuitous logic destined to bring biased results.

As an attempt to see how the experiment would fare without this factor, Jenny Randles conducted an admittedly rudimentary study in which eight people between the ages of 23 and 57, of widely differing backgrounds, four male, four female, and with varying interest in UFOs (ranging from none at all to a practising ufologist) were all placed in the same situation. They were not hypnotized, but in calm, quiet surroundings, alone with the experimenter, were asked the following question: 'I am comparing stories of people who say that they have seen a UFO and made contact with it. Imagine that you are alone in your car in dark, open country. A UFO appears and makes contact with you. What do you see?' No further prompting was given and the accounts of the subjects were taken down. This was not conducted as anything other than a trial for possible future full-scale experiments, but the data is still of interest, in that it matches the Lawson and McCall work up to a point. Not a single person imagined going on board the UFO, although all said the UFO landed and all but two described some form of life. Three out of the four men and one of the women actually said they felt a barrier that blocked them from imagining beyond the point where they see the aliens get out of the UFO. Why was the typical on-board experience that is retrieved under hypnosis never replicated? Why did not one of these eight give even a hint of a medical examination, one of the most common experiences in a type C case, and well known to most people? You may recall that in the study of type C cases the entity was described as 'large' in 60 per cent of cases. In this sample of eight only those with a knowledge of ufology (two people), who tended to go more for the 'three-feet-tall entity', failed to describe taller than normal beings in silvery suits. There were many elements within the stories that were common to one another and also common to supposedly real UFO data, e.g. very bright lights, an unusual calm feeling, an inability to move and no hostility shown by the aliens.

Now of course these features emerged in the stories without hypnosis, a fact which weakens the argument that abduction stories are 'created' by the hypnosis process itself. Some common factor is at work in many minds. This view is backed up by the fact that there are more than a few CE4 cases of type A which involve recall of a completely spontaneous and apparently conscious nature. Such cases show many consistencies and with type C reports, as the following examples serve to illustrate.

Date: Spring 1954
Place: Côte d'Azur, France
Investigator: Gordon Creighton

A single male witness met a landed UFO and two entities, one of whom fired a torch-like instrument at him, emitting a beam of light which paralysed him. The entity came over and inspected him and then gestured that he should follow. The man, still paralysed, did not. The entities re-entered the UFO and the witness lost consciousness but recovered an unknown time later to see the UFO departing. The man recalled all this without hypnosis.

Date: 11 October 1973
Place: Pascagoula, Mississippi, USA

Two fishermen saw a hovering UFO. Two robot-like entities came towards them and physically dragged them towards the UFO. Their memories became hazy in describing this part of the story. Inside, they were examined by a large, eye-like device. Hypnosis was later conducted on the two men, but only confirmed the details consciously recalled.[19]

Date: 16 October 1973
Place: Wellington, Somerset, England

A single woman was driving on a lonely road. The engine cut out as a UFO was seen nearby. She was inspecting the car when a large, robot-like creature grabbed her and dragged her toward the UFO. Her memory became hazy at this point. Inside she was given a medical examination while strapped to a table and raped by a human-like entity. She recovered her memory back in the car and discovered the UFO gone and the engine now functioning. No hypnosis was conducted.[20]

Date: 15 September 1977
Place: Paciencia, Brazil
Investigator: Dr Ann Druffel

A single man met a landed UFO and was approached by three robot-like creatures. He was paralysed by a blue beam of light and lost consciousness. He woke to find himself inside a room. A sample of blood was taken, and he was shown many visual images while being given a message about peaceful alien intentions. He

[19] See R. and J. Blum, *Beyond Earth* (Corgi, 1974).
[20] See J. Randles, *UFO Study* pp. 248–9.

found himself back outside the UFO, feeling ill and unable to account for half an hour of time. No hypnosis was conducted.

Many other examples have been written up in the literature. This implies that the effect of hypnosis is only to distort the pattern, not to create it in the first place. Something else is responsible for the shared features in so many CE4 cases. This may be a root psychological cause, such as Lawson and McCall's 'birth trauma', or perhaps a kind of general yearning for an outside, more powerful form of life which might solve all our problems. But such a psychosis would in itself be a phenomenon worthy of study and the similarities in details need a lot of explanation.

Tales of contact between people and 'alien beings' are not new. Vallée produced fascinating research showing parallels between modern CE4 cases and folklore accounts from many nations about the 'little folk': fairies, elves, leprechauns and so forth. It is hard to escape the extraordinary number of points where these stories do overlap. This may simply mean that the psychosis is not new, and indicates a lasting feature of the human condition, but it could equally mean that there is something alien with which man has always had sporadic contact. Yesterday's fairies are today's extraterrestrials, and who knows what they might be tomorrow?

One psychological phenomenon, and its less respectable but nevertheless real psychic counterpart, may prove to be of great importance in the UFO debate. This is the dissociation of personality and its offspring – psychic possession. A typical case of possession would involve an individual lapsing into an altered state of consciousness – a 'trance' – which bears some comparison with the hypnotic state in which UFO abduction memories might emerge. In this trance the person regarded as psychic will reveal messages which have entered his or her subconscious mind. These are usually assumed to come from the dead, principally because there is occasional evidence that the medium obtains information about particular people who have died, or those still alive, which is not available through ordinary means.

In fact the choice of the word 'medium' will probably prove to have been misleading, because many modern psychic researchers consider it improbable that anyone acts as a go-between in communication from this world to the next. In fact it is more likely that the sensitive individual simply obtains the relevant messages from the memories of the living relatives who are present, perhaps by way of telepathy. A message is constructed by the conscious mind as it struggles to interpret the data coming in from the subconscious. It is heavily influenced by the beliefs of those present, e.g. that any success will demonstrate that there is life after death. Those sceptical of the psychic researchers' evidence will go further and say it is all suggestion and inference from normal psychological cues.

There is a direct comparison here with UFO-contact cases, where it has been suggested that information reaches the hypnotized subject by means of telepathy. The surrounding belief system is now different and so the emergent messages rationalized by the subject's conscious mind would involve life on other planets. This may help to explain the CE4 type C cases, where hypnosis is involved, by doing away with the requirement for an 'external' source for the 'facts' revealed by the subject. But, unless one is willing to assume that all CE4 cases, even where no hypnosis is used, involve altered states of consciousness where telepathy from an unknown source is involved, then this still leaves the case for the existence of aliens undestroyed.

The issue of dissociation has been raised because some psychologists think that it may hold a clue in trying to explain the working of the minds of mediums. There have been documented instances where the consciousness of an individual has temporarily fragmented into several different entities, any one of which can assume command of the physical body at any particular time. These multiple personalities usually conflict with each other, and then often give themselves names. When one of them is in control the person usually behaves in ways quite unlike his pre-dissociation self, 'acting' the character of the currently controlling entity. But of course these entities are not spirits or spacemen; they are sub-layers of the complex psychological matrix which makes up any human being – aspects of the person's personality. The same may be happening, in a way, with mediums who apparently are taken over by spirits. But you may not yet have grasped the significance of all this to UFO contact cases. It is that the alien which is central to their story may actually be a dissociated part of the witnesses themselves, not merely adopting a new name, as is typical of the multiple personality, but in this case also a new planet of origin.

Such an idea would require proper psychological study, but there are indications in UFO reports which suggest there is promise in it. Not least is the banal nature of all messages imparted by the aliens. Never once has a new piece of scientific evidence, a cure for cancer, a new planet in the solar system, or any solution to any of our problems been presented. The information is only in keeping with our own current knowledge and only at the limits of our own imagination, often producing really embarrassing 'information' from aliens such as the existence of a planet behind the moon, or descriptions of journeys of several light years' duration – a light year being a unit of distance rather than time.

Also important is the existence of a fourth type of CE4, which Jenny Randles calls type D. This is rarely studied by ufologists because it involves witnesses who claim mental contact with aliens entirely without physical manifestation. They have been known to produce automatic script which relates dull messages from their alien mentors. Such people seem extremely similar to the various mediums who allegedly produce automatic writings dictated by spirits. The overwhelming weight of the evidence on this kind of case suggests that the 'messages' must emerge from the subconscious mind of the 'contactee'. And if so in these cases, why not in types A, B and C?

One final factor has to be of relevance here. This is something that we know a few ufologists have come across in their hypnotic regression work, but don't seem to have grasped the significance of. This is probably because it points towards an explanation for the close encounter which most investigators have no wish to face. It is possible to question the 'alien' under hypnosis. On the face of it this seems ridiculous, but if one says something like, 'May I speak directly to them?', the subject will probably respond favourably, and a conversation can take place. If a witness is asked to explain how this is done, he will say that the alien relays messages into his mind and transmits the answers through his body as if it were a radio set. Psychologists however might regard the phenomenon as support for the concept that this alien is nothing but a dissociated personality fragment.

This chapter has attempted to shed some light on the mystery of close encounters. Five main points emerge:

1 Reports of UFO close encounters exist as a cohesive, coherent and extensive body of data.
2 They bear unique common features that tend to distinguish them from the root UFO or UAP phenomenon.
3 Their explanation is the aim of much serious, critical and concerned debate among UFO researchers, who are not being carried along by the belief that they must be examples of alien contact.
4 Study of the phenomenon is probably the province of psychologists and sociologists, who seem to be the professionals best equipped to tackle the enigma.
5 In the main, these experts are not yet tackling the subject seriously and consistently; it needs and deserves more research.

It is possible to construct a fictional 'typical' CE4 experience which includes the most common features found in the many hundreds of real accounts in the UFO literature. This may be helpful in showing the problem we face in trying to understand the phenomenon.

Two or three people travelling in a car on a quiet, country road late one might suddenly observe something strange in the sky. They discuss various possibilities, but no explanation seems acceptable so they regard it as a UFO. It seems to come closer and then vanishes. The car's occupants now find themselves in a semi-dream-like state, further along their journey, but with various other differences, e.g. they may be on an unfamiliar road, or the car engine may be switched on, having previously been switched off, or it may be off when their last memory was of it being on. They may notice that their shoes are scuffed, or their bodies hurt. But, without talking over what has taken place or displaying fear or other emotion, they will continue on to their destination. They then learn that a period of time, which may be anywhere between 15 minutes and two or three hours, has

apparently passed without any of them being aware of it. Whatever they do to reconstruct the journey they cannot explain this
missing time.

Over the days and weeks which follow they each try to forget
the incident, and succeed to a greater or lesser extent, according
to their personalities. But probably at least one of them finds it
sufficiently difficult to achieve peace of mind that they suffer
nightmares in which they relive the events, or they become
obsessed with learning more about UFOs. Therefore one of the
party may find his or her way either to a UFO-investigation
group, seeking help or understanding, or less often to a psychiatrist seeking the same thing. The others in the party are either
reluctant to get involved, still preferring to forget it, or are
persuaded to assist in the study of the case.

Crucial at this point is the expectation on the part of both
witnesses and investigators as to what will happen next. The best
investigators will encourage the witnesses not to expect any more
developments, and will simply obtain a coherent account of the
conscious memory, and then wait. It is possible that some spontaneous 'memory' will emerge of what the witness thought took
place during the missing time. It will be difficult to prevent them
sharing this with their colleagues and so muddling the various
independent stories. It is likely that if no proper memory returns
after a few months then none will appear, and the investigators
may resort to regression hypnosis. Ideally, all the witnesses
should be hypnotized separately without there being any possibility of each knowing what the others have said. But this rarely
occurs. When all, or at least most, of the witnesses are regressed,
but do have the opportunity to talk in between sessions, the
memories are usually somewhat consistent, but also individual in
some details. Many events and features are the same, but each
witness usually describes being alone during the events. Almost
never does witness A describe an event which he and witness B
observed together.

When proper separation of witnesses does occur, the above
situation actually hardly changes, although the degree of similarity in the accounts is decreased a little. There are definitely
features which witness A will describe which also come out in the
sessions with witnesses B, C and so on. Overall the implication

that they shared a common experience does seep through, but not overwhelmingly so.

As for the missing memory which emerges, this is extremely consistent. Hypnosis sessions in several different centres have all produced the same repetitive features. Naturally there are individual variations, but the features which are found again and again are so commonplace that a stereotype abduction is easy to construct.

The UFO emits a brilliant beam of light at the moment where conscious memory ends. This seems to calm the witness who thereafter describes a floating sensation in which he or she is not entirely conscious. Memory then tends to be hazy until he finds himself on board the UFO. The memory of being taken on board is one of those least easily retrieved under hypnosis. Within the 'room' in which he now finds himself there is either a table or a bed; it is variously described as both, but is very consistent in its appearance from case to case. There is much equipment and quite commonly a large eye-like device which acts as a kind of probe on the body. The witness gets onto the table or bed, without quite understanding why he does so, as he does not consciously desire to. He then undergoes a medical examination where various parts of his body are studied and blood samples may be taken. There is sometimes pain but this is usually controlled by the beings conducting the examination. These examiners may well be small beings around three feet tall, although commonly they are said to be 'robots'. There is usually at least one tall, human-like figure who oversees the activities. Questions are often asked of the witness via telepathy, an occurrence which is often found stranger than the examination itself. Sporadic, not infrequently silly, information about the aliens' home or intentions is given in response to the witness's own questions. There then follows a further period of hazy consciousness, of which little memory can be retrieved, before the witness finds himself back inside the car, immediately before his return to full conscious recall.

This summary of the CE4 'abduction' experience contains a distillation of many years of research. It is a remarkable phenomenon which one feels must have a psychological explanation. Yet its eerie consistency comes through in case after case to haunt attempts to produce a straightforward solution. There can be no doubt that the CE4 represents a strange part of human experience, a chapter so strange that it is difficult to justify its continued neglect by social scientists.

PART 3· THE FUTURE

11

The Way Ahead

Why complicate things? It is simpler to believe he is telling what happened.

Dr Joseph Jaffe, psychiatrist,
discussing the testimony of a UFO witness

In this final part of the book we must assess what we have tried to explain, and try to look forward to the next few decades of UFO study. What kind of progress should be made? How can we ensure that useful work is done in the subject? Since this book is specifically about science and the phenomenon, we will devote space to a consideration of the potential relevance of the field to a number of individual scientific disciplines. But what about other aspects of human society? How might they better adapt themselves to dealing sensibly with the problem? In many respects we have a three-cornered fight. In one corner sits the UFO enthusiast, with his convictions and his evidence. He must not rest secure in his presumptions. Adaptation to the realities which he tends to ignore must be achieved. In another corner are the government bodies, who have been so influential in shaping public opinion, and tend to discourage any recognition of the phenomenon. The other protagonists are the media. They reflect the phenomenon to the rest of the community, but they can only reflect what they perceive.

Let us first consider the role of the media. A welcome switch in their mood has been taking place recently. The fact that serious news sources can carry UFO stories, without feeling the need to belittle and joke, is an excellent measure of how far we have come. Of course, there is nothing wrong with having fun at the expense of ufology. It is the sort of subject that will always provoke jokes, for it is about the strange and bizarre, and there would be much more to worry about if everyone took all the wildest stories seriously. Scepticism is a sensible precaution when dealing with any subject so difficult to pin down. But the media must continue to recognize that ufology is a genuine and serious field which deserves at least as much critical thought as gentle joviality. It is always a question of balance.

Most ufologists are quite prepared to work with the investigative journalists on serious news sources, but they are not interested in wasting time with reporters who begin with preconceived notions and set out to write light-hearted filler items for the summer's 'silly season'. Some of ufology's crankier 'experts' have done considerable harm by lending their names to articles discussing the latest absurd theory.

In 1975 one of us wrote an article for a US UFO magazine. It discussed close-encounter cases in Great Britain, and was non-controversial. But in the year between the completion of the article and its appearance the magazine was taken over by a new publisher. Since it did not reach Great Britain we had no way of knowing that, in response to falling sales, the truth of any particular story was no longer an issue – so long as it sold copies. The publisher was investing ever-dafter and more ludicrous tales. By the time our article reached the press it was rather too sober for the new format. Of course the text could not be changed because that would have left the magazine open to a lawsuit, but they added a few of their own illustrations. We discovered this when a letter arrived asking what the article had to do with the illustrations alongside it. Our correspondent (and most readers) had assumed the illustrations were the responsibility of the ufologist who had written the article, because the magazine did not say otherwise and the pictures were of Great Britain. They included choice items such as a depiction of an underground room in London filled with computer equipment. The caption informed the reader that this was part of a complex left there centuries ago by aliens! There was also a gravestone alleged to belong to a 'spaceman' at a place called Aurora, England. There is no such place and the publishers knew that very well. They had fabricated all the photographs. While we contemplated legal action (although we were advised our case would not be easy to prove) the magazine collapsed. It over-reached itself by presenting a cover story about the town of Chester, Illinois, which it said was now run by aliens, who had landed and replaced all the key citizens overnight, just like the plot from some 'B' science-fiction film! Unfortunately, they had forgotten to check whether the town of Chester, Illinois actually existed; its key citizens were not exactly amused about the story. Such are the dangers of writing for the media!

For the newshound willing to approach the UFO evidence with an objective mind and write about it seriously there may be many surprises (if not shocks) in store. But such journalists need the support of editors willing to change after years of ignorant assumptions and the reaction against the sillier aspects of ufology. That done, much common sense might finally emerge to swamp the cranky ufologists and prevent the silly stories from the more sensationalist press having the unfortunate impact that they do.

This responsibility is being grasped by the newspapers rather more rapidly than the century's newest medium – television. TV companies' treatment of the UFO subject has generally been decidedly weak. Not a single documentary programme, to which we have been party, has yet done justice to the pro and con arguments. The BBC offering *The Case for the UFOs* (shown in 1982 in the Horizon series in Great Britain and the Nova series in the USA) perhaps comes closest. *The Case for the UFOs* was a rather misleading title, because the programme was very top-heavy with sceptics and debunkers. Nevertheless it performed the task of laying many UFO myths to rest better than might have been expected. It showed the doubtfulness of much photographic evidence. It demonstrated that none of the media-vaunted 'astronauts' UFO pictures' were remotely tenable. And it ably illustrated the fact that a large percentage of UFOs reported turn out to be IFOs, after investigation. None of this will astonish the reader of this book or of any of the serious UFO literature.

However, the BBC programme drew back at this point and left the viewer with the impression that the subject was *all* nonsense. It did not counterbalance with the real hard stuff – the sort of cases working ufologists handle every day. Jenny Randles reviewed the documentary for the BBC saying, 'you have now made a good programme about what UFOs are not – but how about the sequel, what they just might be?' There was no re-action. One day a television producer will realize what a worth-while subject UFOs really are, and make the programme Jenny Randles suggested.

The Rendlesham Forest events (see p. 135) are an excellent example of the way a UFO story can be manipulated. That some primary incident occurred on 27 December 1980 is attested by numerous eyewitnesses (mostly US Air Force personnel). That a subsequent 'landing' occurred on the 30 December is affirmed by an even more impressive list of officials (including the Lieutenant Colonel, then deputy base commander at RAF Bent-waters, himself a witness, a British Squadron Leader, an American Wing Commander, three American base commanders, each one a Colonel, and a plethora of other officers). It is quite the best-supported sighting in recent British history.

Jenny Randles was involved in the investigation, along with Brenda Butler and Dot Street from Suffolk (where the air base and forest are situated). This began in January 1981 with the discovery of a radar tracking of the object at a joint RAF/civilian base near Norwich. It continued for four years and involved battles with both the British and American governments to obtain documentary proof, as well as the tracking down of the various eyewitnesses.

The British government were reluctant to offer any confir-mation and at first attempted to brush the matter off. In April 1983 they did admit that the events had taken place and called them 'unidentified' in a letter to Jenny. But only one sighting was acknowledged at this time and termed merely 'unusual lights'.

Meanwhile, by way of the American Freedom of Information Act, a copy of the preliminary report sent by the base to the British Ministry of Defence was released. This describes *two* landings in clear, unambiguous terms, talks of a structured craft of specific dimensions, details interference to local wildlife, geo-metrical trace marks left in the ground, and excess radiation levels within them and on surrounding trees.

In August 1983 Jenny Randles and her colleagues took this secret report to Whitehall and challenged the Ministry of Defence.

The Ministry confirmed that the report was genuine. They also said that their earlier letter to Jenny was based upon that document, although they would not clarify how they had so grossly misrepresented its content to her. The document certainly did not merely discuss a few unusual lights! At this meeting the Defence Ministry further claimed that, despite the extent of official support, the high calibre of witnesses and the obvious sincerity with which their report was made about an incident half a mile from the end of the runway of a major NATO base, no action was deemed necessary by the authorities.

In October 1983 the British media picked up the story. The popular Sunday paper *News of the World* told its four million readers (and its circulation rose during the currency of the story) 'UFO LANDS IN SUFFOLK:– And That's Official!' The front-page banner headline prefaced a whole month of stories about the incident, mostly quite factual but written up to quite an extent. However, the paper relied totally on the claims of a single witness and one of the more dubious ones at that. It failed to point out any of the real questions raised by the case. In no sense was it an objective view of the situation.

Other newspapers took up the case. A main rival (the *Sunday Mirror*) extracted details from the pre-press issues of *News of the World*, since no serious UFO investigator would talk to them. They got facts upside-down, saying that the UFO had landed on the runway. The whole tone of these sensational newspapers was that an alien spaceship had crashed and the US Air Force had helped repair it, acting as a sort of intergalactic Automobile Association! While some of the witnesses did assert this, those who studied the case recognized the major problems of such a hypothesis and saw several other options which were rather more likely.

The highbrow press went to the other extreme and tried to shoot the case down in flames. A young forestry worker, Vince Thurkettle, suggested that the lights might be those of a lighthouse five miles from the forest which the airmen had simply misperceived. Thurkettle gained overnight fame for this and propounded his theory in *The Times,* on BBC television, and in documentaries about the case in America, Germany and Japan. Yet in October 1984, when Jenny walked the forest with him between takes on a TV film, he admitted that he had proposed the idea half-seriously and was not committed to it all that far. While his argument has superficial attraction, the evidence does not point to the lighthouse as an explanation of the whole complexity of this affair. One simple damning piece of evidence is that witnesses observed the phenomenon from several locations, looking in different directions, enabling rough trigonometrical calculations to be made which place the cause of the events *inside* the forest and not on the coast five miles away.

The point is simply that a great many people preferred not to believe the wild tales of the Sunday press and chose the misperception hypothesis as a more plausible solution to the story. As usual the middle ground was not explored and the truth, as a consequence, was the one thing to suffer.

Questions were asked in the House of Commons by Major Sir Patrick Wall of the Commons Defence Committee. But the media furore and its obscuring of the realities made his task impossible. Nobody took him very seriously. The government minister, John Stanley, stonewalled and said that the government knew all about the incident and saw no defence implications in it. Letters were exchanged between former Home Secretary Merlyn Rees and Minister of Defence Michael Heseltine, and a 'mole', who had been an under-secretary and department head (dealing with UFOs) at the ministry, voiced his opinion that there had been a less than truthful reaction from the authorities.

The UFO investigators, not being involved in this public fracas, continued quietly with their investigations and published the results as a book in October 1984.[1] It laid out the facts of their investigation and assessed the various options. The extremes of the crashed spaceship and misperceived lighthouse were placed in context with other possibilities, such as an exaggerated UFO or UAP event and the testing of an experimental craft or weapon.

The lighthouse explanation continues to find favour with the media. In January 1985 an American TV documentary spent much of its air time showing shots of the lighthouse synchronized with testimony from witnesses. And the *Guardian*, a respectable British newspaper, trotted out the same story with no reference

[1] B. Butler, J. Randles and D. Street, *Skycrash* (Spearman, 1984).

whatsoever to the four years of investigation by ufologists, their research, or the serious suggestions they raised about what might have happened.

Clearly, most of the general public now believe that the events in Rendlesham Forest are either a nonsense, or a crashed spaceship. Neither view is likely to make fair-minded people ask the searching questions still posed by this case and the UFO phenomenon in general, but this is typical of the way the truth gets distorted. Even if the cause *was* the lighthouse, and the ground marks caused by rabbits, and the radiation levels normal background counts, as contended, then the fact that so many senior officers in the British and American forces not only made these errors but later compounded them (in February 1985 the official view of both British and American authorities remains that the case is *not* explained) *must* have defence implications.

It is sad to reflect that Steven Spielberg's film about alien spaceships, *Close Encounters of the Third Kind,* remains far and away the closest the mass media have come to encapsulating some of the key realities of ufology. It is particularly unfortunate that because it was made as fiction, and is rather over-dramatic, to many people the type of event portrayed will remain as unlikely as ever. (It also complicates matters for researchers by so publicizing certain kinds of UFO incident that many people may imagine similar incidents in their own lives.)

To what extent the evolving media position has pleased or displeased governments throughout the world is hard to determine. We have already emphasized the importance of government action in this area. If, as various government and military agencies insist, the phenomenon does *not* have obvious defence implications, then all defence ties with the mystery should be severed. The responsibility for collection of UFO records must be removed from the province of defence ministries and air forces and transferred to that of scientific research agencies. There are government-sponsored and government-controlled science institutes in most countries, which are open enough in the way that they function to fulfil the needs of both government and the people. Governments must retain some connection with UFO study, just in case any discoveries are made which affect defence or other national interests, but they must see to it that there is no more secrecy about UFOs, and no cover-up of extraordinary incidents.

We do not know the truth about the governmental role in UFO study, although we think we appreciate many of the early problems. Some of the released US documents clearly imply that scientific research is going on within government circles under strict security. There is evidently good reason for such research. We have sufficient faith in the major powers to assume that they do what they do with reasons that they can at least attempt to justify. But the reasons for secrecy stretch thinner as each new witness to an inexplicable phenomenon is added to the already lengthy list, only to find himself summarily dismissed, or ignored, by the people he has elected in good faith. There may well come a time when the number of witnesses is so great that governments will have to be more open. If the lessons of the USA are ignored by governments, while 'Freedom of Information' world-wide leads to released documents demonstrating that the pretence of government lack of interest is a sham, then our confidence in governments could seriously be undermined. All we would like from the authorities is a statement like 'Yes, indeed, there do seem to be unexplained phenomena (UFOs). Yes indeed, we have no real idea what they are. But we do not see any evidence that they are a defence threat. We will co-operate in whatever ways we can to aid serious scientific study into these things.'

The community of people interested in UFOs has a much more difficult task. For they are the ones both in possession of the evidence and willing to speak out. As it stands, only they can easily alter public ideas of the UFO which will lead to sensible media coverage and real pressure on governments. But the problems faced by ufologists are not restricted to the nature of the phenomenon itself. They need to work on basic organization, communication and co-operation among themselves. To date all these have proved difficult.

It would be nice to be able to say that this situation is a result of factors outside the control of .UFO researchers, but sadly this is not the case. There has never really been any sort of overall strategy or campaign or any serious willingness to pursue a co-ordinated outline plan or project. Many studies and projects have been embarked upon, but few reach their declared aims. They tend to fade away rather quickly often because of lack of support, interest and cash. Where they do succeed to any degree it is usually only thanks to the dedication and determination of isolated individuals or small groups. Continuity is very difficult to achieve. Another disadvantage of these studies is the lack of communication between them. This allows needless duplication to occur, because not enough people know about the work done by others in the same field. Ufology totally lacks any sort of plan of research. This is a prerequisite of any future progress and it must come about through an informal association of a 'professional' nature, in the manner Hynek has proposed.

Some of the UFO organizations which exist have been around for a long time, e.g. APRO (Aerial Phenomena Research Organization) which was formed in the USA in 1952. However, length of existence does not seem to be proportional to achievement. Indeed, because of the recent growth in serious analytical thinking about UFOs the reverse might almost be true in some cases. People who have taken an interest in UFOs in the past decade generally seem more objective and discriminating in their approach than those who first began to study UFOs when there was only one option – that UFOs were spaceships.

Some psychologists have suggested that early ufologists might have been social rebels, who yearned for the adventure that the subject seemed to promise. Saturnian spacecraft crewed by aliens were a romantic dream with enormous appeal, latched on to and promoted by the media. Early UFO societies had thousands of members. While the confrontation with reality, brought about in recent years, has been beneficial in many ways, it has also decimated the UFO groups. Many have collapsed completely and others survive with tiny memberships and no financial security. Many of their meetings now have to be devoted to economic survival rather than the UFO subject. And the public's interest in reporting UFOs (partly because they have become better educated about potentially misidentified phenomena and partly because of apathy created over years of lack of interest or ridicule) has compounded the problem. Fewer reports mean that UFO groups are less active, which in turn in the end means fewer members. While this decline has come at a time when the media is taking more interest in serious ufology than ever before, the fact that it is happening is bound to be seen as significant by many people – as implying that ufologists are realizing now that there really is no phenomenon to investigate.

As in most voluntary groups, societies and organizations, there is a small, central core of hardworking individuals willing to persevere through adversity. There are also some people whose primary interest seems to be 'role playing', acting the part of 'chairman' or 'publicity officer'. Their involvement in the investigation and research of UFOs is very much less important to them than occupying status positions. Many of those who are most involved in investigation or research shun the bureaucratic manoeuvrings and so avoid the organization's central core. This means that even the best groups can be run mostly by people who know far less about UFOs than those they 'control'.

To the outsider many of the problems of ufology seem glaring. Most stem from the people involved and their approach and attitude towards all phases of the activity – from collection of raw data through interpretation and writing up to communication with the rest of society. It seems that too many ufologists are incapable of seeing the self-inflicted faults of the subject or the fundamental errors in the assumptions of its early days. Too many people are willing to accept that a reported incident will eventually be proven a UFO. Ufologists need to be well trained about typical IFOs. But even an apparently bona fide UFO may well be identified as something else as research techniques improve. Too many people use the label 'UFO' loosely, calling an incident by this name without qualification. The term has been used with so many different meanings that it is now probably safest not to call a phenomenon a UFO until it has been thoroughly investigated and not identified. Claude Maugé, a French scientist, suggests the term 'quasi-UFO' be adopted for such things. Far too many use the argument that UFOs are products of a superior intelligence which wants to remain hidden, thus explaining the lack of proof or evidence. That avoids the question by prejudging the answer – and will never lead to progress.

Since no qualifications are needed to 'become' a ufologist, this produces problems. The vast majority of those involved have no appropriate scientific background. We do not propose that one needs a degree in astronomy to evaluate the extraterrestrial hypothesis for UFO origin, or a doctorate in psychology to make reasoned comment on the birth-trauma theory. However, to make valid contributions one does need informed and realistic background knowledge. It is a major fault in UFO research that those who wish to study the subject fail to realize the extent to which they must learn about other fields. Would-be students should acquaint themselves with a range of topics, including interview techniques, planetary astronomy, major psychological disorders, aircraft recognition, administrative control, current military experimental hardware and geophysics. The list is long and constantly growing.[2]

Eyewitness testimony provides a good case in point. There is a considerable amount of informed discussion on the accuracy of eyewitness testimony within scientific literature. Yet very few of the people involved in the direct extraction of UFO accounts from witnesses have bothered to seek out even the most accessible of this information. When one of us gave a lecture to a gathering of UFO investigators on this topic, the discussion provoked the following comment: 'All this about eyewitnesses confusing detail and introducing inaccuracies is all very well in situations like accidents and criminal acts [cited examples] but the witnesses we deal with *know* what they saw – a UFO – and they won't get confused or exaggerate.'

Far too many investigators are ignorant of the appearance of the night sky and know very little about basic astronomy. Very many ordinary people who see Venus in the sky when it is especially bright, as it is at some point every year, believe it is too 'big' (they equate size with brightness). They insist it cannot be a star (they tend to call planets 'stars' too) and so report it as a UFO. This is a worry to ufologists, but even more alarming are the numbers of so-called investigators who are themselves so unfamiliar with the problems this and other astronomical phenomena can cause that they fail to make the connections and identify the 'UFO'.[3] Similarly, when two astronomical bodies

---

[2] See J. Randles, *UFO Study* (Robert Hale, 1981), for a fuller discussion.

[3] J. Randles, 'A Vendetta with Venus', *Magonia*, spring 1979, discusses a typical case which illustrates all these problems.

happen to lie close together in the sky (as they occasionally do because of the irregular movements of stars and planets), this 'conjunction' is so unexpected, by both public and UFO investigator alike, that the explanation is overlooked.[4] For example, one night in May 1980 two people in Sheffield independently saw an orange blob in the sky for about half an hour. They could not explain it. The investigator thought it was Venus, but that planet was in fact well below the horizon at the time. There was a rare conjunction of Jupiter and Mars which lasted a few days and to observers on the ground could easily have appeared as described.

To a considerable extent one only learns UFO investigation by years of on-the-job experience. But there is such a rapid turnover rate among UFO enthusiasts that the majority of those active today have only been interested for a couple of years. That is just not long enough to be a good investigator, and the general standard of work suffers. This is the justification behind the policy adopted by a few groups (such as MUFORA, on a local level in Manchester, and BUFORA, on a national level in Great Britain) of accrediting investigators, and only allowing people to conduct investigations who can meet the required limits of experience and/or knowledge. This is essential to the future of ufology.

It is clear that ufology tends to perpetuate its own myths, by way of often-cited 'classic cases'. These, such as the Betty and Barney Hill abduction or the landing at Socorro, New Mexico, are held in great esteem. Many of them might well be significant, but they are mostly now old (often 20 years or more), bizarre in nature, and were inadequately investigated at the time.[5] We have tried to show the dangers of this in our discussion of these cases. New cases continue to be elevated to 'classic' status, and this is inevitable, but the subject does not stand by a few choice examples. There is much risk in suggesting that it does. Sceptics can take these isolated instances and pick holes in them, thus implying that if 'Betty and Barney Hill' or Socorro looks even mildly suspect the whole subject must collapse.

Ufology exists as a subject because of thousands of good quality reports, the majority of which are without notoriety.

[4] See the report by N. Watson in *FSR*, vol. 24, no. 5, 1979.
[5] For the Betty and Barney Hill abduction, see J. Fuller, *The Interrupted Journey* (Souvenir Press, 1980); for the Socorro landing see R. Stanford, *Socorro Saucer in a Pentagon Pantry* (Blueapple Books, 1976).

These represent the real evidence about UFOs. Ufologists must start to realize this and emphasize it more. When Ronald Story compiled a book of 'best' cases he wrote to a number of leading investigators throughout the world, asking them to nominate the one case they felt was the classic of classics. In this way the aim was to produce a 'top twenty' listing and write these up as the prime evidence. Story had to choose the cases himself, because virtually every long-standing investigator approached would not put his money on to one case. The sceptics used this to advantage, but in fact it shows that ufologists are cautious enough to know the problems they face. It also shows that ufology is built upon a very wide base – something not often realized.[6]

As ufology has grown more complex, so ufologists have begun to specialize, often in certain types of case. But this is not infrequently done by people who frankly have no experience in, or deep knowledge of, these chosen fields of interest. A prime example, growing in popularity, is the study of apparent UFO abductions. So far *not one* of the books on this topic has been written by a psychologist. Instead, excellent though some of them are, they are produced by individuals with no such background knowledge. In many of these cases hypnosis is employed in an effort to retrieve memories. The hypnosis may well be (and often is) conducted by a qualified doctor or psychologist. But the investigator then goes on to draw his conclusions after a wholly inadequate consideration of the suggestibility that hypnosis is known to induce. Much has been written by specialists about the nature and problems of hypnotic regression, but far too few UFO investigators have read any of this. They use hypnosis like a new toy, often so eagerly that no conventional investigation ever takes place.

Self-inflicted problems of this kind abound in ufology. They need to be corrected, because they fundamentally weaken the case for a genuine phenomenon. It is much too easy to believe something rather than prove it, and ufology relies to far too great an extent on belief. It may be comfortable simply to accept that UFOs exist, but what is needed is the painstaking work of constructing arguments from link-by-link chains of evidence

[6] See R. Story, *UFOs and the Limits of Science* (NEL, 1981).

which can stand up to the criticism that must be expected. The
statement, which we still hear all too often, 'I believe in UFOs',
has no place within the subject. If any real advance is to be made
it must be after weighing the evidence for and against each
hypothesis, and then advancing logically to the next one. Scientists cannot accept any theory that cannot be proved wrong. That
is why it is totally unscientific to argue that UFOs are aliens who
are trying to deceive us. Any evidence that does not fit will be
regarded as part of the deception, and so the theory can *never* be
disproved!

Consider a UFO abduction case where the subject has been
unable to account for a period of time. The memory (however it
is obtained, or some would say 'created') is of a visit to a UFO
base somewhere. It is remarkable how many ufologists would
respond to that situation by leap-frogging over the obvious and
necessary stages. They would use hypnosis hoping to get the
witness to direct them to the UFO base or to describe the UFO
propulsion system they 'recall' having been shown by the aliens!
This sounds strange, but when it happens it seems natural to the
investigator. They will justify it by saying that if they can be
directed to the base, go there and find it, then they will prove the
reality of UFOs. Realistically they must know the futility of this
hope but romanticism drives them onward. Clearly the first stage
in the investigation should be to examine precisely what the
witness saw that he *thought* was an alien craft. It is *just* possible
that he really did see a genuine craft and get taken in it to some
base or other, but the alternative possibilities are so much more
likely that they must be studied first. Every investigator's experience tells him that, more often than not, people see UFOs which
are explicable as incorrect interpretations of mundane events.
The balance strongly favours any single case being an IFO, not a
UFO. But when the case is exciting they forget all this experience.

Few of those involved at the sharp end of UFO research
acknowledge that the social sciences can contribute as much as
the physical disciplines. We believe that recognition of this by
ufologists is yet another essential prerequisite of long-term progress. The relevance of psychology is an anathema, not just to
investigators but particularly to the witness, who after seeing

his UFO not infrequently joins the search for the solution to the UFO mystery in some way or another. They misconstrue the suggestion that a psychologist be called in as meaning that the investigators think they (and other witnesses) may be crazy.

Can a witness to a close encounter exercise objectivity in the investigation of other people's close encounters? It is a controversial topic. Active British ufologist Nigel Mortimer commented to us that when he began investigation after his close encounter in November 1980 he was at first constantly looking for parallels between what he had seen and any new sighting. At first he was unaware of it, but then he recognized that he was biasing the version of events that he presented in his case reports by focusing on certain elements he believed to be important. With effort, this 'Mortimer effect' can be minimized. But can it ever be removed? It probably applies not just to UFO witness turned investigator, but to investigators who have developed theories about UFO origins (as any serious thinker is bound to do). And yet who is better qualified to know which *are* the key facts to look for in a report than someone who is prepared to accept his limitations, but who has himself had an unexplained encounter? Would a botanist feel he was more or less able to do his job if he never got to see the plants he studied, but only received other people's descriptions of them?

As ufology has expanded a new problem has evolved with it. We now find investigators looking at events which, at best, are possibly relevant to the mainstream. At worst, these may be so irrelevant as to be positively misleading. But how does one decide? An observation of a strange light in the sky is an agreed component of the UFO phenomenon, as are landed UFOs and 'humanoids'. But what about isolated 'humanoids', described in the same way as UFO entities but where no UFO (flying or otherwise) is seen with it? A witness recently reported to us that as he was walking his dog past a deserted US Army base in the middle of the night, figures in strange silver suits stood on the runway gesticulating wildly at him to go away! Could this have been a UFO event of any description? Some might say yes and others no. But if the figures had risen into the air and flown away or walked through a solid wall (both of which acts *have* been reported), then do we reassess our opinion?

Some UFO investigators will examine claims of teleportation, where people say they suddenly found themselves hundreds or thousands of miles away from home. They might have been flown by a UFO, they argue. If so, this would be a sort of UFO abduction. But they might very well have got there by Greyhound bus – in which case the problem is one of simple memory lapse or fraud and of no interest to ufology. What about showers of frogs falling from the sky? They might have been picked up for alien experimentation and dumped back to Earth afterwards. There are some serious proponents of this idea. Some people are willing to consider animal mutilations, lake monsters, Bigfoot, coincidences, chunks of ice falling out of the sky, unexplained loud bangs and mysterious humming noises emerging from the ground as all likely to be related to UFOs.

There is something to be said for *not* excluding potentially valuable data, but when the floodgates open it is much harder to shut them again. Just where do you draw the line? We too have been guilty of such ramblings, for in truth this is what they usually turn out to be. But the moment has come to stop wasting valuable time with rather peripheral problems.

The dangers of excluding certain types of case can be illustrated, though, by the following example. It was discussed at length during a meeting which one of us attended in early 1984, at which a decision on whether or not to investigate was taken. See if you can decide what that decision was.

A woman had reported that she had been driving along when she saw a figure by the roadside flagging down a vehicle as it slowed down and stopped. The woman was curious about this and so continued to watch, only to find to her astonishment that both vehicle and figure vanished 'between one blink and the next'. She told workmates about this incident when she reached her destination, but met with a great deal of ridicule and did not discuss it again until she met one of the UFO group in a social situation.

On the face of it this has nothing to do with UFOs. The vehicle was a car, not a UFO. The figure looked human enough. And the woman was aware of no time lapse in her memory. Yet there have been UFO abductions where the time lapse was first indicated by sudden leaps in reality such as this. To those interested in abduction cases there was a possibility (faint but real) that the woman had been abducted when she saw the car by the roadside. Her memory returned an unspecified time later, when the vehicle had moved off from its stationary position. To the unwitting abductee this had appeared as an amazing disappearance by the car, but regression hypnosis might show otherwise. The investigator who had discovered this 'case' was proposing that the group sponsor regression hypnosis on the witness. But if that had been done and a memory of a UFO event produced, how should we treat it? Would it be the uncovering of a remarkably well-hidden memory? Or would it be the creation of a totally fictitious fantasy? Nobody would know.

The question is extremely difficult, but the group decided against hypnosis. Common sense is needed by everyone involved in UFO investigation, but it is in short supply in a subject that is dreadfully complicated, and concerned with 'uncommon' phenomena. The call sometimes goes out to both sceptic and believer to have an 'open mind', and the sceptic needs to be willing to face the distinct prospect that they are unexplained events. But the committed UFO believer has to realize that his 'open mind' is often so wide open that he will swallow anything at face value all too reminiscent of an open hangar door!

12

The Importance of UFOs to Science

These thousands of reports, this world-wide body of human testimony, constitute a very formidable case for the UFO.

Dr Richard Sigismund,
social psychologist

Astronomy and Cosmology

In the earliest years of UFO study most of the few scientists involved came from the field of astronomy. This is because the dominant view of UFOs was that they were extraterrestrial in origin. Thus, by inference, astronomers were the only scientists who were qualified to comment on them. This is no doubt part of the reason why Hynek, an astronomer, became the chief civilian consultant to the US Government UFO projects. But another factor was of equal (and probably greater) importance. The need to explain UFO reports, many of which turned out to be IFOs, demanded the attention of relevant experts. Since a large proportion of the potential solutions lay in astronomical fields (e.g. stars, planets, meteors, etc.), the astronomer was the best choice if budgets were limited.

Since those days the percentage total of astronomers in all scientists involved has fallen sharply. But the subject has still attracted at least mild interest from this direction and from cosmologists. They are less concerned about observation of the universe and more with the theoretical nature of the great unknown. UFOs, to some, seem possibly relevant. But it would be fair to say that this apparent relevance has declined as new suggestions for UFO origin have grown in popularity.

In the event of UFOs being in any real sense extraterrestrial, the implications would affect many more people than just space scientists. They would fundamentally affect our social cultural thinking. The scientific demonstration that advanced, intelligent life existed elsewhere in the universe would be regarded by most people (scientists and non-scientists alike) as one of the single most important discoveries in the history of mankind. The repercussions are so wide that we cannot attempt to spell them out. At the very least, astronomy, cosmology and the developing fields of astrogeology and exobiology could benefit enormously from such a discovery. Astronautics would be transformed; our billion-dollar space projects would be superseded and outmoded overnight as we learnt of technologies far more advanced than our own. The social and cultural implications are mind-boggling.

We do not here intend to argue over the evidence for and against UFOs being extraterrestrial. We have demonstrated what we regard as strong negative evidence elsewhere.[1] Generally speaking, and especially in its most simplistic form, the ETH (as the extraterrestrial hypothesis is widely called) just does not work. Those who propose that all, or most, UFOs are spaceships are not supported by the bulk of the data.

However, there are various considerations to bear in mind. Most of our presumptions about what is and is not possible stem from our current position in the history of science. Allen Hynek frequently reminds us that there *will* be a twenty-first- (and indeed a twenty-second-) century science. Barring any catastrophic disaster, all we can reasonably conclude about that science is that it will be both unrecognizable and unpredictable to our present way of thinking. To assume that something is impossible because we have not yet conceived of a way to do it is perhaps one of the most naïve but widespread modes of thought we are prone to. Also, while it is patently unreasonable to argue that the majority of UFOs are alien in origin, we must pose

[1] J. Randles and P. Warrington, *UFOs: A British Viewpoint* (Robert Hale, 1979), pp. 185–96; J. Randles and P. Whetnall, *Alien Contact* (Spearman, 1982), pp. 172–5.

another question: what if one or two, out of the thousands of seemingly genuine reports, do describe (for want of a more precise term) spaceships? This is a more tenable suggestion. The UFO records, while certainly not probative of that by any stretch of the imagination, leave the door of possibility open a crack. Furthermore, we might speculate that a more subtle form of alien involvement is represented by the phenomenon.[2] This soft-option alien approach is again more equitable with the evidence before us. It demonstrates the need for flexibility in our thinking about the possible relation of the UFO phenomenon to astronomy and cosmology.

In studying some kinds of astronomical incident it is important to have access to eyewitness data regarding transient events. Meteor and space debris re-entries are two examples. While modern surveillance and monitor equipment reduce the need for eyewitnesses, much of this is used by the military and not available to the average civilian scientist. Ufologists receive many reports of sightings every year that unquestionably refer to meteors or space-debris. It is generally easy for them to isolate these out of the mass of reports, and there is scope here for fruitful co-operation between ufologists and astronomers.

For example, in early 1984 the National Investigations Committee of BUFORA agreed to compile a special report for the fire-ball section of the British Astronomical Association. This referred to an unusual type of fire-ball that was invariably reported by witnesses as a UFO. Ufologists had become adept at identifying these when they were reported and under ordinary circumstances would not have investigated the incidents any further. But only they had access to the data which the astronomers needed, and so they co-operated in the interests of science. This is something most ufologists would be delighted to continue.

It is possible that some UFO reports actually concern rare phenomena which might be of value to astronomers. Ufologists lack the expertise to identify what is responsible in these cases, and scientists, by regarding all UFO data as valueless because of their preconceived ideas about UFO enthusiasts, may be missing

---

[2] J. Randles, *UFO Reality* (Robert Hale, 1983), pp. 213–25; J. Randles, *The Pennine UFO Mystery* (Granada, 1983), pp. 222–34.

out on something of great interest. That this can occur is shown by the number of civilian 'UFO' reports which emerged from the Soviet Union and were reproduced in Western UFO journals. It took space writer James Oberg to demonstrate that these were observations of secret Russian space launches from their Plesetsk launch site.[3] Not only did this co-operation explain problematic UFO sightings, but it also gave insight into the Soviet space programme.

Earth Science

Until recently it would have been considered very odd to suggest that UFOs could have any relevance to geology or geophysics. UFOs, by definition, were *flying* objects in the atmosphere and possibly travelling from beyond it. What could the earth have to do with them? The work of the French ufologist Lagarde (connecting UFO reports with fault-line distribution), the theoretical concepts of Persinger and their experimental support from Brady, and the latest theory and research from Devereux, McCartney and his Project GAIA team (see references in chapters 8 and 9), have all contributed towards establishing the role of earth science within ufology. This has not occurred without controversy, but few would now deny it as a valid area of study.

It is not surprising that most earth-science research into earthquakes has centred on countries where such disasters are common. It matters to many Americans if the next slippage of the San Andreas Fault can be predicted, and similarly, in China or Japan, the destructive effects of tremors are always at the back of people's minds. So therefore money and scientific research are expended on the problem. It may be because of the lack of eyewitness testimony regarding earthquakes, or it may be our increased tendency to rely upon technology, but the developed nations have tended to ignore the accounts of 'earthquake lights', seen painting the sky like displaced aurora, and the many references to animal anticipation of an imminent tremor. As has happened with many breakthroughs in science, it might be that major progress in earthquake research will only come when we

[3] Letter to *FSR*, vol. 28, no. 1, 1982.

begin to take notice of something which has been right under our noses for ages.[4]

Geologists beginning to take an interest in these phenomena may not at first realize that data on them lies in the files of researchers into the paranormal. For when an ordinary person witnesses something which lacks an obvious reference, and which science renounces both knowledge of and interest in, then he turns to the student of mystery. He may well get a rather curious response and be offered wild theories to explain his observations, but at least he is listened to.

There is one specific branch of the literature on the paranormal which sometimes includes information on anomalous animal disturbance, reacting as if to some unseen energy field, and strange light effects in the atmosphere. That field is, of course, ufology. Any scientist interested in earthquake epiphenomena really needs to examine the UFO data. It is not really particularly strange that geophysical processes might affect the atmosphere. The slippage of fault lines creates a considerable release of energy. It is not correct to assume that would only be kinetic. Sound energy is known to result, producing assorted weird noises at the onset of a quake. Energy in other parts of the electro-magnetic spectrum (such as very low frequency waves) is quite feasible. Evidently something must account for the disturbance to local animal life.[5]

Many theories have been put forward about the lights in the sky which are often mistaken for UFOs or UAPs, but ionization, in some form or another, seems to be favoured by the majority of researchers. Persinger and Brady argue that quartz crystals in the rock vibrate under strain, squeezing out a piezo-electric signal which ionizes gases in the atmosphere. Devereux and McCartney doubt this, and Dr Helmut Tributsch calculates that insufficient energy would be produced in this way to produce the lights

[4] See H. Tributsch, *When the Snakes Awake* (MIT Press, 1983).

[5] See the work of Michael Persinger: (with G. Lafrenière) *Space-time Transients and Unusual Events* (Nelson Hall, 1977); and articles in R. Haines (ed.), *UFO Phenomena and the Behavioural Scientist* (Scarecrow Press, 1979) and *Fortean Times*, vol. 41, winter 1983. The former assesses typical energy releases from earthquakes; the latter presents results of a comparative study of earthquakes in Britain and UAP events.

people describe. Instead he postulates that this piezo effect acts within the interstitial spaces between rocks, where it triggers an electrochemical reaction in the liquids that are present. Gas is given off, some of which leaks out into the atmosphere, glowing, and also giving rise to strong odours as the gases dissipate. Many UAP reports *do* refer to either nitrous or sulphurous smells which may suggest that the Tributsch idea is right.

As for the animal behaviour, Tributsch has also suggested that free-floating ions close to the ground might be breathed in by them, producing changes in the level of the hormone serotonin within the bloodstream, which cause unusual behaviour in the animal. This might occasionally happen to humans who breathe in the ions and UFO researchers can certainly testify that some witnesses seem to undergo traumatic character changes both during and after an encounter. Many UAP reports could be interpreted by Tributsch's ideas.

A typical case is that of the UAP briefly mentioned on page 37 in connection with the 'green fireballs'. This phenomenon was observed in February 1975 by a postal worker on a beach near the Sizewell nuclear reactor in Suffolk. The UAP emitted a noxious odour and the man's dog became severely disturbed, running away in complete terror. The man himself suffered subsequent nightmares and personality disorders so severe that he had to resign from his job.[6] Tributsch might not find this story too extraordinary – some of the most damaging British earthquakes have centred on faults in this part of East Anglia.

One couple in Cornwall spent time in hospital after a close encounter with an almost identical UAP. They underwent a battery of tests for the illness they both suffered from (which had symptoms similar to those of radiation sickness). No explanation was found and the problems cleared up in due course.[7]

Obviously, if severe physical effects are possible from UAP encounters (as the records of ufologists indicate), then scientists (including doctors) should be examining the problem. It seems, on present evidence, that earth science offers the best current

[6] See the report by Peter Johnson in *FSR*, vol. 21, no. 6, 1976.
[7] See the report by Terry Cox in *FSR*, vol. 24, no. 1, 1978.

hypotheses to explain much of this sort of data, so the geo-physicist has a key responsibility.

Such phenomena as lights and animal disturbance, however they are caused, may well have an important warning role with regard to earth tremors. By properly understanding the warning signs and perhaps designing equipment to detect changes in atmospheric ionization at potential earthquake sites, sufficient notice of a tremor might be given to save many lives by timely evacuation. The evidence suggests that this possibility is worth investigation. Another possibility arises from the fact that UAP glows tend to occur in the build-up period *prior* to an earthquake. In Great Britain, where large tremors are rare, they seem to act as safety valves, leaking away the strain slowly as it builds towards an otherwise destructive quake. A 'skyquake' (an un-explained bang or explosion in the sky) sometimes indicates the final discharge, and is much less dangerous than a major earth-quake. An example of this happening in connection with UAPs occurred in the Pennine Hills, by the Craven Fault, in April 1982.[8] If we can find out why some quakes discharge slowly, but others suddenly and with violence, then we might find ways of controlling and neutralizing some of the numerous tremors that occur throughout the world.

If the scientific study of an enigma offers hope (however faint) that it might help predict earthquakes, and perhaps eventually help prevent some of them from happening; if it also offers hope of curing the severe physical effects on humans of a natural phenomenon; then surely this enigma must be seriously investi-gated.

Physics

Many questions raised in the study of UFO phenomena have a bearing on physics. It has even been claimed that a proper understanding of ufology could provide a breakthrough not dis-similar to the quantum-mechanics revolution of a few decades ago. Scientific UFO pioneers, such as Allen Hynek, have even been portrayed by the media as latter-day Galileos! This is no

[8] Randles, *Pennine UFO Mystery*, pp. 229–30.

doubt gross exaggeration, but by how much we cannot yet say. Obviously a great deal depends on what UFOs turn out to be. If some of them prove to be 'dimensional interface phenomena' (i.e. instrusions from a different kind of reality), which is a theory with some support from scientists (including Hynek), then the significance to theoretical physics could be immense. There is even a 'time-anomaly' theory, which postulates that UFOs are visionary encounters with our own future selves, whose ultra-advanced technology creates a time-slip side-effect providing their temporary appearance in our era. Again, if this is anything other than wild speculation, the importance to physics is obvious.

The fact that UFOs as a single type of phenomenon probably do not exist increases the likelihood that physical science may be able to interpret at least some of the phenomena, and thus make significant advances. It is almost certain that some of the UAPs are atmospheric phenomena on our present threshold of understanding. Ball lightning, as we have seen, is a typical UAP-like event just about becoming accepted by science. Other UAPs will no doubt be similarly explained in due course. More importantly, because the characteristics of ball lightning are inadequately understood and most non-specialists are unaware of it, it may still get reported as a UFO and thus continue to crop up in UAP records.

What of the UAPs which can not be explained as ball lightning, or any other known phenomenon, but which are still consistently reported? From the files of any organized UFO group one can classify UFO types. To a biased UFO thinker these types will represent different models of spacecraft, from diverse planets or with special purposes. To the less convinced they may better be seen as a whole range of UAPs – in other words yet-to-be-explained terrestrial physical phenomena. For example, one classic UFO shape is that of a child's spinning top. This is usually thought to be a machine and its descriptions (it has been seen all over the world) are closely alike. A general outline would be: wider in the middle than at the top or bottom, glowing with a bright fluorescent fuzziness (often orange in colour), having a dark band of 'blotches' in the centre (frequently called 'portholes' or 'windows' by witnesses). Normally it rotates and is heard to emit a faint humming sound.

Another very different UAP is what we might call the 'pawn-

broker sign'; a triangle of three glowing spheres usually apparently stationary in the sky. This has been observed both in
daytime and at night, and so is unlikely to be explainable in terms
of sun- or moon-related optical effects. The majority of people
describing it had no idea that anyone else had seen it before. It is
so far removed from the popular idea of what a 'spaceship' should
look like that it attracts much less publicity. This is a positive
boon, and the fact that a number of very similar, very clear
descriptions of it are on the files must strongly argue in favour of
its reality.

Viewed simply as eyewitness accounts of interesting phenomena, these now numerous stories could be computer crossmatched and physicists might then be able to start explaining just
what they are. But our tendency to outline what they are – to see
them as alien spaceships – has been an effective block on this
research. It will not happen until ufologists are honest about the
data and scientists are willing to ignore what the newspapers
think and worry about what the phenomena might in fact turn out
to be.

Just one more type of UAP will make the point. On 6 June
1977 a young motorcyclist was overtaken on a hill in Durham by a
car. It was pouring with rain. Suddenly his engine lost power and
he could see that the car in front of him was having the same
problem. But neither vehicle stopped; instead they were 'pulled
up' over the hill, quite without their own power. Glancing upwards, the motorcyclist saw a large oval shape which was surrounded by a very strange purplish/pink colour with fuzzy edges.
This vanished suddenly and his bike's power returned. On stopping to discuss the experience with the car-driver, the motorcyclist noticed that all the water had evaporated from his machine
and his leather jacket was bone dry and wrinkled. When he got
home some minutes later he felt weak and nauseous and had a
sunburn-like rash all over his hands and face.[9] This is by no
means a unique report. The physiological effects described by the
witness are surprisingly common and the strange colour around
the UFO (which may well be ultraviolet emission) has also been
recorded several times.

Of course, many ufologists would argue that this 'car-stop' case

[9] J. Randles, *UFO Study* (Robert Hale, 1981), pp. 245–6.

and others like it (see chapter 8) are the effects of an alien UFO. It is at least equally possible that it is a form of UAP that has escaped explanation because of the alien connotations people have attached to it. Either way, this kind of case is one of the most significant challenges to physics and has exercized the minds of researchers for three decades without solution. One of the problems about car stops is the variation in the effect. Sometimes engines and lights fail, at other times one or the other. They may completely cease operation or merely be impaired. Most extraordinary of all are the seemingly reliable reports of occasions on which the engine allegedly restarts on its own! The 'truck-stop' scene in *Close Encounters,* entirely based on real reports of UFOs, shows witness Roy Nearey almost leaping out of his skin at the departure of the UFO, when his headlights come back on, his torch regains life after having been extinguished, and the truck ignition fires of its own volition.[10]

The search for an electromagnetic-field effect that might produce all these symptoms has not been successful, although certain cases, where a vehicle with spark plugs suffers interference while a diesel engine runs on, suggest that this approach may be correct. Many investigators believe that the effects derive from temporary impedence of the flow of ions in an electrical circuit, but it will take research and experimentation by physicist to solve this baffling little mystery.

Another problem is that of 'solid-light'. We mentioned this earlier in discussing the UFO event at Brockworth (see p. 3). There is now quite a body of testimony concerning this strange effect. The 'beam' looks like ordinary light, as might emerge from a torch, but it displays properties wholly inexplicable in current scientific terms. It can penetrate solid objects (e.g. the body of a car) and come out the other side. It has been said to bend through right angles and pass round corners. The most common manifestation is of it dropping down from a UFO like a rope ladder or snail's feelers (both terms which have been chosen by witnesses). It has in some situations allegedly entered a room and behaved

---

[10] See reports by M. Rodeghier, *UFO Register,* 1976, subsequently published as a full computer study by CUFOS in the USA; A. Pace and C. Lockwood, *Vehicle Interference Project* (BUFORA, 1979).

like a solid probe, poking about.[11] This effect is frequent enough
in the UFO records to require careful thought by physicists. It
may simply be argued that such things cannot happen, and that
witnesses are wrong about what they saw. But had a laser beam
been demonstrated without explanation to a scientific audience
50 years ago they would have reacted the same way. If these
reports of solid light beams are correct, as there is every reason to
suppose, they seem to describe a phenomenon that demands
examination.

We could cite more examples of physical problems posed by
UFO stories. For example, how can a phenomenon be seen to
leave an area at a speed in excess of that of sound (or be detected
on radar demonstrating the same velocity) and yet do so totally
without sound? What happened to the sonic boom that should
have been created? And what about the 'Oz-factor', which we
have described before? Is this a physical or psychological effect?
What kind of physical phenomenon might produce the sensation
of isolation, calmness and sensory deprivation in the witness? As
with quite a few UFO epiphenomena, researchers suggest that
atmospheric ionization at the focal point of the experience might
be the cause.

Physics, especially atmospheric physics, is one of the most
obviously important areas of science for the progress of ufology.

Psychology

By this stage any critical reader must have appreciated how
relevant psychology is to UFO investigations. The reason for this
can be simply stated. We do not have bits of a UFO to examine
under a microscope. We do not have alien languages to transcribe
into English. We do not often have hard scientific data to scruti-
nize. What we do have is a very large collection of accounts by
human beings of something they have observed and found
strange and inexplicable. These accounts stem from observations
by the physical senses of the individual witnesses, which are
interpreted in their mind, decoding an original stimulus event.

---

[11] See *FSR*, vol. 23, no. 5, 1977, for a typical solid-light case.

That this process is not a clear, straightforward and untainted one is evident from the alarmingly high percentage of misidentifications. The very fact that 90 per cent or so of the UFO accounts do *not* arise from a genuine UFO stimulus points to the extreme importance of psychology in the UFO field.

The question of the reliability of eyewitness testimony is much discussed in ufology.[12] Related psychological experiments could be applied directly to the subject and psychologists working in this area could benefit from a study of the collated in-field experience of ufologists. They face a situation where an anomaly has been thrust before a whole range of people with assorted psychological backgrounds, under a number of varying external influences and pressures. It is a tailor-made opportunity for research, whose rich potential is being overlooked.

This is only one aspect of ufology which opens up new vistas to the psychologist. Other aspects are equally interesting and could add considerably to psychologists' understanding of the human mind and its workings. Just why does a witness describe a domed UFO with windows and definitive alien control, when the origin of this experience can be demonstrably shown to be mundane? We are all familiar with the full moon. It is seen so regularly by us that to anticipate its misidentification as a UFO, on anything other than a very rare occasion, seems ridiculous. That is why this problem was not recognized until the last few years. It happens remarkably often, and it does not always involve a single witness in an isolated location. There are cases on record where half a dozen people have compounded each others' beliefs and grossly distorted the moon into a 'spaceship'. The UFO enthusiast is partly to blame. He does not exactly rush to the psychologist with this information because it is counter-productive to his argument that UFOs are alien in nature.[13]

The experienced ufologist has learnt something about certain psychological processes that can cause ordinary things to appear extraordinary. He will know, for instance, that 'autokinesis' is the

---

[12] See, e.g., W.K. Hartmann, 'Process of Perception, Conception and Reporting and M.W. Rhine, 'The Psychological Aspects of UFO Reports', in E. Condon (ed.), *The Scientific Study of UFOs* (Bantam Press, 1969).

[13] Two interesting examples of moon misidentification can be found in Randles, *UFO Reality*, pp. 33–6 and 76–8.

tendency of the brain to invest stationary lights with motion. But the solutions to UFO sightings do not always lie within a few well-defined areas. The number of things which can create distortion during the passage of sensory information from the external stimulus to the mind is vast. Only a psychologist is likely to recognize most of them, and so be able to offer a reasonable verdict on whether a UFO account really does stem from an extraordinary UFO event.

On another level, we also need to know if there are reasons why certain kinds of people observe certain kinds of thing. Is there any connection between UFO-contact claims and psycho-pathic disorders? One clinical psychologist, Dr Alexander Keul, thinks there is, basing this hypothesis on a detailed Rorschach test study of many close-encounter witnesses. Other uninvolved psychologists we have spoken to on this point disagree with his view, and think the evidence is interesting but points the other way! The controversy needs a resolution. In 1984 BUFORA agreed to participate in an experiment, including a detailed personality questionnaire, designed by Dr Keul and operated by experienced investigator Ken Phillips. This is working concur-rently with investigations by the National Investigations Com-mittee and may add valuable new data. There is obviously scope for more joint experimental studies by ufologists and psychol-ogists.

Investigators specializing in 'missing-time' contact cases, where hypnosis is used to try to produce 'memories' of a hidden UFO event, naturally have a close working relationship with both psychiatrists and clinical psychologists. It is part of the Code of Practice adopted by BUFORA and other British groups that any such experiment *must* only occur under correct medical super-vision, but these safeguards are sadly not yet applied in every country. Generally ufologists find that psychologists become ex-tremely interested in the work once they see the consistency of the evidence and the extreme emotional responses of witnesses. Many other psychologists remain ignorant of a truly fascinating mystery which is clearly within their domain.

Psychologists do not *only* have a role to play in the extreme alien-contact cases; they should not overlook the problems gen-erated by more ordinary UFO or UAP events. These remain observations made by human beings and not by precise scientific instruments. They need unscrambling. One day we may be able to by-pass the human element by studying UAP events via instruments. But at present almost all we know about UAPs is distorted by this human element, and if we are to outline plans and principles for future study we need psychologists to help in our interpretations.

Another interesting thing about UFO-witness psychology is that the questions it raises often touch on areas on the distant borders of traditional study. Psychologists themselves still know less than they would like to about hallucinations, hypnagogic and hypnopompic imagery, the way we distinguish between dream and fantasy, and whether, as we grow up, we learn to distinguish what is real from what is not real, or unlearn how *not* to distinguish (an important difference). A recent case we have investigated involved a witness who told us that one of the post-encounter effects she suffered was being unable to tell whether one particular memory she possessed was of a dream or a real event.

Children seem particularly prone to weird UFO encounters.[14] And people we might term psychically aware often have repeated UFO encounters. In other words, those who profess to experience phenomena of an incredible diversity (e.g. seeing ghosts, having precognition, experiencing telepathy, etc.) also have more UFO encounters than people who are psychically 'blind'. We may choose to interpret this as meaning simply that that such people are more gullible or hyperimaginative, or we may, at the other extreme, suggest that these individuals are tuned into another dimension (which Jacques Vallée calls 'Magonia'[15]). Certainly for children the difference between what is an internal subjective phenomenon and what is external and objective is less easily seen. The same applies to some people with certain mental disorders, e.g. forms of schizophrenia. Possibly at an early age we have not yet educated ourselves about how to make such differentiations. This would be the case if the differences are an actual part of how the universe really is. But what if this diffusion of

[14] Randles, *Alien Contact.*
[15] J. Vallée, *Passport to Magonia* (Tandem Books, 1975).

borders, with which we seem to be born, represents a more accurate (rather than inaccurate) picture of the way things are? What if it is merely convenience which makes us force ourselves to delineate sharply between 'real' and 'unreal' phenomena? Until we understand a great deal more about the mind and its relationship to the external world both possibilities remain. The woman mentioned earlier, who could not distinguish between dream and reality after her UFO encounter, was not regarded as schizophrenic or medically disturbed by the psychologist who examined her as part of the UFO investigation. Nor was she a child: she was 26 at the time.

Whatever the ultimate answers may prove to be, in particular about UFO close encounters, they seem to point up a basic uncertainty about the nature of reality. They are maverick phenomena which we cannot pigeon-hole. Perhaps they will be shown to be subjective and wholly internal experiences. Or perhaps they may help us to discover a far more flexible link between material 'reality' and the human mind than we currently believe in. The people best equipped to tackle this particular problem are psychologists, who must work closely with physicists in these investigations. It is probable that, whether we like it or not, the ufologists of the future will tend to be psychologists. Adaptability and tolerance will be needed on both sides of this merger of interests. However, ufology is unlikely to make much progress until more psychologists become professionally interested in the phenomenon of UFO sighting and its associated effects. Courage will be needed both from them and from the ufologists who must recognize how relevant psychology is to the subject they are studying.

Sociology

The UFO phenomenon provides an excellent experimental device, which one might think could only have been invented by a sociologist! A very bizarre stimulus with highly emotive overtones, virtually guaranteed to polarize views, is introduced to the world in such a way and with such media fanfare that it is almost impossible to avoid hearing of it. This represents a useful set of conditions for social research. UFOs are instantly recognizable, and everybody has heard of them and has an opinion. Perhaps the most obvious question for sociologists to investigate is the one about which least seems to have been done. The people concerned in the subject who most affect the world's idea of UFOs are the ufologists themselves. Unlike the witnesses, they have *chosen* to become involved. It would certainly be interesting to discover why.

Shirley McIver undertook an attitude survey of ufologists in BUFORA, as part of her Ph.D. project at York University. However, she concentrated on the 'fringe' groups because to a sociologist they are much more fascinating. Such fringe groups include the semi-religious Aetherius Society (see p. 70). Their popularity does much to set back the cause of serious ufology, and is a source of great irritation to the cautious worker. But it is undoubtedly of sociological interest to know why their extreme (and usually insupportable) claims can attract great followings, while the more reasonable pleas of the serious UFO worker are ignored. Oddly, some of the best studies of these extreme 'cult' groups have come from amateur writers rather than sociologists.[16]

So far as the less exuberant ufologist is concerned little is known. The McIver study of 218 members of BUFORA came up with some interesting facts, showing that the field is male-dominated (about 70 per cent men to 30 per cent women).[17] The percentage of the group studied who had no formal education after school-leaving age was 28; 18.3 per cent had been to university. She found that surprizingly few people become interested in ufology after a personal encounter, although quite a number do enter by this route (19.3 per cent). Most people seem to be persuaded by reading books (35.3 per cent). A TV programme or media coverage was cited as the stimulus by 21.2 per

[16] C. Evans, *Cults of Unreason* (Corgi, 1972); P. Grant, *The Directory of Discarded Ideas* (Corgi, 1982).

[17] Basic sex-stereotyping, which inclines boys more to interest in space and technology, was thought to be the reason. A summary of the results of Shirley McIver's work was published in both issues of the *Journal of Transient Aerial Phenomena*, 1983.

cent. This discovery may go some way towards explaining the
slow progress of the subject. Most UFO books give a rather false
impression of the realities. They create the illusion that there is
strong evidence of alien invasion, when the evidence (such as it
is) is conflicting and contradictory. The discovery of this inevitably brings disillusionment, and an early crisis point at which the
ufologist decides either that the subject is a sham and gives up, or
that a problem remains, though it is different from his original
idea of it, and adapts his views. Most working ufologists are only
involved in the subject for two to three years. Shirley McIver
found 44 per cent of her respondents thought 'physical extra-
terrestrials travelling in vehicles' were the most likely explanation
for UFOs; 19.3 per cent went for 'as yet unexplained natural
phenomena' and 11.9 per cent 'psychic events'. She also asked
whether respondents believed that major governments of the
world are in contact with extraterrestrials and are keeping this
secret. A high percentage, given the popular image of ufologists,
did not believe this – 47.7 per cent, as against 26.1 per cent 'don't
know' and 23 per cent who believed in the cover-up.

The sociological work undertaken so far is patchy. We still do
not know why a typical ufologist becomes one, why he stays or
leaves or what he hopes to achieve. The motives of ufologists are
bound to be reflected in the way the subject is presented to the
rest of the world, and in their methods and conclusions.

A sociologist might also take up the challenge of media interest
in UFOs. Is there a significant correlation between the number of
UFO stories in the press at any time, and the numbers of
sightings? Is there a cause-and-effect relationship? Which type of
media, serving which type of audience, treats UFOs fairly or
unfairly, seriously or light-heartedly, and why? Many other questions need to be tackled too.

The most important member of the UFO community is the
witness himself. There is something to be said for studying
witnesses as a social sub-group. Some experiments, usually (so
far) conducted by ufologists, have not found any obvious patterns. Witnesses come from a broad spectrum of social groups,
although there are sociological factors that inhibit UFO reporting
in some quarters. This is another problem that could do with
investigation.

Perhaps certain kinds of case are witnessed by certain kinds of people? In recognition of this, modern investigators are laying more stress on the collection of social data from a witness. Some sections of recent case reports almost read like the diary of a family social worker, with information on interpersonal relationships, marriage problems, and so on. The inclusion of this material in UFO report files is another reason for the introduction of a code of practice. The investigator now has a greater responsibility to protect witness confidentiality.

We would add, with some trepidation, one further aspect of the UFO problem that the sociologist could usefully study. In this book we have looked at many aspects of the relationship between science and UFOs. Often we have found that the subject is not being rejected through sound scientific reasoning but that sociological factors concerning the way scientists work create the problems. A reappraisal of scientific methods, motives and expectations, conducted by sociologists, may be in order. This would not be simply for the benefit of UFO research, because scientists will encounter other enigmas in the future, and they may lose out by treading the same paths again.

In *The Truth About Astrology*, Professor Michel Gauquelin tells a tale that is sadly familiar to the working ufologist. Of course, the very fact that a psychologist is delving into astrology is sufficient to turn most scientists away in horror. They would not even want to open the book and confront Gauquelin's evidence and information (the amount of experimental data he has amassed and published is immense).[18] It is not relevant that the psychologist has apparently proven his case (which is *not* that astrology is correct but simply that a relationship between the position of certain planets in the sky at birth and certain psychological traits in the individual is indicated). He seems to have done this at least to the point where other scientists should take him seriously. It also does not seem to matter that he has laid down many challenges to his detractors, providing all his data and results and making his methodology clear so that they may prove him wrong. Nobody has so far done so, although arguments have raged for years. Apparently replication attempts have not dis-

[18] M. Gauquelin, *The Truth about Astrology* (Basil Blackwell, 1983).

proved the 'Gauquelin effect'. Regardless of whether Gauquelin is actually right or wrong, what matters is simply the fact that astrology is impossible. Every scientists *knows* it to be a collection of superstitious nonsense. They know this despite never having studied it. They judge the subject on what they see in their morning newspapers, the horoscopes which, as Gauquelin shows, are the astrological equivalent of our own Aetherius Society. The problem is very similar to that of ufology. The evidence is presented by unscientific, often unreliable people; it does not fit current scientific theory; therefore it *must* be totally wrong.[19]

Gauquelin has responded in exactly the same way as most serious UFO researchers. He has renamed his subject, insisting it is not really astrology. Ufologists have invented the term UAP to replace UFO in the same endeavour. Gauquelin has also criticized (sometimes harshly) many of the ideas of traditional astrology, such as the signs of the zodiac, in his efforts to prove he is not an astrologer. But he works with astrologers and attends their conferences. Some UFO researchers lead this curious double life too.

We have asked a few scientists why they think it is so hard for subjects like ufology to be accepted. Surely the potential for new discoveries that these fields offer ought to go some way in compensating the scepticism which cautious scientists must feel? One researcher told us it might be because UFO research had no money behind it, and scientists (like everybody else) go where the money is, but this seems a circular argument: the money would be forthcoming if the scientists could persuade their backers that investigations would be worthwhile.

Scientists are wrong to ignore the pleas of serious ufologists on the justification of lack of evidence (there is plenty of evidence, though not evidence of alien spaceships), the lack of theories (there are several, as we have seen, and they could certainly provide more once they worked with the data) or the apparent lack of commercial application (it is not difficult to envisage them for some of the theories put forward so far).

There is also the question of public relations. If the public see a

[19] Articles by proponents and detractors (including Gauquelin himself) have appeared since 1981 in most issues of *Zetetic Scholar*.

mystery, they expect – and rely on – scientists to study it and search for explanations. Scientists can be rather dogmatic in deciding what is or what is not worthy of study, and in telling members of the public what they have or have not 'really' seen. This attitude can only do harm to the scientific professions, while it persists.

We hope this chapter has given some indication of the areas of ufology in which scientists (social *and* natural) should, to their own benefit, get involved.

An Important Note

We feel the time has come for a reputable scientific institute to get to grips with the UFO phenomenon. There is no reason why, with relatively modest expenditure, a major pilot project cannot be launched immediately. A university would be ideally suited for this work. Multidisciplinary talent is vital for an adequate study. There would be no shortage of volunteer workers from the student population. Equipment would be available for the collection and analysis of data. It would be a very useful exercise in multidisciplinary research which could be stimulating and ground-breaking – and quite a challenge to do well. Ideally, several similar projects should begin at universities and science institutes around the world so that results might be compared.

So far as Great Britain is concerned, there are several areas where UFO and UAP sightings seem to occur more frequently than elsewhere. There may be physical, geological, environmental or sociological reasons for this. Perhaps all. Any project would have to be broadly based to do its job properly. But using one of these areas (e.g. the Pennine hills on the Lancashire/Yorkshire border), a field study could be conducted with a good chance of obtaining hard data.

Two projects, at Missouri State University, USA,[20] and around Hessdalen, Sweden,[21] have already been conducted. The

[20] H. Rutledge, *Project UFO* (Prentice-Hall, 1983). See also Rutledge's article in *Probe Report*, March 1983.

[21] J. Allen Hynek, 'Swedish Project Review', *International UFO Reporter*, Jan./Feb. 1984; H. Evans, *The Evidence for UFOs* (Aquarian Press, 1983).

Missouri scheme involved only the University Physics Department. The Swedish study was basically a private research team
with some university scientific support. Neither was anything like
as extensive and broadly based or scientifically orientated as the
project we consider necessary. However, both have produced
persuasive evidence of UFO and UAP activity, including a large
number of photographs taken by the researchers themselves. We
are critical of many of the interpretations placed upon these
results. Some of the workers seem to have set out to try and prove
that alien craft were responsible for the sightings. We also feel
that insufficient attempts have been made to obtain additional
useful data, e.g. spectrographs of UFO emissions, psychosocial
profiles on observers or details of the geological conditions of the
area. However, this work does represent a starting-point and
suggests that any multi-disciplinary team undertaking a serious,
in-depth study would stand a real chance of making scientific
progress.

Any readers, particularly those with a scientific background or
skill, interested in joining a thorough, scientific research project
into UFOs and UAPs are welcome to write to us. We would also
be happy to hear from people who have seen a UFO or had a
close encounter. If you would like a reply, please provide a
stamped, addressed envelope.

Write to: 8 Whitethroat Walk, Birchwood, Warrington,
Cheshire WA3 6PQ, UK.

Appendix: Code of Practice for UFO Investigators

Over the years UFO investigators have given some consideration to the methods of their occupation and some groups have published 'Investigators' Handbooks'. However, little emphasis has been placed on the methods and conduct of an investigator during an investigation, despite the obvious importance of such matters. Do not forget that we are dealing with a very emotive subject,. one which is frequently misrepresented to the public, and often we are a party to this misrepresentation. Witnesses whom we confront may have undergone harrowing physical and psychological traumas as a result of their experience. In this sense we have a role to play which stretches far beyond the extraction of a witness's story.

Ufologists have not had a good record for co-operation, and much of our internal strife has been counter-productive. It has also worked against the interests of the person we should consider most – the witness. However, early in 1981, various groups of investigators met to discuss future co-operation, and the first positive result was the creation of a working party to plan what was variously termed a 'code of ethics' or 'code of conduct' and which has now emerged as a 'Code of Practice'. This was formulated at meetings in Nottingham, London, Swindon and Bristol between March 1981 and February 1982. The final draft was then vetted by a solicitor before presentation to ufologists and the world at large.

This code is a triumph of co-operation, and shows what can be achieved by concerted effort, but, as it stands, it merely sets out principles which should be followed during an investigation. Unless followed by investigators it will mean nothing. We hope it will be adopted by all UFO researchers and organizations.

The code was drafted by the following organizations:– British UFO Research Association (BUFORA), UFO Investigators Network

(UFOIN), Northern UFO Network (NUFON), Nottingham UFO Investigation Society (NUFOIS), Manchester UFO Research Association (MUFORA), Swindon Centre for UFO Research and Investigation (SCUFORI) and PROBE Research Group (Bristol). Contact UK and British UFO Society (BUFOS) also participated in some stages of the discussions. The principal groups involved in the formulation of the code have joined together to create a Supervisory Body for Great Britain. They resolved that members who investigate on their behalf *must* sign an undertaking to follow the code. The public are invited to make specific complaints regarding any abuse of the code (though we hope, of course, that such complaints will be few and far between) to the organization concerned, and such complaints will be passed to the Supervisory Body. They will decide what action should be taken against the investigator (or group) concerned, if they are found to be in breach of the code of practice.

Introduction

1   The Code is intended to regulate the investigation of UFO phenomena by UFO groups and organizations, and by lone investigators.

2   This Code of Practice is based on proposals discussed by representatives of leading national and local UFO organizations on 28 March, 25 April, 13 June and 14 November 1981.

3   UFO groups, organizations and lone investigators are equally invited to subscribe to the Code of Practice.

4   Investigators who are members of, or acting under the auspices of, a UFO group or organization which subscribes to the Code of Practice, must themselves subscribe to the Code.

5   A Supervisory Body, with its members drawn from several leading UFO organizations, should administer the Code of Practice.

Definition

Preamble
Except where specifically stated, words shall have the commonly accepted meaning, all cases of doubt to be resolved by reference to the *Concise Oxford Dictionary*.
(a) 'Investigator' includes both lone investigators and UFO organizations.
(b) Reference to the singular includes the plural, and vice versa.

Directive verbs
(a) 'Must' indicates mandatory action on the part of the investigator.
(b) 'Shall' or 'should' indicates strongly recommended (but discretionary) action by the investigator.
(c) 'Desirable' indicates preferable action by the investigator.

Reports
(a) 'Original': report made and filed by the investigator. (May contain confidential material.)
(b) 'Edited': report cleared for general distribution and publication; may have been edited or rewritten. (Must *not* contain confidential material.)

Classification
'Confidential': information not to be disclosed generally.

Publication
Publication includes UFO (and other) periodicals, newsletters, circulars, news media hardcover books, paperbacks, etc.

This Code of Practice consists of three sections:

1 Responsibility to the witness
2 Responsibility to the public
3 Responsibility to ufology.

Section one: *Responsibility to the witness*

1.1 The identity of a witness to a UFO event is *confidential* and *must not* be disclosed unless written consent is obtained from the witness to release such information. (Sect. 3 para. 4 refers.)

1.2 The witness *must* be advised of the consequences which may arise if the information specified in clause 1.1 is released.

1.3 Insofar as is practical, all interviews shall be by prior appointment.

1.4 It is desirable that all interviews shall be conducted by two investigators, and in the event of the witness being a woman or child (under 16 years), that one of the investigators shall be female.

1.5 All requests by the witness (or, in the case of a minor, a parent or other responsible person) for a third party to be present during an interview *must* be honoured.

1.6   If the witness categorically refuses to co-operate in any way, or to meet another investigator, he or she *must* not be approached further, the option for further contact resting with the witness.

1.7   An investigator *must* not enter or attempt to enter any private property without the permission of the owner, tenant (or occupier), or authorized agent.

1.8   Any damage to property caused by an investigator during the course of an investigation (for which the investigator admits liability) shall be made good by that investigator.

1.9   Specialized techniques or equipment *must* not be used during the interviewing of a witness other than by the written consent of the witness and the use of any such aid, or aids, shall be restricted to interviews conducted by fully qualified practitioners. The use of hypnosis shall only be under the guidance of a medically qualified psychologist.

1.10   The witness is entitled to be informed of the conclusions reached if he so requests.

1.11   Due consideration should always be given to the health and welfare of the witness.

Section two: *Responsibility to the public*

2.1   All investigators *must*, so far as is practicable, co-operate fully with the police and any other official body, particularly in circumstances which may affect national security. (Sect. 3 para. 4 refers.)

2.2   If, during any investigation, a situation is encountered which is, or is liable to become, dangerous to the general public, or result in damage to property, the investigator *must* without delay notify the police or other responsible body, and take all reasonable steps to protect public and property.

2.3   No information gained during an interview shall be made available prematurely to the news media.

2.4   The investigator shall not issue unsupported statements to the news media concerning any case.

2.5   Investigators are reminded that they have no special privilege, and may be required to disclose confidential information to the courts.

Section three: *Responsibility to ufology*

3.1 The free flow of information shall not be restricted for personal gain; where possible the investigator shall make data available promptly to accredited investigators, with due credit being given to the source of that information.

3.2 All interviews regarding cases of high strangeness shall be electronically recorded unless the use of a recorder is objected to by the witness (or other responsible person in the case of a minor).

3.3 All reports should indicate the persons present during interviews, and their status.

3.4 Any information, confidential because of factors inherent within this Code, *must* not be made available in the *edited* report. Only the *edited* report should be made available for external use. (Note: unless released by witness, the witness's identity is confidential and *must* not be included in the *edited* report. To protect fully witnesses in sensitive occupations, it may be desirable to restrict details of the time, place and circumstances of the incident to such UFO researchers as 'need to know'.)

3.5 An investigator should not discuss his personal theories with a witness during the course of an investigation.

February 1982

DECLARATION of the ADOPTION of the CODE of PRACTICE for UFO INVESTIGATORS

I, the undersigned, have read and understood the CODE of PRACTICE for UFO INVESTIGATORS (February 82) and state that:

1   I wish to be registered as a subscriber to the above Code of Practice.

2   I will conform to the clauses and principles of the Code of Practice when engaged in UFO investigation or research.

3   I understand that I may be required to give account to the Supervisory Body of any failure to conform to the Code of Practice for which I am responsible.

Signature ....   Date ....

Name (in block capitals) ....   Address ....

....   Group or society ....

Certified that I have received DECLARATION as copied above

....   Group Sec.

....   Date

Bibliography

The following books may be useful to those who wish to take UFO study further. Some are still in print, others will only be available at libraries. Most national UFO groups (e.g. BUFORA in Britain, and CUFOS in the USA) operate a loan system with their extensive collection of books. The Newcastle-upon-Tyne Central Library in the UK houses a fine collection of all the major UFO books and full runs of many of the UFO periodicals referred to in this book, including *FSR* (*Flying Saucer Review*) and *Northern UFO News*.

Barry, James Dale, *Ball Lightning and Bead Lightning* (Plenum Press, 1980).
   A recent book, it covers the subject very comprehensively and includes details of virtually every claimed photograph of the phenomenon. It also has an exhaustive bibliography.

Bourret, J.-C., *The Crack in the Universe* (Spearman, 1977).
   Translated into English by UFO scholar Gordon Creighton. This is a detailed transcript of a long series of programmes transmitted on French national radio in 1974. Various UFO experts and scientists discuss UFO cases and theories, and the book contains a transcript of the interview with the French Minister of Defence in which he admitted that UFOs exist.

Bowen, Charles (ed.), *The Humanoids* (Spearman, 1969).
   Bowen was the longest-serving editor of *FSR*. The book brings together material from all over the world, and is the first book ever given over entirely to close encounters of the third and fourth kinds, i.e. those involving alien entities. It came early in the study of such cases, before the use of regression hypnosis took root (although the first abduction case on record is fully detailed). Widely considered a classic in alien contact research.

Clark, Jerome and Coleman, Loren, *The Unidentified* (Warner, 1975).
A book by two then 'psychic' ufologists, who sought to marry psychic
phenomena with UFO close encounters. The book attempts to explain UFO events in a social, psychological and psychic sense – and is
one of the most successful and readable attempts at humanistic
ufology.

Condon, Edward (ed.), *The Scientific Study of UFOs* (Bantam Press,
1969).
The 1,000-page dossier which resulted from the US government-
funded project at the University of Colorado. Try to leave the
conclusions (at the front) until after reading the book.

Corliss, William (ed.), *'Sourcebook Project'*. PO Box 107, Glen Arm,
Maryland, 21057, USA.
Corliss is in charge of 'The Sourcebook Project,' at Maryland, USA.
His contribution to anomaly research is inestimable. In dozens of
volumes he has collated records from scientific journals (some obscure, some not so obscure) and bound together brief accounts of
phenomena on the fringes of understanding. Books are determined
by broad area of study and sub-defined within. 'The Handbook of
Unusual Natural Phenomena' is but one of many useful to ufologists.

Devereux, Paul, *Earthlights* (Turnstone Press, 1982).
This has stirred up more controversy than any in recent UFO history.
Devereux outlines the research which led to his thesis that all UFOs
are atmospheric phenomena induced by geological processes capable
of being moulded in form by witness psychokinesis. Important to all
students of UAPs.

Evans, Hilary, *The Evidence for UFOs* (Aquarian Press, 1983).
A slim book which attempts to do as its title suggests. Its author is an
experienced UFO researcher. He makes a brave attempt at an impossible job in such small space. One of the best general introductions
on the market and very up to date. A new work in process by Evans,
to be published as *Visions* by the same publisher, promises to be an
invaluable analysis of witness-centred close-encounter cases.

Fawcett, Larry and Greenwood, Barry, *Clear Intent* (Prentice-Hall,
1984).
By researchers in the US 'Freedom of Information' group, CAUS,
this book describes the fight through the US courts to obtain UFO
documentation from their government. It discusses many reports,
memos, papers and files that have been released and those tantaliz-
ingly still held back. Essential to anybody interested in the relationship of governments to ufology.

Foggarty, Quentin, *Let's Hope They're Friendly* (Angus & Robertson, 1983).
Foggarty was a TV reporter caught up in one of the most widely publicized UFO encounters of recent times. He flew with a New Zealand cargo plane crew to film a reconstruction of their earlier sightings, when UFOs reappeared. The film was screened throughout the world and has spawned a book by the pilot (*The Kaikoura UFOs*) and more 'explanations' than any previous case (ranging from squid boat lights to moonlight on cabbage patches). This is one of the most honest UFO books on record. It does not shirk from analysing the social effects (including the money-making) which this 'overnight sensation' produced.

Fowler, Raymond, *Casebook of a UFO Investigator* (Prentice-Hall, 1982).
Fowler is one of America's most respected investigators, with a long track-record of work in the field. This book well illustrates both the typical social role of a ufologist and the fact that most of the time he is not involved in dramatic cases but in fairly mundane encounters.

Fuller, John, *The Interrupted Journey* (Berkley, 1966; Souvenir Press, 1980).
Fuller is a journalist who has written several books on UFO cases. This is an in-depth look at a UFO abduction involving an American couple who met UFO entities in the New England mountains in 1961. Much of the story was retrieved by hypnosis (the first time it was ever used in UFO research). Lengthy transcripts and comments by the psychiatrist who treated the couple build the book. Anybody interested in alien contact cases or the use of hypnosis in UFO study must read this. It brought global publicity for the case, and led to a film (*The UFO Incident*). Newer editions contain updated material and a further hypnosis session held some years later.

Haines, Richard (ed.), *UFO Phenomena and the Behavioural Scientist* (Scarecrow Press, 1979).
A collection of articles by specialists in the field, particularly psychologists and sociologists. Many contain original research. The only book of its kind yet to appear.

Hendry, Allan, *The UFO Handbook* (Doubleday, 1979; Sphere, 1980).
Hendry, an astronomy graduate, was employed as full-time investigator for CUFOS, the American group. This book chronicles his time there, and includes a statistical study of more than 1,000 cases studied. The author bends over backwards to be critical and has

earned the respect of both sceptics and believers with this book. Especially important for its detailed examination of IFO cases (where the witness was convinced a UFO was the cause but Hendry found a mundane stimulus).

Hopkins, Budd, *Missing Time* (Merek, 1982).
Famous American artist becomes UFO investigator, after a personal encounter. This is a detailed study of alien contact stories involving time lapse, almost all retrieved by hypnosis. Significant patterns emerge from the work. None of the cases are well known in UFO circles, all being discovered and worked on by Hopkins and psychiatrist Dr Aphrodite Clamar. Not a scientific book, but the only serious attempt to present a research file on this sort of investigation.

Hynek, J. Allen, *The UFO Experience* (Regnery Press, 1972; Corgi, 1974).
First book by the scientist who has had the longest involvement in UFO investigation, through his role as scientific consultant to the USAF projects. This classifies cases and creates the terminology 'Close Encounters of the first, second and third kind'.

Hynek, J. Allen, *The Hynek UFO Report* (Sphere, 1978).
With the release of the Project Blue Book files under Freedom of Information Hynek was free to speak about the investigations he participated in for the US government. This book discusses some of the key cases and shows Hynek's insights into US government policy.

Hynek, J. Allen and Vallée, J., *The Edge of Reality* (Regnery Press, 1975).
Little publicized or available, it comprises a series of transcribed conversations between the authors and scientific colleagues on various thorny UFO questions.

Jacobs, David, *The UFO Controversy in America* (Signet, 1976).
The only serious attempt to study the social basis of ufology in a historical sense. It begins with the wave of 'airships' in the last century but ends before release of government papers through Freedom of Information. Their subsequent appearance merely confirms how perceptive Jacobs was.

Jung, Carl, *Flying Saucers* (Routledge & Kegan Paul, 1977).
First published in 1959; one of the great psychologist's last works. This was the first book studying UFO witnesses instead of UFO events. It drew heavily on dream material and was too early to

incorporate the work produced when serious ufology really got under way in the following decade.

Keel, John, *Operation Trojan Horse* (Abacus, 1973).
Journalist Keel has spent many years chasing the stranger UFO cases and written several speculative and controversial books, often involving personal confrontations with the phenomenon. Certainly UFO witnesses often claim the wild things he writes about, but he is the only ufologist brave enough to say so with sufficient restraint to make them plausible.

Klass, Phillip, *UFOs: The Public Deceived* (Prometheus Books, 1983).
Klass, another journalist, has a reputation in US UFO circles as second in notoriety only to the devil. The 'deception' is, he claims, by the ufologists who seek to mislead the public for their own ends. He is always determined to solve cases and explain away the UFO. Sometimes he makes a good point. Often he goes much too far. This latest work, in which he looks at the US government's released files and some recent cases (including the Kaikoura, New Zealand, films) is a little more restrained – and thus his most effective attempt yet.

Michel, Aimé, *The Truth about Flying Saucers* (Spearman, 1958).
France has always been at the forefront of UFO study. Michel was, until his recent retirement, one of the most intelligent theorists in the field. As a science writer he always stuck to scientific principles. Most of his work was published through his magazine *FSR* in the sixties and seventies, but he wrote several of the earliest serious UFO books which first brought the complexity and strangeness of the phenomenon to the public's attention.

Michel, John, *The House of Lords UFO Debate* (Pentacle, 1979).
No relation, Michel (the Englishman) is most noted for his books about earth mysteries and archaeology. Here he presents an annotated transcript of the debate forced by Lord Clancarty in the British House of Lords in 1979. Michel explains the peers' references to ufology and elaborates on things they talk about or miss. Nothing of great moment was said in the debate, which led to the creation of the House of Lords All-Party UFO Study Group.

Oberg, James, *UFOs and Outer Space Mysteries* (1982).
Oberg, a NASA writer, is a UFO sceptic who describes himself as 'benevolent'. Certainly he writes about UFO cases with the aim of explaining them, but unlike his colleague, Klass, he is not afraid to admit it when he cannot do so. This book destroys through careful

investigation all the hyped-up claims published in several uncritical UFO books that astronauts saw and photographed UFOs during space missions.

Page, Thornton and Sagan, Carl, *UFOs: A Scientific Debate* (Cornell University Press, 1972).
A collection of articles based on the papers given at the 1969 American Association for the Advancement of Science UFO debate, superbly balanced and compiled and edited by two famous scientists who neither believe nor disbelieve. There is no single theme and the papers cover varying topics. But there are some invaluable ones, such as Hynek on scientific approaches to UFO study, McDonald on radar/visual cases and Baker on UFO films under scientific analysis. Far and away the most scientific UFO book, must be read by any scientist interested in the subject.

Pugh, Randall and Holliday, F. W., *The Dyfed Enigma* (Faber & Faber, 1979).
In 1977 there was a wave of UFO reports in rural south Wales. This spawned massive publicity and several books. Pugh was the local BUFORA investigator and so on the spot with both experience and facilities. These facts are reflected in this record of the wave, easily the most sober and accurate published. However, it displays certain biases. Holliday died before it was published (his previous books had been about demons and monsters!). Pugh became persuaded by personal experience (*after* the book) that UFOs were of demonic origin and burnt his files. The book does give a fascinating insight into the way a UFO wave develops.

Randles, J., *UFO Study* (Robert Hale, 1981).
Subtitled 'A handbook for enthusiasts', this is designed as a 'teach-yourself' course in UFO field investigation.

Randles, J., *UFO Reality* (Robert Hale, 1983).
Subtitled 'A critical look at the physical evidence', this is based on over 1,000 personally evaluated UFO cases collected between 1975 and 1979. Chapters take the study through types of effect (e.g. physiological, psychological, electromagnetic), giving statistics and examples in each case. All kinds of physical (i.e. scientifically testable) evidence for UFO reality are studied.

Randles, J., *The Pennine UFO Mystery* (Granada, 1983).
Using the theoretical concepts defined in *UFO Reality* this applies theory by examining the UFO phenomenon in one small area (the Pennine hills). It suggests a two-part (UAP and close encounter) explanation for the events described.

Randles, J. and Warrington, Peter, *UFOs: A British Viewpoint* (Robert Hale, 1979).
The book looks first at the social background to the phenomenon in Britain, moves to a type-by-type study of the reports on record (nearly all from our own investigations) and analyses the extra-terrestrial hypothesis. Ideas are proposed for building a new witness-centred theory.

Randles, J. and Whetnall, Paul, *Alien Contact* (Spearman, 1982).
Part I is a stylized account of a series of UFO encounters claimed by one Welsh family, involving abductions and even trips to other planets. It is very much a 'beyond the fringe' UFO story. Part II analyses the claims and compares them with other UFO phenomena. A psychological theory (with psychic overtones) is developed as the most satisfactory solution to the problems raised by the case.

Rimmer, John, *The Evidence for Alien Abductions* (Aquarian Press, 1984).
Rimmer is editor of *Magonia* magazine, devoted to psycho-social theories of UFO origin. In his first book he summarizes the evidence for and against the reality of contacts with UFO entities. Despite lack of space the book is a useful attempt and provides a good basis for more detailed study. The conclusions are strange, but good insight into the problems of regression hypnosis is demonstrated. An ideal first book to read for those wanting to delve more deeply into the alien contact side of UFO phenomena.

Ruppelt, Edward, *The Report on Unidentified Flying Objects* (Ace Books, 1956).
The first important UFO book to be published. Ruppelt, as head of the US government's own UFO study, became convinced of UFO reality and defied secrecy rules to publish this history of the early years of government involvement. Many classic cases (later explained without comment in the official records) are reported from the inside by the man who led the investigation. Sometimes they are explained, and he shows how. Often they are not, and he says so openly. A number of cases later covered up are also discussed in this book.

Saunders, David and Hawkins, R., *UFOs? YES!* (Signet, 1968).
Saunders was fired from the Condon Report staff late in the study, as this book explains. He reflects the opinion of at least half the project staff that Condon was grossly mistreating his scientific responsibilities. It is intriguing to see how Saunders puts forward a totally opposite appraisal of the cases which Condon uses to dismiss ufology. This book must be read in conjunction with the Condon Report itself.

Seargent, David, *UFOs: A Scientific Enigma?* (Sphere, 1978).
When the film *Close Encounters of the Third Kind* was released a glut of UFO books flooded the market. Most were unhelpful and unwelcome. This one by an Australian investigator with a penchant for psychological theory was not. It aims to prime interest, but it demonstrates such a deep insight into the complexities of close encounter UFOs in particular that it leaves many more pretentious books standing.

Steiger, Brad, *Project Blue Book* (Ballantine, 1976).
Steiger has written several strange UFO books with extreme speculations in them. This is his one useful contribution to the field. Written to coincide with the release (under Freedom of Information) of the USAF files, it traces the history of air force involvement from 1947 to 1969, reconstructing cases from the released papers. It also includes important documents, such as the final reports of Project Sign and Grudge. In historical and governmental senses the book is invaluable.

Story, Ron (ed.), *The UFO Encyclopedia* (NEL, 1980).
A huge volume which contains entries written by many ufologists (mostly American). It serves to summarize leading cases, theories, figures and related facts. Biographies of the hundred or so people Story considers to be the world's leading UFO experts are included, with each contributing a short 'position statement' outlining their views on UFOs. It is as well to remember that these statements were written several years ago. Quite a few have changed their views.

Thomas, Paul, *Flying Saucers Throughout the Ages* (Tandem, 1973).
An uneven book which should not be taken too literally. It aims to show that UFOs have been seen for millennia. Its attempts to link biblical stories with UFO encounters may seem strained, but the summary of the more recent history of the UFO phenomenon is worth examining.

Watson, Ian, *Miracle Visitors* (Gollancz, 1978).
Watson is a science-fiction writer and this is a fictional story. It begins with a UFO encounter in the Yorkshire Dales and regression hypnosis to uncover memory. Watson is noted for being an 'ideas man' and this book (which we know from Watson himself is meant to be taken as serious ufology) contains some of the best new ideas of recent years. Its theoretical concepts about the UFO phenomenon bear contemplation.

Useful Addresses

Great Britain

BUFORA (British UFO Research Association),
30 Vermont Road, Upper Norwood, London SE19 3SR.

(Publishes *BUFORA Bulletin* and *Journal of Transient Aerial Phenomena.*)

NUFON (Northern UFO Network),
8 Whitethroat Walk, Birchwood, Cheshire WA3 6PQ.

(Publishes *Northern UFO News.*)

USA

CUFOS (Center for UFO Studies),
PO Box 1621, Lima, Ohio 45802.

(Publishes *CUFOS Newsletter* and the bimonthly *International UFO Reporter.*)

APRO (Aerial Phenomena Research Organization),
3910 East Kleindale Road, Tucson, Arizona 85712.

MUFON (Mutual UFO Network),
103 Oldtowne Road, Seguin, Texas 78155.

Other publications referred to in this book

FSR (Flying Saucer Review)   FSR Publications, Snodland, Kent
ME6 5HJ, UK.

Fortean Times   96 Mansfield Road, London NW3 2HX, UK.
Magonia   64 Alric Avenue, New Malden, Surrey KT3 4JW, UK.
Quest   68 Buller Crescent, Leeds LS9 6LJ, UK.
UFO Register   48 Crown Road, Wheatley, Oxfordshire, UK.
UFO Research Australia   PO Box 229, Prospect, South Australia 5082.
Zetetic Scholar   Department of Sociology, University of Eastern
  Michigan, Ypsilanti, Michigan, USA.

Index